BEAT COP
TO TOP COP

BEAT COP
TO TOP COP

A Tale of Three Cities

JOHN F. TIMONEY

Foreword by Tom Wolfe

PENN

University of Pennsylvania Press

Philadelphia

THE CITY IN THE TWENTY-FIRST CENTURY
Eugenie L. Birch and Susan M. Wachter, Series Editors

Published in collaboration with the Penn Institute for Urban Research

Published by University of Pennsylvania Press
Philadelphia, Pennsylvania 19104-4112
Printed in the United States of America on acid-free paper

10 9 8 7 6 5 4 3 2 1

Library of Congress Cataloging-in-Publication Data
Timoney, John F.
    Beat cop to top cop : a tale of three cities / John F. Timoney ; foreword by Tom Wolfe.
      p. cm. — (The city in the twenty-first century)
    Includes index.
    ISBN 978-0-8122-4246-1 (hardcover : alk. paper)
    1. Timoney, John F. 2. Police—United States—Biography. 3. Police—United States—Case studies. I. Title.
HV7911.T563A3 2010
363.2092—dc22
[B]
                                                              2009046955

To Noreen, Christine, Sean, and lovely Leah:
It's the cop's family that makes the real sacrifice.

CONTENTS

PART III. MIAMI

FOREWORD

Tom Wolfe

Ecce facies! Behold the face!

That face, belonging to John Timoney, has become a legend in its own time. In the 1970s, Timoney was a young New York City police officer assigned to street patrol in the South Bronx, the worst skell hole on earth. Everybody else on earth got an eyeful of the Bronx's skell-bent misery in the movie *Fort Apache, the Bronx*, starring Paul Newman, and the television miniseries *The Bronx Is Burning*. "Skell" is cop slang for a lowlife with the IQ and humane fellow-feelings of a virus.

All a policeman in the South Bronx had to do was cast his net, anywhere, anywhere at all, and he could haul in a wriggling, writhing, rattler-fanged tangle of toxic felons. Catching them was one thing. Taking them into custody was another. As cop lore had it, in Manhattan you could tell some skell he was under arrest and say, "We can do this the easy way or we can do it the hard way—it's up to you," and he would at least know what you were talking about. In the South Bronx you got ready to roll in the dirt from the git-go. Every police officer assigned to street patrol had that problem . . . except for John Timoney. According to the legend, Timoney never once had to draw a weapon to arrest a felon and take him in. He just gave him a good look at . . . *that face* . . . and even the most obtuse and poisonous viper became a mewling little pussy . . . and that face became a legend in its own time. Like most legends, I am sorry to say, this one is not entirely true. At one point Timoney was reduced to drawing his gun and engaging in a shootout before managing to bring in two drug dealers who had just fulfilled the dream of a lifetime in their line of work, found the pot of gold at the end of the rainbow, laid hands on enough treasure to retire in posh style and cover themselves with honor by collecting Pre-Raphaelite paintings, if they wanted to, and donating them amid posh pomp to the Metropolitan Museum of Art: namely, one hundred pounds of pure, uncut heroin.

By the time I ran into Timoney ten years later, he had risen to inspector, the third highest rank in the New York Police Department. Another four years, and he would become, at age forty-five, the youngest four-star chief in the department's history. Even someone in the grandstand, like me, could read the lines incised in that face, punctuated by a blunt nose, and immediately make out the words "tough Irish cop." Timoney was the platonic ideal-typical incarnation of the breed. He was the *real* real thing, born in Dublin to working-class parents who, when their boy Sean—as they called him then—was thirteen, emigrated to New York with him and his younger brother, Ciaran. The boys grew up streetwise, as they say, or at least wise in the ways of the Studs Lonigan–style streets of Washington Heights, a neighborhood in far northern Manhattan right across the Harlem River from the South Bronx. Both boys joined the police force. Among sturdy Irish lads, it was as natural as breathing.

I remember asking Inspector Timoney if the NYPD still recruited Irish policemen. "Yeah," he said, "we recruit them, but now they all come from the suburbs . . . and to tell the truth, a lot of them are cream puffs. These days if you want a real Irish cop, you hire a Puerto Rican."

By now, Timoney had turned into a fitness fiend. He had begun running at least five miles a day, and that led to fifteen marathons and so many half marathons, more than two dozen, he and everybody else lost count. After he resigned as deputy police commissioner in New York in 1996 and became Philadelphia's police commissioner in 1998, the fiendish fitness obsession did wonders for the legend—*just like that.* A week after being sworn in as Philadelphia's top cop, amid heavy press coverage, Timoney happened to be on his daily run and had just reached the city's toniest downtown residential area, Rittenhouse Square, when an excited citizen cried out, "Hey! I know you! Aren't you the new guy—the new police commissioner?" Timoney stopped, smiled, and went over to shake hands. But the excited citizen didn't have time for that. He pointed across the street and said, "You see that guy there? He just stole that lady's purse!"

The new commissioner, forty-nine years old but a fiend afoot, exploded into a hundred-meter dash, ran the skell down, overpowered him, showed him that face, and hauled him in.

Now we're talking about . . . *press!* One week on the job! Fights crime . . . *Himself!* Philadelphia's love affair with John Timoney began at that moment and never cooled in the slightest. It only became more ardent . . . especially the day in 2000 when demonstrators out to disrupt the Republican National Convention in Philadelphia got out of control, and *Himself!* rode a bicycle head-on into the mob and launched *Himself* airborne from his bike seat, yodeling an old Irish war cry—"Fuck you!"—as he tackled a rude, self-righteous rowdy boy and smashed him to the ground. *Le tout* Philadelphia loved it all, ate it up.

So went the heroics. In fact, what really reduced crime in Philadelphia so dramatically under Timoney were tactics he had worked on in New York with Police Commissioner William Bratton: pro-active patrolling (spotting—and hassling—the skells *before* they strike); Timoney's specialty, which was daily CompStat statistics (keeping track of precisely where they have been striking); and Bratton's specialty, "quality-of-life" arrests. The theory was that if you made it a policy to crack down on minor offenses, fare beating, brown-bag drinking on the streets, boom-box noise violations, truancy, graffiti, vagrancy masquerading as homelessness, teenage rowdiness, and random vandalism, you would erase the skells' impression that this town is Open City for far worse. It worked in New York, and Timoney made it work in Philadelphia.

If anything, all the skell quells, shootouts, and yodeling *Himself*-missiles distracted the press and the public from the secret weapon located immediately behind *that face,* namely, what the test pilot Scott Crossfield, upon the advent of digitally computerized flight controls, placed his bets on: "a chemical analog computer of vast power, easily reproducible by unskilled labor, known as the human brain." Timoney had been awarded practically every honor a street-combat policeman could receive, including the Medal of Valor, but there is no question that brainpower was responsible for much of the speed of his rise through the ranks of the New York Police Department. The department brass put a heavy emphasis on higher education, so much so that they were flexible when it came to an officer serving on the force and going to college at the same time. Any ambitious policeman was going to take advantage of the opportunity, especially since he could not rise beyond the rank of captain without a bachelor's degree. Timoney graduated from the John Jay College in Manhattan at twenty-six and didn't stop there. He received a master's degree in American history from Fordham two years later and a second master's, this one in urban planning, from Hunter College four years after that.

The public's first glimpse of the tough Irish cop's intellectual side came in 1987 when the *New York Daily News* revealed that Timoney and five other policemen had formed a book club. Every month they met to discuss a particular book—always a classic such as *Crime and Punishment* or *Madame Bovary,* if not a classic among classics on the order of *The Iliad.* Now that the word was out, he was invited to Mount Holyoke College to lecture on *Crime and Punishment.* An exegesis of this, the most psychological subtle of Dostoyevsky's novels, coming from . . . *that face* . . . so wowed Mount Holyoke students and faculty, he was invited to give the same lecture at Amherst. *Crime and Punishment*'s climax comes when a police detective's interrogation of the main character, Raskolnikov—strictly verbal, I should stress, in light of what was about to happen—so thoroughly dismantles the young intellectual's philosophical self-justification of his crime that he is overcome by guilt and confesses that, yes, he was the one who murdered his landlady.

In the question period after the lecture, a student, a girl, young and pretty as a morning glory opening to the first rays of the sun, asks Timoney, "Chief, how many killers turn themselves in because of pangs of conscience?"

Oh-oh, the chief has a problem here. He has just spent an hour holding forth on exactly that. He doesn't want to disillusion the tender young flower's virginal—he assumes—view of human nature by telling her the truth, which is, "I can't remember one . . . ever." So he . . . *uhmmmmm* . . . shades things a bit and says, "Ohhhh. . . . about 5 percent."

Without a blink, the flower says, "And how many do you have to beat a confession out of?"

Stunned, Timoney says, "None, I hope! Whatever gave you that idea?"

"Oh," the little morning glory says brightly, "I watch *NYPD Blue*."

NYPD Blue? "If I were your parents," says Timoney, "I would ask for my tuition back!"

In real life, however, real blue knuckle sandwiches were among the offenses that brought Timoney to Miami in December 2002 as chief of police (the top cop, since Miami had no office of police commissioner). America is a wonderful country. Only in America could people from a foreign country, with a foreign language and a foreign culture, have taken control, via the voting booth, of a metropolitan area the size of Miami's in one generation. I am talking about Cuban refugees from the Castro regime, whom the federal government welcomed to Miami by the hundreds of thousands from 1959 on. By now, December 2002, the mayor was Cuban, the police chief was Cuban, his top brass was heavily Cuban—in fact, the entire force, all the way down to street patrolmen, was heavily Cuban. So were those cops most commonly accused of excessive use of force, outright brutality, and outrageous lying and cheating. The bitterest accusers were the American black residents of Miami's two big slums, Liberty City and Overtown. They regarded the Cubans as foreigners who had suddenly dropped from the sky like paratroopers, taken over the police force, started shoving them around . . . and giving them blue knuckle sandwiches. . . . By the time Timoney arrived, thirteen officers were on trial in a sensational case

charging them with planting guns at crime scenes and otherwise rig-
ging evidence and concocting stories to cover up for themselves and
their brother blue knucklers. The mayor, Manny Diaz, and the city
manager, Carlos Gimenez, saw Timoney as a man who could reform
the police department with a free hand. He had no political or natural ties in Miami. An Irishman born in Dublin? In Miami, by 2002,
he might as well have been from Mars. Quite aside from the Cubans,
Miami had become a polyglot of immigrants from Central and South
America and the Caribbean. Since 1980, Haitians had poured in, legally
or otherwise, in huge numbers.

Timoney made Mayor Diaz look good. *That face* snapped the police force to attention, reassured the American black population, and
soothed the souls of the entire polyglot lot. Right off the bat he made a
meet-and-greet tour of Liberty City and Overtown and listened face-to-
face as people complained about the police department. He gave them
all the time they wanted and promised them fair treatment from now
on. This business of police officers planting guns and dreaming up
other fraudulent evidence? Timoney did more than put an end to it. He
established a strict protocol regarding the use of weapons. During one
twenty-month stretch, nobody in the entire Miami Police Department
fired a single shot—and the city's rate of violent crime, one of the highest in the nation, dropped steadily.

In the process, Mayor Manny Diaz and Police Chief John Timoney
became the Diaz & Timoney Duo . . . masters of defusion. Whenever
any group in Miami's simmering immigrant stew began to boil over,
Diaz & Timoney would appear before them, and Timoney would say,
"I'm John Timoney, chief of police. I'm an immigrant from Dublin, Ireland. And this is our mayor, Manny Diaz. The mayor is an immigrant
from Havana, Cuba. What can we do for you?" After that the—

Well, I could tell you Timoney tales from now until the sun comes
up, but the book before us is not John Timoney's personal memoir.
And I say, thank God for that. A memoir—*anybody's* memoir—is like
Wikipedia: some of it may be true. Timoney does something far more
valuable. He takes us inside the world of police work in three big cities:
New York, Philadelphia, and Miami. He shows us metropolitan cops

in action, their strategies, their sensitivity to public opinion, and, most fascinating of all to me, the political games they have no choice but to play.

Believe me, you have a treat on your hands, the product of the sharp eyes and insightful Irish utterances of . . . *that face.*

INTRODUCTION

Be Careful What You Wish For

In January 1984, New York City mayor Ed Koch named Ben Ward the new police commissioner, succeeding Bob Maguire, who had held the position for the prior six years. Maguire's administration had been devoted to fixing the damage done as a result of the fiscal crisis of the mid-1970s, when the city had gone bankrupt. Staffing levels in the department had dropped from around thirty-one thousand sworn personnel in June 1975 to just under twenty-one thousand by the end of the decade. Not surprisingly, 1980 had the highest overall crime rates in the history of the New York Police Department (NYPD). Clearly, the number of police officers matters. By the time Ben Ward took over, the staffing level was around twenty-five thousand, which was good compared to 1980 but still far from the thirty-one thousand of the early 1970s.

While Ward had also been a high-ranking official in other city agencies, his background was all cop. He started his career as a foot officer in Brooklyn during the 1950s, then became a detective, and later reached the rank of lieutenant. In 1972, Police Commissioner Pat Murphy appointed him to serve in Murphy's "reform" administration. By 1984, as he took command of the NYPD, Ben Ward had a strong résumé to lead the organization.

And lead it he did—early on. In the first months of his tenure, Ward announced a sweeping anticrime, antidrug initiative called Operation Pressure Point. This action sent hundreds of uniformed and plain-clothes officers as well as detectives into the Manhattan neighborhoods of the East Village and the Lower East Side. These areas were crime infested. Residents and visitors (tourists and drug purchasers) were all equal-opportunity victims. I discovered this myself on February 12, 1978 (which happened to be my seventh wedding anniversary). I was executing a drug search warrant when I was involved in a gun battle with a local drug dealer. My partner was hit by a bullet aimed directly for his heart. His bullet-resistant vest saved his life, but he was seriously injured by the blunt trauma.

Shootouts like this and other assorted violent crimes made this neighborhood ideal for Ward's new operation. In addition, there was growing demand from the public, especially from the new urban pioneers who were beginning to gentrify the fringe neighborhoods of lower Manhattan, for the police to do something.

Operation Pressure Point was an immediate success. The quality of life in these neighborhoods dramatically improved. The open-air drug bazaars were reduced in quantity and quality, and much of the drug trade was taken indoors as opposed to the corner of Eighth Street and Avenue B, to name just one of the more notorious corners. Crime, and especially violent crime, was reduced significantly. To no one's surprise, the success of Operation Pressure Point led to calls for the Ward administration to replicate the operation in other neighborhoods.

Operation Pressure Point 2 appeared in Harlem, and by the end of 1984 it was also implemented in other neighborhoods. There was a real feeling within the NYPD that the organization was fighting crime in a serious manner. I remember a colleague, Mike Tiffany, remarking that Police Commissioner Ward was the first commissioner since we had joined the NYPD (in the late 1960s) to make fighting crime our number one priority. It was true, and it felt good.

By the third year of his administration, Ben Ward and his team were on top of the world. Ward's chief of department, Robert J. Johnston Jr., was the four-star chief responsible for all day-to-day operations.

Johnston was not only in charge but he looked like he was in charge. A silver-haired, barrel-chested man, Johnston began to epitomize the NYPD—a no-nonsense, take-charge organization. Behind the scenes, the day-to-day running of the huge bureaucracy fell to Patrick Murphy, the first deputy commissioner. Murphy was a kind, self-effacing man with a wealth of experience and brains to match. He had been the four-star chief of department under Bob Maguire but had been elevated to the number two position by Ben Ward.

While Ward and his team had great success in fighting crime, they also dealt in a serious fashion with other issues facing the department, especially use of deadly physical force and dealing with emotionally disturbed people.

But policing is a very volatile business. Things go wrong all the time. It's the nature of the business. In mid-1986, a police corruption scandal exploded in the newspapers. It was known as the "77th Precinct Scandal," and the tabloids, led by *Newsday* columnist Mike McAlary and *New York* magazine's Michael Daly, told stories of drug rip-offs by cops and other crimes by police officers in full uniform. How could this happen? Where were the bosses? What was the top command at One Police Plaza doing? Who would be held accountable? Didn't Internal Affairs see the dots they should have connected? Headquarters, quite literally, was under siege. Something had to give. Heads had to roll. Things had to change.

As this scandal erupted I was a young captain assigned as the commanding officer of the 5th Precinct in Chinatown. The 5th Precinct was one of ten precincts in Patrol Borough Manhattan South, which encompassed everything south of Fifty-ninth Street in Manhattan. The commanding officer of Manhattan South was a two-star, Assistant Chief Gerry Kerins. Kerins was a respected NYPD veteran with a great sense of humor and tremendous streets smarts and experience. He was also a veteran of World War II, having served his time in the South Pacific. He despised lawyers and often said that had he known at the end of the big war that one day the NYPD would be run by and controlled by lawyers, he would have stayed in the South Pacific.

Kerins and his fellow one-star, two-star, and three-star chiefs were all summoned to One Police Plaza for a tongue-lashing by the top bosses for allowing the scandal to erupt. The session lasted over an hour and was one of those "career-threatening" sessions. The message to the attending chiefs was simple and clear: Get back to your commands and make sure your captains understand that this shit is serious and that careers will be made or broken depending on how it is handled.

When Chief Kerins got back to his office, he summoned all his captains and inspectors to his conference room. "Gentlemen," he began, "I have just returned from a session with the Divine Trinity [the police commissioner, first deputy commissioner, and chief of department]. They are like cornered rats ready to strike out at anything or anyone that causes them problems. They are serious and they are scared. They think their jobs are in jeopardy. And if their jobs are in jeopardy, your job is in jeopardy! We need to make sure our corruption skirts are clean and that we have the proper integrity programs in place. In case you all forgot, CORRUPTION is your number one priority! Finally, gentlemen, the commissioner reminded us that neither a political administration nor a police administration has ever been taken out as a result of a rise in crime. However, a corruption scandal can take out both!"

After the meeting we all knew that corruption would once again become the top priority for everyone in the NYPD. Careers would be made and broken on how the individual midlevel and senior officers dealt with it. I think we all knew that with corruption now the number one priority, our gains in fighting crime would wane.

It didn't take long. With the advent of the crack epidemic and the loss of our focus, crime rose, and for the remainder of the decade, it rose dramatically each successive year. By 1990, New York City reported its highest homicide rate in its history, with 2,245 people killed. To put those statistics in context, let's compare them with the sectarian killing in Northern Ireland. "The Troubles" began in 1969; by 1990, some 3,000 people had been killed. In twenty-one years of sectarian violence a total of 3,000 were killed, while New York City came close to matching those numbers in one year, 1990.

The final irony was that while police corruption was now the number one priority, that didn't mean there would be no more corruption.

In fact, corruption continued, and a series of scandals in the early 1990s resulted in the new mayor, David Dinkins, establishing another commission to investigate police corruption—the Mollen Commission (after Judge Milton Mollen, the commission's chairman). This followed New York City's familiar pattern of establishing such a corruption panel every twenty years or so.

The Mollen Commission, like those before it, conducted its investigations, held its very public hearings, assembled its self-congratulatory press conferences announcing this or that arrest, made its predictable recommendations in voluminous detail, and facilitated the future careers of the commission staff. Everyone won. The politicians could feel good because they had "finally" dealt a deathblow to police corruption. The press gloated over its role in "uncovering" police corruption and exposing it to the public. The commission and its supporters took satisfaction in their efforts to end, once and for all, police corruption. The top brass won by surviving another corruption commission and could breathe a little easier. As I said, everyone won. Or did they?

How did the public win when crime seemed to be out of control? How did the hardworking men and women of the NYPD win when they were told their first priority was police corruption? When they signed up to be police officers, they thought their top priority would be fighting crime and improving the quality of life for the average New Yorker. Talk about mission incongruence!

Watching all of this, I had said to myself on more than one occasion, "Boy, if I ever get to the top, things will be different. I will make sure that the number one priority for every police officer and his boss is to fight crime and improve the quality of life. Police corruption? I'll deal with it, but it will not be my top priority." Be careful what you wish for.

PART I

New York City

1

Getting on the Job

Jesus, Mary, and holy St. Joseph, he wants to be a cop.
—CATHERINE TIMONEY

Sometimes, when a chief of police or other high-ranking police official is interviewed regarding his career, he will say that he always wanted to be a police officer. Not me. I never gave much thought to becoming a cop. In fact, I was not very fond of police officers while I was growing up in Washington Heights, a working-class neighborhood in northern Manhattan. Police officers, like parents or teachers, told you all the things you couldn't do. Police officers and their authority were resented and to be avoided.

However, just as I was getting ready to graduate from Cardinal Hayes High School in the summer of 1967, one of my childhood friends, Brian Nicholson, convinced me and about six other guys to take the police officer exam one Saturday morning. Back then, the NYPD gave "walk-in" exams; no prefiling was required. You just walked into a local high school, filled out some papers, took the exam, and went home.

After partying the night before (typical Friday night partying back then was drinking beer in Highbridge Park, hopefully out of sight of the local police), we all got up early and took the downtown A train to lower Manhattan to the exam site. After a few hours, with the exam complete, we took the uptown A train back to Washington Heights and bragged to the rest of our friends that we were all going to become cops! One minor detail remained, however: Did we pass the exam? No problem. We could just tune in to WOR AM radio on Saturday night when an announcer would read out the "official answer key" to the various civil-service exams that had been administered earlier in the day.

That afternoon I had announced to my mother that I had taken the police officer exam and was going to be a cop. First, she looked at me in disbelief, then bewilderment, then amusement, then finally with maternal support. We sat at the kitchen table that night and listened to the announcer read off the answers in an unemotional, matter-of-fact manner: (1) a, (5) c, (17) d, (89) b, and so on. Before I knew it, all of the one hundred answers had been given. I needed to score a 75 to pass.

I added up the score as my mother watched over my shoulder. Yep, I passed! I scored a 76, which was more reflective of the Friday night beer drinking and lack of sleep that it was of my mental acumen. Or so I convinced myself.

My father had passed away a year before, but I am sure he would have been proud of his son becoming a New York City police officer. A month after I graduated from high school, my mother and sister, Marie, moved back to Ireland. We had come to the United States in 1961, but my mother never adjusted to the fast pace of New York City, even though we had grown up in Dublin, not exactly farmers. My mother had begged my younger brother, Ciaran, and me to return with her, but he and I were having none of that. While I had just graduated high school, Ciaran was only beginning his junior year at Cardinal Hayes High School. So he and I stayed together in the same apartment, and I worked numerous jobs while he attended high school and worked after school in a butcher shop. Things were just fine, if precarious.

Three months after graduating high school, I entered the NYPD as a police trainee, since I was not twenty-one yet, the required age to be a full-fledged police officer. Police trainees wore gray uniforms and did clerical and administrative work throughout the seventy-six police precincts and at other administrative offices, including police headquarters. But these were not nine-to-five jobs. Just like regular police officers, we worked "around the clock"—one week of 8:00 A.M. to 4:00 P.M., followed by a week of 4:00 P.M. to midnight, and then a week of midnight to 8:00 A.M. This shift work was actually beneficial to me since it allowed me to work another job during the day (before a 4:00 P.M. to midnight, and after a midnight to 8:00 A.M. shift), which augmented my miserable biweekly salary of $112 as a police trainee, not nearly enough to pay the rent and support Ciaran and myself.

In early October on a cold, wet morning, I took the subway downtown to police headquarters on Centre Street in the heart of Little Italy. A massive four-story gray building, New York Police Headquarters was legend and had been the backdrop for many movies and television series. I was quickly sworn in with a few other lads by the then city clerk Louis Stutman, a little Jewish man who had been born into this position, or so it seemed. I would later learn that the city clerk was a very powerful position in the city. I would also learn what a great and understanding man Mr. Stutman was, as he was one of the men who would decide whether or not I successfully completed my twelve-month probationary period as a police officer in the NYPD.

After I was sworn in, I was directed to report to my new command (whatever that meant), the 17th Precinct, located on the east side of Manhattan, near the United Nations and other landmarks, such as St. Patrick's Cathedral. The 17th Precinct was known as the "silk stocking" district. It certainly could never be mistaken for the "woolen sock" district, if such a district ever existed!

Up to this point in my life I had been inside only two police stations, the 34th Precinct (my neighborhood precinct) and the 30th Precinct (where my old CYO—Catholic Youth Organization—basketball coach worked). Both the 30th and 34th precincts in northern Manhattan were old, drab gray-brick buildings whose interiors looked worse than their exteriors. My new command, the 17th Precinct, was nothing like those turn-of-the-century monsters.

The 17th Precinct is located on Fifty-first Street between Third and Lexington avenues on the ground floor of a high-rise office building. There is a large glass window in the front with a glass door at the entrance that allows full view of the interior of the precinct, specifically the desk officer. In the back, out of view, were the cells, about eighteen in total, which temporarily housed prisoners while they waited to be transported to court. The 17th Precinct Detective Squad was located on the second floor, which is typical of the majority of precinct detective squads throughout the city.

My first two weeks as a police trainee in the 17th Precinct were a bit of a fog, especially because I was working in an entirely new and foreign environment. As I said, I was not particularly fond of police officers as a teenager, and so this was a strange situation. However, within three or four weeks, I began to get the idea of policing and to get used to being around police officers, and I was getting more excited by it, even though I was a mere paper pusher or telephone-answering service. I started to like what I was doing and soon began to love it. I was "in the know." Initially, all the police officers shied away from talk-ing to me, but as a few got to know me, the rest followed. These were incredible guys! After a while they included me as they shared their cop-on-the-street stories.

While the uniformed cops were the regular guys, the fun guys— the really cool guys—were the detectives from the 17th Squad. They dressed in suits, wore pinky rings, and carried themselves with a cer-tain swagger. They were commanded by a gregarious young sergeant who would always let me know which detectives were "catching" (as-signed to investigate the cases that came in during the evening) and the restaurants where they could be located in the event of an impor-tant case that needed their immediate attention or an incident that they needed to respond to. It was clear to me that these detectives had the world by the balls.

While the detective squad room was on the second floor, the really interesting offices in the building were on the third floor, which housed the office of the Third Division Plainclothes Unit. These plainclothes of-ficers worked for the division inspector (two ranks above captain) and were responsible for the enforcement of the vice and gambling laws as well as assorted other laws, especially those involving the illegal sale of alcoholic beverages. Their job was to enforce those laws, in the words of Mr. Dooley (the fictional character created by the nineteenth-century satirist Finley Peter Dunne), "meant to control the pleasures of the poor."

As a police trainee I learned pretty fast that plainclothes officers were different from other police officers. They only worked nights, and not every night. So on a Thursday or Friday, they would enter the station house at one o'clock in the morning escorted by three or four ladies of the night who were wearing bracelets, but not the sort you buy in a jewelry store. They would deposit their charges in the holding cells and then proceed to the "124 room" (the clerical office) to type their reports. I watched this routine on a regular basis from my seat behind the telephone switchboard, where I answered calls from citizens who, at that time of night, were mostly inebriated.

After a few months on the switchboard, I was assigned to the 124 room one night because I could type. (I had taken typing at Cardinal Hayes High School.) That night, a couple of plainclothesmen entered the station with their female charges. They secured the arrested women in the holding cells and then came into the 124 room to type their arrest reports. Or so I assumed.

One of the plainclothes detectives came in wearing rings and assorted pieces of other jewelry and an open-collar shirt.

"Hey, kid, I can't type. Can you knock off these reports for me?" He put two dollars next to the typewriter. I dutifully typed the reports (six 5 x 7 sheets of heavy card stock alternating with carbon paper) and other assorted paperwork. When the reports were finished, the plainclothes officers retrieved their paperwork and their girls and headed outside to a waiting prisoner wagon for a trip to night court.

With the two dollars in hand, I walked over to my lieutenant, a silver-haired old Irishman with over thirty years in the department, who was barely awake and seemed bored by the whole arrest routine. When I showed him the two dollars, he responded, "Don't worry about it. They'll make that back in overtime."

Some weeks later, the same plainclothes officers entered the station house at 5:00 A.M. This time they had in tow three or four guys who wore the same bracelets the ladies of the night had worn. In addition, they brought in box after box of liquor bottles and multiple cases of beer. They informed the lieutenant that they had just hit a "bottle club" on Third Avenue. The lieutenant nodded and handed them a stack of vouchers (property inventory reports) in addition to the normal arrest reports. A plainclothes officer came into the 124 room, where I was once again assigned, with the arrest reports and vouchers and placed five dollars next to the typewriter. He said, "Hey, kid, can you knock these off in a hurry? We gotta get to court before eight." For a guy making $112 every two weeks ($1.40 per hour), a five-dollar tip for typing someone else's report was astonishing.

The Third Division Plainclothes Unit was probably the most infamous plainclothes unit in the city. It had a long and storied history dating back to before the Depression. In December 1968, at 157 West Fifty-seventh Street, two people (a man and a woman) were shot and killed and a third was seriously injured inside an apartment in this luxury building. It was believed that the victims were involved in some kind of prostitution ring and that the shooter was a member of the NYPD—Bill Phillips, a former Third Division plainclothes detective. Phillips was later tried, convicted, and sentenced to life in prison for the crime.

Also in late 1968, an address book was found inside a telephone booth and then turned over to a newspaper reporter. A front-page story with the names and addresses of bars and restaurants that were listed in the address book and that had given payoff money to the police appeared in the next day's paper—"proof" there had been a "pad." (*Pad* was the slang for *payoff*. Those using police vernacular would refer to this guy or that place being "on the pad.")

When the story broke, a duty captain was visiting the precinct and engaged the desk lieutenant in conversation regarding the address book. Half jokingly, he said to the lieutenant, "Look here, it says this restaurant paid a hundred dollars, yet the son of a bitch told us he was only getting fifty from that place. The lying bastard was holding out!"

Sitting there at the telephone switchboard and listening to the conversation, I was amused and yet a bit shocked at the casualness of the captain's conversation. But I must admit I was not surprised. The whole idea of pads and payoffs just seemed part of the everyday culture of the

NYPD, and even a young, impressionable police trainee was privy to such conversations.

A few years later, the hearings of the Knapp Commission on police corruption were televised. The hearings featured numerous NYPD personalities, including the famous Frank Serpico. The plainclothes officers of the Third Division were also featured prominently in these hearings.

The net effect of the Knapp Commission changed the NYPD forever, and for the good. By and large, the recommendations of the commission were the right ones, including the notion of paying police officers better salaries and encouraging the education of young police officers. However, there was one particular downside to the recommendations. It made sense to recommend the elimination of plainclothes officers and the corruption they bred by establishing a centralized unit for narcotics and vice enforcement called the Organized Crime Control Bureau. But the unintended consequence of this recommendation was that local police officers were discouraged from enforcing narcotics, gambling, and other quality-of-life violations. This led to troubling situations where open-air drug markets flourished because, in order to prevent police corruption, uniformed police officers were strongly discouraged from making narcotics arrests. The irony is that average citizens, particularly those in tough neighborhoods, who observed open-air drug dealing going on even as police car after police car drove by, reached the understandable conclusion that the cops were being paid off to look the other way. Over the next twenty years, I must have heard that complaint at community meetings at least a hundred times.

The commission's recommendation to remove the NYPD from regulatory enforcement of the ABC (Alcohol Beverage Control) laws was aimed at ending the corruption potential from licensed and unlicensed premises. However, the unintended consequence of this allowed licensed and unlicensed premises to run amok and engage in more serious criminal violations, such as assaults, shootings, and drug dealing. This seemed to me not the best way to run a police department. Because we were fearful of corruption, we prohibited and discouraged police officers from engaging in activities at which they could be corrupted; yet we still had periodic episodes of corruption. The point is that police departments should never shy away from enforcing the law due to a fear of corruption. The bottom line is that you enforce the law, and if there is a corruption problem, you deal with the corruption problem. Years later, this would become one of the central tenets of Commissioner Bill Bratton's administration.

What I most remember of these early days was the atmosphere of the time, the zeitgeist of the late 1960s. The Vietnam War was in full bloom and with it the antiwar protests in every major city, especially New York City. In April 1968, Martin Luther King was killed, which resulted in civil unrest in most major cities across the United States. Months later, Bobby Kennedy was also killed.

The protests and civil unrest preoccupied the NYPD to the detriment of ordinary policing. It was policing by crisis. Hundreds or thousands of police could be handling antiwar protests in Midtown Manhattan, then head up to deal with the unrest and riots at Columbia University, and then later head to riots in the various African American neighborhoods in the city. There was a real feeling that Armageddon was at hand.

The Police Academy

Civil unrest and protests affected not only the ordinary policing of the neighborhoods but also training at the police academy. In February 1969, I was transferred from the 17th Precinct to the police academy to begin my six months of training to become a full-fledged NYPD police officer. The academy didn't have the feel of a regular school or college. Rather, it looked and felt more like a military boot camp mobilizing for war. Thousands of officers were going through the training, and the facility's capacity was always an issue. Incredibly, the academy operated seven days a week, from 6:00 A.M. to midnight. It was not uncommon to be doing calisthenics on the gym floor at 11:00 on a Saturday night or to be in the classroom at 9:00 on a Sunday night. The overcrowding had a huge, negative impact on the quality of the training. And the quality of the training was dramatically reduced by the protests going on out on the streets. I often found myself on the back of a flatbed truck delivering wooden police barricades to a disturbance on a college campus or to a demonstration in Midtown, as opposed to listening to a lecture in the classroom. But we still finished our police academy training on time, even if we were not fully prepared.

The irregular hours of the academy, while not good for training, were better for me, personally, because I could work my side job of driving a Coca-Cola truck to augment my salary. With my brother still in high school and rent to be paid, I needed both jobs. Unfortunately, the Coca-Cola job impinged on my class work and my participation in class. I often found myself dozing off from lack of sleep. At the end of the six months of training, my academic instructor, Sergeant Corrigan, made note of my less-than-stellar participation in the classroom as he gave a verbal evaluation of each student's career potential. When he reached me, he stated, "Timoney, you will amount to nothing because you're lazy and you keep falling asleep in class." I was too tired to tell him about my Coca-Cola job.

The biggest lesson for me from my academy days was not what I learned in the classroom but what I observed in and around the academy. When the civil unrest broke out after Martin Luther King's assassination, the NYPD—like a lot of other police departments across the country—hired a large number of new police officers. They were immediately assigned to the streets after meeting the bare minimum qualification for firearms proficiency: they were required to shoot fifty rounds of ammunition.

These officers received no other training, and so when things quieted down in the winter of 1968–69, these officers were sent to the police academy for their formal training. Some of them had been involved in gunfights over the past nine months, and others had made great arrests and had been involved in other hair-raising experiences. In other words, many of these officers were seasoned "vets"—not exactly prime candidates for instruction at the academy. To make matters worse, if that was possible, most of these officers finished their probationary period within their first or second month of the academy. That meant that no matter what they did or refused to do, the police department had little recourse. The officers were off probation and had job security, which the department could not take away, except in the case of those caught committing a very serious violation of department rules and procedures or a criminal act.

The massive hiring of thousands of police officers in 1968 and 1969 provides one of the most valuable lessons for any police chief or mayor contemplating such an action (most cities across the United States have engaged in such practices over the past few decades, with similar results). While emergency hiring may work in the short run, bypassing thorough background checks and providing inadequate training can mean only trouble in the long term.

The new hires can be valuable in the short term—putting down riots, stopping an awful crime wave—but eventually the police officers who have slipped through the cracks will come back to haunt the department. Within a few years, many of officers from the 1968 and 1969 classes got into trouble. Some, including a classmate of mine, were arrested for a variety of crimes—ranging from drug dealing and ripping off drug dealers to murder. As these cases garnered headlines, police administrators and politicians openly questioned the fitness of the members of the classes of 1968 and 1969. The cops responded with typical gallows humor by creating T-shirts emblazoned with I SURVIVED THE CLASS OF 68/69 or I AM A PROUD GRADUATE OF THE 68/69 CLASS. While the T-shirts may have been funny, their reference was anything but.

2

The South Bronx

Hey, kid, to get a locker here it's gonna cost you five dollars.
—*"HOLLYWOOD" SID CERILE, POLICE OFFICER*

In July 1969, I turned twenty-one years of age, was sworn in as a full-fledged police officer, and was assigned to the 44th Precinct in the Highbridge section of the South Bronx. I had actually gone to Cardinal Hayes High School in that part of the Bronx, so I was somewhat familiar with the neighborhood. I also lived just across the Harlem River in Washington Heights, so I could see my apartment building from the front steps of the 44th Precinct Station House. The precinct house, located on Sedgwick Avenue, which ran along the Harlem River on the Bronx side, was affectionately referred to as "Sedgwick by the Sea," a sobriquet replaced in 1975 by the more damning name, the "Murder House," after a prisoner was beaten to death inside a holding cell.

The 44th Precinct was one of eleven precincts in the borough of the Bronx (there are now twelve). While New York City is composed of five boroughs—the Bronx, Brooklyn, Queens, Staten Island, and Manhattan—the NYPD is made up of seven police boroughs, with Manhattan and Brooklyn both divided into "North" and "South" boroughs. The borough commander is a two-star assistant chief, with a one-star deputy chief as his executive officer.

The 44th Precinct covered a large land area, stretching from 149th

Street in the south to Burnside Avenue (or 180th Street) in the north, and from the Harlem River to the Grand Concourse. In 1969, it was a neighborhood in transition, as poorer residents began to move into the area, replacing the largely Jewish population along the Grand Concourse. Within a few short years the transition was almost complete. The 44th Precinct went from a "sleeper" house to one of the busiest precincts in the city, and by the mid- to late seventies it was the busiest.

I arrived in the 44th Precinct in mid-July 1969 at the height of the mayoral campaign. Mayor John Lindsay was running for reelection against the Republican John Marchi from Staten Island. During the 1960s, the issue of crime and social order had become the number one concern nationally. It had also become a huge issue locally, and Marchi was running on a law-and-order platform. Clearly, Mayor Lindsay felt vulnerable in this area and believed it threatened his reelection, which would have brought to a halt his ultimate intention of running for president. As a result, he sent a clear message to the NYPD as to how it could contribute to his reelection campaign: make arrests, and lots of them—especially narcotics arrests.

Traditionally, a police officer could earn a day off on the books as a result of a good arrest—for example, an armed robbery of a liquor store or a burglary arrest. However, during the mayoral campaign, the criteria for a good arrest/earned day off became watered down. I learned this from my two childhood friends, Pete Dunne and Tommy Hyland, who had been assigned to the 44th Precinct a few months prior to my arrival. "Timoney, you're not going to believe this. They're giving us a day off for bullshit narcotics arrests," bragged Tommy, who was only ten months out of the police academy but carried himself as if he were a ten-year veteran. "As a matter of fact, they'll give you four hours off if you bring in an asshole with a hypo!" It seemed incredible to me, but who was I to argue? So I jumped on the gravy train and accumulated as many days as I could in my "time bank."

Once the mayor was reelected, the generosity ceased and the qualifying standards were raised once again. By the early 1970s, police managers began to realize that giving police officers time off for doing their job was bizarre and wasteful. The qualifications for earned time off were then restricted to special categories like those who were named Officer of the Month or individuals who had performed some genuinely heroic act. Nonetheless, I had managed over the prior three years to accumulate a great deal of earned time on the books. In fact, I had so much time accumulated, I was almost able to take off the entire summer that year.

I must admit that earning a day off for a good arrest did create an incentive above and beyond the call of duty. Sometimes, you took unnecessary risks to get to the scene first. One day, I was filling in for Mel Pincus, whose partner was Tom Fitzgerald. Pincus was a tall, good-looking Jewish guy who looked Irish. Fitzgerald was a five-foot-nine Irish guy with a rotund figure who looked Jewish. In fact, the old Jewish residents on the Grand Concourse would refer to Fitzgerald as Officer Pincus and vice versa.

While on routine patrol, Fitzgerald and I were directed to an address on Woodycrest Avenue regarding "shots fired" on the roof of an apartment building. The buildings along Woodycrest were generally five- or six-story walk-ups. We raced to the location. I was the driver, and my heart was pounding in anticipation of my pending "gun collar." Before the police car had even come to a stop, I jumped out, ran into the building, ran up six flights of stairs, and emerged onto the rooftop by myself. After a cursory search, I found nothing. I then started to catch my breath as Tommy Fitzgerald emerged onto the rooftop, holding out the keys to the police car. He said, "Hey, kid. This is the South Bronx. You leave the keys in the car, when you come back, there's no car. Oh, and by the way, there's an elevator in the building. Look at you! You're huffing and puffing. What if there had been somebody on the roof? What the hell could you have done in your condition? Wait for your partner, asshole."

Deadly Stereotypes

During my first year in the 44th Precinct, I learned another lesson: stereotypes can fuel crime. The predominantly Jewish area of the 44th included the Grand Concourse and its surrounding streets. By 1970, the Jews who remained there were largely elderly, many of them Holocaust survivors. Unfortunately, young thugs in the area believed that "the old Jews had lots of money." For a three- or four-year period, a number of these elderly Jews were the victims of nasty crimes, including push-in robberies, where the elderly person would be followed to his door and then pushed into his apartment, where he was then robbed and sometimes gratuitously assaulted, especially if he said he had no money. As a detective explained, "One group of thugs used to remove the shoes of their elderly victims because it was a known fact that is where they hid their money."

The borough commander of the Bronx at the time was a two-star chief who happened to be Jewish. He devised a Borough Robbery Report mimeograph form that all reporting officers had to complete, in addition to the regular crime report, whenever a robbery was committed. The Borough Robbery Report asked for the age, race, and, more important, the religious identity of the victim. To the best of my knowledge, nobody ever asked why we were required to fill out the additional borough report. We were cops and did what we were told.

The rationale behind the Borough Robbery Report became clear one Saturday morning while I was walking my assigned foot beat along 170th Street. I received a call from the desk officer of the precinct directing me to report to the borough headquarters, which was located on the second floor of the 46th Precinct, just north of the 44th. When I arrived, I joined a group of more than a half dozen young officers who had come from the other precincts in the borough. We were there to meet with the borough commander—a two-star chief! This was unusual, to say the least.

The borough commander instructed us to go through our precincts' Borough Robbery Reports and compile a chart, by religion, of the victims of the robberies. Once I finished the chart for the 44th Precinct, the numbers spoke for themselves: Jews had made up a disproportionate share of all robbery victims for the prior three years. From speaking with the other young officers, it was my sense that all of the precincts with significant elderly Jewish populations were similar. Once we finished, we were directed to return to our various precincts. Nothing more was said. Nothing more needed to be said. It was apparent that the Jewish two-star chief was just trying to confirm his suspicion that the old Jews around the Grand Concourse neighborhoods were disproportionately the victims of certain violent crimes.

Two years later, I was assigned to the 44th Precinct Anti-Crime Unit. This was a select group of officers in civilian clothes assigned to make robbery arrests on the streets of the South Bronx. While I was in this unit, the borough chief's suspicions were corroborated. Sometimes after we made a robbery arrest, while debriefing the prisoner, we would ask him, out of curiosity, why he had committed the crime. At times these young men would be quite honest in their rationale. The reason they targeted their victim was because he/she was Jewish and "you know the Jews have money!"

Another lesson I learned while patrolling the South Bronx was just how powerful individual police officers are and how they often don't even realize it. As a young police officer in 1969, like other young officers in the city, I was given the less desirable assignments: watching over a DOA (dead on arrival), taking an emotionally disturbed person—an EDP—to the hospital, or guarding the broken window of a store that had been burgled. Every once in a while, on the day or evening shifts, I would get to ride in a car with a partner, and it was like being a "real cop."

However, due to personnel shortages on the overnight shift (midnight to 8:00 A.M.), I almost always got to ride in a police car with a partner. After a few months of riding on the late shift, a few things became apparent. First, after about 1:00 A.M., just one hour into the shift, the radio went dead. There were very few calls for service, and thus the next seven hours were often boring, with nothing to do. Idle hands are the devil's handiwork, my mother used to tell us. Second, one night I was riding with another young officer (he was probably the same age as me, twenty-one). Sometime during the shift he turned to me and said, "Can you believe this? Here we are, just the two of us, and WE ARE IN CHARGE. Jesus!" It was true. While there was a sergeant working with us, we rarely saw him or knew where he was at any given moment. Thus, two young men, still wet behind the ears, were in charge of a rather large geographical area. We could take a life or make an arrest or just make someone's life miserable. What power!

This notion of the power of the officers working the graveyard shift took on more sinister and damaging implications as the NYPD moved to the practice of "steady tours" of duty. As I mentioned earlier, when I first entered the NYPD, police officers assigned to police precincts worked rotating shifts, three in all, around the clock, each week a different shift. Thus, an officer never became "too comfortable" in any one shift. Clearly, however, working weekly rotating shifts was difficult, and some officers would take almost a week to recover from the graveyard shift.

In the mid-1970s, police human resources experts began to make arguments for "steady shifts," particularly in reference to the graveyard shift. The NYPD responded by creating a "steady late shift" (graveyard shift), and a second rotating shift for 8:00 A.M. to 4:00 P.M. and four P.M. to midnight. In other words, a police officer would work one week of 8:00 A.M. to 4:00 P.M., followed by a week of 4:00 P.M. to midnight. These new working "charts" seemed to please most. Now you had individuals who worked the graveyard shift because they chose to.

However, the unintended consequences of a good idea were realized some years later as scandal after scandal erupted within the NYPD. The vast majority of times these scandals involved officers working the steady graveyard shifts. Not only did these officers have the power to do good, they also had the power to do bad. And there was plenty of time to do either, since the police radio became quiet after 1:00 or 2:00 A.M. Additionally, there was less supervision on these shifts. While sergeants and sometimes a lieutenant were assigned to these shifts, it was very unlikely that a police officer would run across a captain or other high-ranking official at 3:00 in the morning. At 3:00 in the afternoon it was, however, always possible to encounter a high-ranking boss, even one from another precinct or headquarters unit.

With this power and lack of supervision, some of the officers on the graveyard shift began to fall into cliques. Often, they seemed to develop a *Lord of the Flies* mentality with their own mores and code of conduct, with informal leaders and followers. It sometimes appeared to me that these officers even looked "different" from the regular officers who worked during the daytime hours. They seemed pale and tired, either from working their second job during the daylight hours or, more likely, from spending hours sitting in a courtroom waiting for their case from the previous night to be called.

Some years later, in the mid-1980s, police human resources began to argue for "steady shifts" for all shifts. Thus, a police officer would work steady 8:00 A.M. to 4:00 P.M., or 4:00 P.M. to midnight, or midnight to 8:00 A.M. Human resources argued that such a system would be beneficial. Productivity would increase. Morale would increase. Sick time would go down. These arguments were bought hook, line, and sinker, and the "steady shifts" were implemented.

A few years later, in 1990, Inspector Mike Julian, assigned to the Research and Planning Division, conducted a short study on the benefits of these shifts. None of the supposed benefits was evident. In fact, it could be argued that the direct opposite happened. Productivity, in terms of arrests, went down. You started to find police officers who were scheduled to get off work at 4:00 P.M. going home to watch their children while their wives went to work at night. Stories were legend of police officers not getting "involved" in anything near the end of their shift (from about 2:00 P.M. on) for fear they would get "stuck" with an arrest that would interfere with their babysitting responsibilities. Other police officers found second jobs that they worked prior to coming in for the 4:00 P.M. to midnight shift. And so it went. In some instances, the police job became the "second job."

The most detrimental effect of the "steady shifts" was a loss of camaraderie. Officers on one shift literally did not know officers who worked an opposite shift. In addition, there was a loss of familiarity with the ways in which the character of a specific geographical area could vary depending on the time of day or the day of the week.

Take, for example, the 47th Precinct. This was a mainly residential precinct with a large working and middle-class African American population. There was also an Irish section in the northwest part of the precinct called Woodlawn. During the day, the precinct was a typical quiet residential area. However, at night, when people were home from work, it looked quite different. Then on the weekends, there were bars and clubs that were very active in the evening and early-morning hours. Finally, two large hospitals brought outsiders into the area either as patients or visitors. At night, the air was permeated by the sound of ambulance sirens as they raced to and from the hospital carrying shooting and stabbing victims. Depending on the time of day or the day of the week, an officer might find himself investigating a stolen trash can cover or questioning a person with multiple gunshot wounds in the hospital emergency room.

Years later, in 1994, when I was the chief of department, I was conducting roll call at the 47th Precinct. The difficulty with the steady shift was well illustrated when a very young officer informed me that he had been out of the police academy for only one year and was working a steady shift of 8:00 A.M. to 4:00 P.M., with weekends off. There were two immediate problems with this. First, the notion of a new police officer working banker's hours seemed incredible to me. In the past, a police officer would have had to have ten years under his belt before ever being considered for a steady day shift. Second, and more important, when I asked the police officer if he had ever been in the precinct at 11:00 P.M. on a Friday or Saturday night, he replied that he had not. That was an eye-opener. Here we had a police officer whose training was one dimensional. He knew only how to deal with a quiet residential precinct; his most serious encounter during the course of a shift was to issue tickets to parked cars for not obeying the alternate side parking regulations so the sanitation workers could clean the streets.

The Strike

In January 1971, a court ruled against the police union, the Patrolmen's Benevolent Association (PBA), in a case regarding pay and work conditions. The ruling led to an immediate wildcat strike that began in the 43rd Precinct and spread to other precincts in the Bronx and then to all of the precincts throughout the city. Police officers refused to go out on the streets for a full five days. Normally, such an action might have been effective in persuading the city to come to the bargaining table and do the right thing. Unfortunately, this strike was one of the great lessons of all time for most police officers. When things that can go wrong do go wrong, it is referred to as Murphy's Law. In the case of this police strike, another law was at work—"O'Toole's Law"—which stated that Murphy was an optimist!

A few things made the 1971 strike a complete disaster and affected the way police officers would react in future labor disputes, all to the benefit of the city. First, the PBA is one of five police unions, and it represents only uniformed police officers. Another union represents detectives; another, sergeants; another, lieutenants; and another, captains and those with higher ranks. Thus, the additional four unions' membership was available to fill in for the striking police officers. Second, uniformed police officers who were still on probation, over a thousand in all, did not have to take part in the strike or job action since they could have and would have been fired. Third, there were some police officers (a few very brave officers) whose conscience did not allow them to take part in the job action.

When we began the job action, the city reacted immediately and put all the detectives, sergeants, lieutenants, and nonparticipating police officers on twelve-hour shifts, with no days off. Under normal conditions, the 44th Precinct put on the streets about ten two-officer cars, a few foot beats, and a few special posts. During the strike, they were able to deploy about twelve sector cars and fill all the foot patrols and special posts, which meant more officers than normal were working the streets. At the same time, the temperature for that week never went above twenty degrees. Not only was there no crime, there were no people on the streets to "miss" their regular police officers.

The job action lasted five days, and we returned to work with our tails between our collective legs. But the city was not finished with us. The city invoked the New York State Taylor Law, which forbids police officers from striking. We responded that it hadn't really been a strike, since all officers had shown up for work, stood roll call, and then merely stayed in their station houses during their shifts. The city's position that it was a strike was upheld, and we were docked two days' pay for every day we did not hit the streets. For police officers, most of whom live payday to payday, it was a hard, expensive lesson that would affect us the rest of our time on the job. For me, it was particularly hard. I was to be married a few weeks later to Noreen Carroll, whose father was a sergeant in the 28th Precinct in Harlem.

In addition to loosing two weeks' pay, the job action caused huge friction between those officers who, out of conscience, refused to participate and those who did. There was some ugliness and some vandalism to the conscientious officers' lockers. That ugliness remained my most significant memory and proved quite valuable when I had to handle another police "job action" in 1986, when I was the commander of the 5th Precinct in Chinatown.

Stopping the Dougie Walshes

In 1971, Patrick Murphy, the new reform police commissioner, put together a group of top police executives that included his deputy commissioner for community affairs, Benjamin Ward. The group was asked to study the issue of police use of deadly physical force, specifically when police officers discharge their weapons in the line of duty. Police shootings were the matches that lit the fuses of much of the civil unrest that occurred in city after city throughout the United States in the 1960s and early 1970s. The committee came up with a series of recommendations, which were then put into a police directive.

The directive set up the procedures for how and who would conduct an investigation whenever a police officer discharged his weapon, regardless of whether or not he wounded/killed someone, and whether or not it was intentional or accidental. The directive also listed certain situations in which an officer was forbidden from discharging his weapon. The most controversial of these new guidelines prohibited a police officer from "discharging his weapon at or from a moving vehicle, unless the occupants of the other vehicle are using deadly physical force against the officer or another person, by means other than the vehicle." In other words, a police officer could not shoot at a vehicle that was coming toward him unless the occupants of the vehicle were using deadly physical force (shooting at the officer). If the officer felt his life was in danger from the approaching car, then he should get out of the way!

While the policy was crafted and ready to go, it was never implemented for fear of a backlash from the police union. Into the early 1970s, police officers were being gunned down in the streets on an almost regular basis. Therefore, the union would have had little problem rallying the public, press, and politicians to support their cause. Six years earlier, the police union had roundly defeated a voter referendum on the establishment of a civilian complaint review board.

It is important to note that there is never a good time to implement a controversial policy. However, implementing controversial policies after a controversy is sure to generate more controversy.

In August 1972, an eleven-year-old African American boy was shot and killed by an NYPD officer while he was fleeing a stolen car in Staten Island. The media ran with the story, and as a result, racial tensions reached a boiling point. The police commissioner directed Ben Ward to go to Staten Island to gauge the temperature of the community. Ward spent two days listening to and speaking with community residents and leaders, assuring them that an appropriate investigation would follow.

In 1985, while discussing the issue of police shootings with Ward, who was now police commissioner, he informed me that upon his return to headquarters from those two days in Staten Island, he reported his findings to the police commissioner and recommended the implementation of the deadly physical force policy that had been developed a year prior. The police commissioner, looking to relieve the public pressure, concurred. In less than two weeks, the policy was announced to the public, and it went a long way to assuage the concerns of the black community. Meanwhile, the police union objected strenuously, feeling that the NYPD had caved in to community pressure and, as a result, was jeopardizing the ability of police officers to defend themselves. They also feared that the top brass had "rushed through" the creation of a radical policy in the days following the shooting of the eleven-year-old boy.

The irony was that the policy had actually been developed in 1971, a full year prior to the shooting. But because the top brass feared that then was not the right time to institute the policy, they sat on it, waiting for the right time to arrive. There is almost never a right time to institute radical policy change: you just institute it. However, there can always be a wrong time—such as immediately following the shooting of an eleven-year-old boy. In situations like that, people are invariably going to allow their own ideas and prejudices to influence their opinion of the change.

The development and implementation of the deadly physical force policy has two final lessons: First, if you've taken the time to study and discuss a new, radical policy change then decide not to implement it, that needs to be explained. Second, when you implement radical policy change without explanation and rationale, do not be surprised if the recipients of that information (police officers, the public, and the press) all come to entirely different conclusions concerning that policy.

Many in the black community felt that the policy would help reduce the number of African Americans killed by police; many in the white community felt that the police department was succumbing to community pressure and jeopardizing the safety of its officers. The media, depending upon their political leaning, came up with their own understanding of the policy.

The "don't shoot at a vehicle" part of the new directive was discussed ad nauseam among the officers in the 44th Precinct. The one thing we all agreed upon was that the cause of the policy was Dougie Walsh. Dougie had a habit of shooting at cars that drove toward him. Also at cars that drove away from him. What we didn't realize is that every precinct in the city had a Dougie Walsh who shot at cars on a pretty regular basis.

The other much-discussed part of the directive dealt with forbidding officers to shoot at fleeing felons. The wisdom of this particular section was upheld in 1985 when the Supreme Court of the United States, in the landmark decision *Garner v. Tennessee*, forbade shooting at unarmed fleeing felons. The court justices used the NYPD policy as part of their legal rationale.

I did not appreciate how effective the policy was until the early 1980s, when I was assigned as a young lieutenant to the Chief of Operations Office at police headquarters. In 1983, there was a series of congressional hearings on police brutality regarding deadly shootings by members of the NYPD. The hearings were racially charged, and my boss, the chief of operations, asked me to do some research on the recent history of police shootings in the city. When I looked at the numbers, they were startling, especially the effect of the deadly physical force directive that was sent out in August 1972.

In 1971, the last year before the firearms directive was issued, the NYPD recorded more than eight hundred incidents of a police officer discharging his weapon, whether a person was wounded/killed or not, whether the discharge was intentional or accidental. Ninety to one hundred people were killed as a result of police bullets.

The firearms discharges for the first eight months of 1972 (about two-thirds of the year) look similar to the numbers for 1971. However, when you track the firearms discharge numbers for the last four months of 1972 (after the directive was implemented), there is an immediate and dramatic decline of somewhere around 40 percent. For 1973, the first full year of the firearms directive, overall shootings were reduced to between five hundred and six hundred, with about sixty-six civilians killed as a result.

Over the next thirty-five years, the shooting numbers continued to decline to the point where the number of civilians killed by police officers is around 12 per year and the number of overall shootings has dropped to fewer than 150. The bottom line is that when an organization produces a good, sound policy on a critical matter—in this case, deadly physical force—and combines the policy with other changes such as training, the results can be remarkable.

I am sure there are some who would argue that the restrictive shooting policy implemented by the NYPD was specific to New York City and that the policy may not work in other police departments. Some years later, I would get to test that theory as the commissioner of the Philadelphia Police Department and later still as the chief of the Miami Police Department. The policy worked as intended; it reduced police shootings and killings dramatically.

Fourth Platoon

When the new shooting policy hit the streets, I was a member of the 44th Precinct's Fourth Platoon. The Fourth Platoon was started two years earlier as an effort to address the increase in violent crime in the late 1960s and early 1970s. Up until that point, police officers worked three rotating platoons: 8:00 A.M. to 4:00 P.M., 4:00 P.M. to midnight, and midnight to 8:00 A.M. (the "late tour"). There were equal numbers of officers in all three platoons, so the same number of officers were on at 2:00 in the afternoon as were on at 2:00 in the morning, even though the workload and demand for police service was completely different at those two times.

The Fourth Platoon consisted of about forty volunteers from the three rotating shifts. This platoon worked from 6:00 P.M. to 2:00 A.M., as an overlap shift, to get additional police officers on the street during the peak crime hours. On the first day of the Fourth Platoon, TV cameras showed up at precincts throughout the city to film the roll calls to great fanfare and public interest. The Fourth Platoon was going to be the silver bullet that drove down crime and assuaged people's fears. How many times over the next thirty years did I participate in unveiling new anticrime initiatives that were hailed as the silver bullet to end this or start that? The reality is that in policing there is no silver bullet. What is required to reduce crime is hard work and creative thinking.

In any event, after joining the Fourth Platoon it became clear to me that while we looked very good in uniform out on the streets, I was not so sure we were very effective as "crime fighters." Twenty to thirty of us would attend roll call, get our assignments, and then drive our private cars to our foot beat, sometimes as far as a mile away from the precinct. (By the way, riding in a private vehicle while in uniform was a violation of the NYPD's policy and procedures that everyone engaged in.) There were no handheld, portable radios at that time, so you walked your beat and checked in with the station once an hour using the police call box at your post. For example, I was given patrol post 27, with a ten ring and a 2100 meal. That meant I walked 170th Street from Jerome Avenue to the Grand Concourse. I would ring the station house at ten past every hour. And at nine o'clock (2100 hours, military time), I would take a meal. You were expected to be on your post for the entire eight hours (except during the meal period). However, your supervising sergeant would let you know when he would be coming around to see you. He would say, "Timoney, I'll give you a 'see' at 8:30 P.M., so you had better be on your post."

Since there were no portable radios, the only crime you could fight was what you saw in front of you or what a resident of the neighborhood brought to your attention. I often found myself noticing three or four police cars (which were equipped with radios) speeding past with sirens blaring and lights flashing, responding to a robbery in progress at, say, 169th Street and Walton Avenue, one block from my post. But it could have been thirty blocks since there was no communication. Nonetheless, the appearance of police officers in uniform on foot had a greatly reassuring effect on the general public.

The lack of portable radios and the danger that entailed became quite evident in 1970 and 1971 when a number of police officers were shot and killed by members of the Black Liberation Army (BLA). The BLA was determined to overthrow the government of the United States and used the killing of police officers as a means to its end. As a result of these shootings, the police department rushed to acquire portable, handheld radios, and within a year or so they became part of our daily equipment. Although the 44th Precinct received a supply of portable radios, we never had enough to go around. The allocation of the radios was not based on priority or danger, but rather the idiosyncratic nature of the various police officers. Those who were lazy and didn't want to be bothered refused the radios for fear of being assigned "jobs" during the course of their eight-hour shifts. The younger officers, me included, were eager to get the portable radios so that we could fight crime, not just on our beat but on the adjoining beat as well.

For management, portable radios had a downside, since they compromised beat integrity. Police officers could hear what was going on around their beat and away from their beat. This created in some the temptation to leave their beat for greener pastures, where they felt they could make an arrest. If 170th Street was quiet after 9:00 P.M. when the stores closed, an officer could always drift over to 167th or 168th

Street to make a narcotics arrest. In some cases, officers became really creative by using their private cars to drive to locations, sometimes ten or fifteen blocks from their beat, to answer a call in progress. Beat integrity went to hell in a handbasket. But that was the upside for police officers like me; we were able to use a high number of arrests to get into the newly established Anti-Crime Units and work in plainclothes.

The Knapp Commission

One of the advantages of working the Fourth Platoon was that it allowed me to go to school during the daytime. Another unintended advantage was that I was able to watch the live television coverage of the Knapp Commission hearings on police corruption. Witness after witness testified to the ubiquitous corruption within the NYPD. The stories were gripping, but the picture they created was ugly. After watching the hearings during the day, my partners and I would patrol the streets of the South Bronx at night, often hearing derogatory comments and sometimes outright cursing about the NYPD and its officers. It was not a good feeling, and it certainly was a hard lesson—the notion that when a few cops screw up, everybody pays. One night, one of the veteran sergeants, Nick Sforza, was conducting roll call, and he tried to explain to us what we could expect in terms of the public's attitude and demeanor as we patrolled the streets. He told us we would be angry and would want to strike out at the civilians, but he explained that we had to take it. It was the nature of the business. We had to have thick skin. To prove his point, he told us that when a lawyer or a doctor screws up, you never hear the public condemning the entire profession and those within it. The idea that everyone pays for the mistakes of the few is one I was to hear repeated far too often over the next thirty-plus years of my career.

I've heard all sorts of rationalizations and justifications trying to explain the phenomenon. One long-time cop explained to me, "You see, kid, we're always in the business of telling people to their face when they've done wrong. Whether it's some junkie we arrest for a burglary or some housewife we issue a citation to for rolling through a stop sign, there are lots of people with pent-up frustration and anger toward the cops. When they get the chance to vent, they do." I don't know if that is true or not, but it is as good as any other explanation I have heard.

One major gripe police officers had concerning the Knapp Commission was how it seemed to focus almost entirely on the police department, paying little attention to other parts of the criminal justice system that they knew to be just as corrupt. For example, in the late 1960s and early 1970s, lawyers roamed the halls of the Bronx Criminal Court at 161st Street and Third Avenue looking for clients. There seemed to be no rhyme or reason to the cases they took on, and there seemed to be no standard fees except the cold cash that happened to be in the defendant's pocket. It was not uncommon for a defense attorney to ask a judge for the postponement of a case because one of his witnesses, "Mr. Green" (that is, the money), hadn't arrived yet. The judges understood and acquiesced to these and other such requests.

One day I was standing outside the courtroom waiting for my case to be called on a gun arrest I had made a week earlier. The defendant's lawyer, who was probably the most famous of the hallway lawyers, was engaged in conversation with the defendant and his family on the other side of the corridor. Out of nowhere, the lawyer approached me and asked, "Patrolman Timoney, what time is it?" I replied sarcastically, "What are you, nuts?" and indicated the large clock overhead. He just thanked me and returned to the family. Frank Gaffney, a veteran cop from the 43rd Precinct, came up to me and asked, "What did he want?" I told him he wanted to know what time it was, even though there was a huge clock right here. The veteran cop replied, "You've just been set up. He's gone back over and told the family that he has spoken to you, that the fix is in, but it will require another hundred dollars to pay Timoney." I replied, shocked, "You gotta be fucking kidding me." That was life in the criminal court of the South Bronx, and I am sure it existed in the other four county courtrooms in the city as well.

The Knapp Commission did make a series of recommendations that were solid, including more formal education of police officers. The commission also decried the poor wages police officers received and recommended increases, which all officers overwhelmingly endorsed. The pay issue was brought home to us one day at roll call. The Seventh

Division inspector stopped in to speak to us before we hit the street. He talked about the Knapp Commission's findings and recommendations and then got to the issue of the pay raise and said, almost matter-of-factly, "Listen, you guys, we're gonna be giving you better pay, so there's no need to steal."

The Knapp Commission hearings affected me directly when the Bronx district attorney, Burton Roberts, held a press conference. Roberts was a larger-than-life figure with a boundless ego; he did not suffer fools lightly. As the police department was being bashed day after day in the press, Roberts decided to hold a press conference to show that in the Bronx, at least, there were good cops who did not succumb to theft and bribery. He decided to call the press conference with Bronx police officers who had made bribery arrests the prior year. Two dozen police officers were assembled in a conference room, and I was one of them. The plan was for all of the officers to form a semicircle around the D.A. while he made his announcement and pontificated on how there were many brave and honest police officers in the Bronx. Before the conference, I figured out the best position to be in to get my mug on television, since I did not have a speaking part (our role was that of blue potted plants, a role I would play on numerous occasions throughout my career). I maneuvered for a position next to and slightly behind the D.A. while the officers took their positions. When I gathered all of my friends that night to watch the press conference on TV, there was a great shot of the D.A. with my left hand slightly to the right of his face. As the camera zoomed out to get a panoramic view of all those assembled, it panned to the left and showed all of the fine officers to my right, missing Patrolman Timoney, who stood to the right of the D.A. That was my first appearance on television. As the years passed, I would manage to get other parts of my body in the picture and even every once in a while have a speaking part.

Plainclothes in Anti-Crime

The Anti-Crime Units were regular patrol officers who were assigned to wear plainclothes within the precinct. Their main job was to deal with crime, specifically violent crime and burglaries. There was a quid pro quo deal between the anticrime officers and the police department. We got to work in plainclothes and use our private cars, and the police department had to supply only the gas At the time, I was driving a 1966 blue Volkswagen Beetle with a sunroof and a rotted floor in back. You could actually see the ground under the car as it was moving. On more than one occasion I had to put prisoners in the back with the admonition to keep their feet raised so that they didn't fall through the floor.

My two partners in the Anti-Crime Unit were Joe Rooney and Richie Sabol. Sabol was the senior man on the team and was considered by most to be one of the top and toughest cops in the 44th. He was a veteran of fifteen years, having spent seven of those as a cop in Yonkers before joining the NYPD. Sabol had entered the Marine Corps at age seventeen and served a two-year stint during the Korean War. He had an easy-to-understand policing philosophy: "Our job is to protect the most vulnerable: the very young and the very old." Joe Rooney was a blond-haired, blue-eyed cop with less time than I had on the job. While I had spent my first two years as a police trainee, Joe served those years in Vietnam. He was a very good street cop with a bit of a temper. Fortunately, Sabol controlled the worst tendencies of both Rooney and me.

In 1973, my brother, Ciaran, entered the NYPD, and after six months he was assigned to the 44th Precinct. Ciaran's class was the first in the history of the NYPD to have a significant number of females who trained next to their male counterparts in preparation for all aspects of policing. Prior to this, women in the NYPD had been assigned to specialized units such as the Juvenile Aid Division or had performed matron duties like handling female prisoners. Now, women were to become full and equal partners with their male counterparts.

When Ciaran was assigned to the 44th, I was a little surprised; I had thought that there was an unwritten rule that brothers were not assigned to serve in the same precinct. There was the so-called Sullivan rule, based on the World War II military tragedy of the five Sullivan brothers who were assigned to the same ship and who were all killed when the ship sank. I should not have been surprised, though, because in the 44th at that time there were two other sets of brothers and a father and son who were both assigned to the 44th Precinct.

The rationale for the Sullivan rule became apparent to me shortly after Ciaran started work at the 44th. I was assigned to the Anti-Crime Unit with my partner Richie Sabol and we were on the lookout for robbers and other miscreants. I knew the patrol post where Ciaran and his partner were working. The radio had been quiet when all of a sudden Ciaran's partner got on the police radio hysterically screaming, "Officer needs assistance!" Since I didn't hear Ciaran's voice, I assumed the worst. I drove my Volkswagen like a maniac through the streets of the South Bronx, mounting sidewalks to get through traffic. I eventually arrived at the location: 1430 Grand Concourse. This address consisted of six seven-story buildings surrounding a huge courtyard. It was referred to derisively by the cops in the 44th as "jungle habitat." About a year earlier I had responded to this location only to have a burning mattress, heaved from the roof, barely miss my partner and me. "Airmail garbage! Incoming!"

When I entered the building where Ciaran and his partner needed the assistance, I found him on the second floor, as cool and calm as could be, with his prisoner handcuffed. When I asked him, "What the hell happened?" he just head nodded toward his partner, saying, "He panicked."

A few hours later, discussing the whole incident with my partner Richie, we concluded that the Sullivan rule, if it didn't exist, should be implemented and enforced. I had risked not only my life and Richie's life but also the lives of those pedestrians whom I almost ran over in my highly emotional state. In any police response to an officer needing assistance, the heartbeat will always increase, as will the tension and the desire to get to the location as quickly as possible. When it's your brother, the heart rate goes off the charts. The blood rushing to the head clouds your thinking, and the results can be disastrous.

Tommy Ryan

The most profound lesson I learned in my eight years in the 44th Precinct, and, in fact, probably in my entire career, related to an incident that took place while I was on vacation in Ireland in July 1975. Upon returning from vacation, I received a phone call from my plainclothes partner Richie Sabol, who was now a sergeant in Brooklyn. "Did you see the papers?" he asked. "Your friend Ryan's in trouble." While I obviously was not working the night of the Ryan incident, I learned enough about what took place from my fellow officers.

On the evening in question, two police officers were dispatched to an apartment building on Nelson Avenue in the Highbridge neighborhood regarding "men with guns." Upon arrival at the scene, the two officers confronted three men exiting the building; when they frisked them, they discovered the men were armed with illegal handguns. It was a very good arrest. Other units responded to "back up" the initial two officers, but when they arrived, the three bad guys were already in custody. Some of the responding officers were curious to see what apartment these three men had come from. The three arrestees were obviously reluctant to talk. Enter Officer Thomas Ryan.

Tommy Ryan was a friend of mine with whom I played football in the Bronx. Tommy, like me, was a police trainee; he was assigned to the 44th Precinct when I came through the door in 1969. When Tommy turned twenty-one and became a full-fledged police officer, he was assigned to the 41st Precinct (known as "Fort Apache") in the South Bronx. The 41st Precinct had a reputation as a "wild" precinct, and many of the officers assigned there tried to live up to that reputation. Tommy was no different. After a short time in the 41st, Tommy ran afoul of police brass and was transferred to a precinct in the North Bronx. He didn't last too long there before he again came to the attention of the police brass and was transferred once more, this time to the 44th Precinct. Tommy had come full circle.

Right around this time, after Richie Sabol was promoted to sergeant, I was back on a uniform post. One day I was summoned to the precinct commander's office and informed that Ryan had been assigned to the 44th Precinct. The commander knew Tommy and I were friends and asked me to work with him and to "look after him." I partnered with Tommy over the next few months on a semisteady basis. Tommy was a guy with a big heart, but he also had an unorthodox way of policing, which irritated many of the veterans to no end. He was a handful. And that's putting it mildly.

The night of the incident on Nelson Avenue, Tommy Ryan took one of the three prisoners back into the building to ascertain which apartment he had come from. Ryan took the prisoner to a top-floor apartment and had the guy stand in front of the door. Ryan then knocked on the door.

Inside the apartment were a man and a woman. The man had just been "ripped off" by the three other males who had been arrested fleeing the apartment building. The man inside the apartment looked out through the peephole, saw one of the men who had just robbed him standing there at the door, got a gun, and fired at the door. Officer Ryan, who was standing to the side, heard the shot and told the other officers nearby that the person inside was shooting at him. The officers forced their way into the apartment and arrested the man inside. Everything was fine up to that point. What happened next is not quite clear, but it goes something like this.

When the officers got inside the apartment, the man who had been shooting was roughed up and injured, but apparently not too seriously. The prisoner and the occupant of the apartment were taken from the apartment to the street, where the other two guys were still in handcuffs. All four were then transported by police vehicles to the 44th Precinct station house, about ten blocks away.

It was alleged that, while being transported to the station house, the man who shot through the door was punched about the body. It was further alleged that, over the next few hours in the station house, the male was again beaten by police officers, specifically by Tommy Ryan. The man was eventually taken to a local hospital, where he lay on a stretcher for a long period of time before he was taken into the emergency room. But it was too late. The male died from internal injuries as the doctor was working on him.

As you can imagine, a huge investigation was undertaken by the Bronx District Attorney's Office. Ryan was indicted for murder, and three other officers were indicted for assault. Eventually, the charges were dropped, correctly, against the three other officers. Ryan, however, fled the jurisdiction for a few years (allegedly to Ireland), then surrendered, stood trial, and was sent to jail.

The damage this case did to the esprit de corps of the 44th Precinct is not to be underestimated. Police officers testifying against other police officers . . . not a pretty sight. Police community relations were severely damaged, and there were protests by community members against the officers assigned to the "House of Murder."

In the immediate months after the initial incident, police officers were reluctant to discuss this case with other police officers. Nobody wanted to be involved. However, every once in a while, I would be assigned to partner with an officer who had been working that night and, though he may have gotten to the scene a little late, still had some insight into how this could have happened. The stories among the officers I spoke to were remarkably consistent in the details, and there was almost unanimous agreement on what went wrong, and who failed to do his job.

The sergeant who was working that fateful night was a joke. He fancied himself as "one of the boys" and always thought he was funny. In fact, some officers opined that, during the night of the arrest and beating, he found the whole thing somewhat amusing. The problem was that he failed to do his job. He was the one person who could have stopped the nonsense, but he didn't. While I never tried to make an excuse for Tommy Ryan's actions that night, he was not the only one at fault. The patrol sergeant failed—big time.

There are certain unwritten rules in the police world. While it is never excused, there is an understanding that sometimes, in the heat of battle or in a highly emotional situation, a police officer might loose his cool. However, it is up to other officers, especially those not directly involved in the situation, to intervene to stop any conduct that is counter to good policy and procedures. Sometimes it is a lot to ask of an officer to step in and break up these situations, but good cops do it all the time. When it comes to a sergeant, however, it is his job. He *must* stop the conduct forthwith. The sergeant working in the 44th the night in question failed miserably, and there is some anecdotal evidence that he, in fact, encouraged the misconduct. Yet he went unpunished, turning state's witness against his own officers.

What I learned from this event is something I continue to put into practice even today: *It is the responsibility of the sergeant to get police officers to do their job, and while the officers are doing their job, the sergeant must also make sure to keep them out of trouble!* Sometimes keeping the cops out of trouble might mean sergeants have to do unpopular things: confront the cops, including their informal leaders, and sometimes even impose discipline. In paramilitary organizations, discipline is the glue that holds everything together.

Layoffs: Cops Matter

In the spring of 1976, New York City was going through a profoundly difficult fiscal crisis. There were threats of layoffs for city workers, including police officers. To avert layoffs, the police union made an agreement with the city that all officers would work an additional five days over the following twelve months. The deal never made sense to me, since I did not understand how working an additional five days (the officers got to choose which days) over the next year would put money in the city's coffers. But I had a brother who faced a layoff and, being a good union man, I went with the program.

We began working the extra days almost immediately. In June of that year, the city did not get the assistance from the federal government that it had anticipated. One of the city tabloids ran a headline regarding President Gerald Ford's refusal to give money to the city—"Ford to City: Drop Dead." On June 30, 1976, the last day of the fiscal year, the city laid off five thousand police officers, my brother, Ciaran, included. However, the police officers who remained were still held to the bargain of working those additional five days, even though five thousand officers had been laid off. It was surreal.

It became more surreal for me about a month later when I was working one of my additional five days. I was with my partner when I spotted a kid, about seventeen, in a car that looked suspicious. As soon as I made eye contact with the kid, he took off, so I chased him with the police car, using lights and siren. After a few blocks, the kid dumped the car and took off on foot. I was quite fast at the time and actually liked foot chases. I chased the kid for about two blocks and eventually caught him. No harm, no foul. Or so I thought. A few police officers who came to back me up in the chase cursed me out: "Timoney, you jerk! What the hell are you doing? They laid off your brother, Ciaran, and here you are, working for nothing but a broken promise. And to make matters worse, you're making collars! You're an asshole!" My only retort, which probably seemed lame at the time, was that we were still police officers and we had to enforce the law even when it didn't seem to be in our own personal best interest.

The real eye-opener with the layoffs was the police union's reaction, or lack of action. Five thousand officers were laid off in one day, and the effete union could do little but protest. The lessons of the 1971 strike were fresh in every officer's mind, including those heading the union, and we were not about to pay any more fines under the Taylor Law.

There was an even greater lesson for me personally as a result of these layoffs—that you could lay off five thousand police officers and not expect there to be a dangerous downside. You really had to believe that the number of police officers does not matter. You had to subscribe to the theories coming out of the 1960s that there was little the police could do about crime because the police did not address the underlying causes of crime: poverty, racism, unemployment, homelessness. There was also the notion, since the Knapp Commission, that police officers should not deal with drugs, disorderly bars, and other so-called quality-of-life issues. Enforcement in these areas, it was assumed, only bred corruption; there was no nexus between low-level quality-of-life crimes and "real crime." Finally, there was the idea that low-level quality-of-life enforcement, especially in ethnic minority areas, was an example of being judgmental and unfair. Enforcing minor violations such as open-container drinking, illegal social clubs, and low-level drug use (marijuana) was wrong. The police needed to be more sensitive to other cultures rather than engaging in strict enforcement. And there was the recognition that enforcing low-level quality-of-life violations was labor intensive and therefore distracted police from real crime. For example, if a police officer made an arrest for violation of the marijuana law, it meant that that police officer had to come off the street and be stuck in the station house, and then in court, when he could have been more viable out in the street.

Only with a mind-set like this could five thousand police officers be laid off without a whimper. Worse still, in addition to the five thousand laid-off officers, another five thousand officers were lost through attrition over the next five years. By 1980, the NYPD had only about twenty-one thousand police officers on payroll, as opposed to the thirty-one thousand officers it had had in the mid-1970s. During all of this time, I do not remember any high-ranking police official speaking out against or resigning in protest of these layoffs. They, too, had bought into the idea that cops don't matter—that crime and disorder are beyond the ability of the police to affect.

With this thinking, is it any wonder that by the end of the decade New York City had the highest crime rate in its history? The police leadership failed to understand the direct connection between low-level, quality-of-life violations and serious crimes. They didn't understand that the failure to break up and arrest a small group rolling dice on the corner could prevent a homicide later that night when the loser of the game took back his money at gunpoint. They didn't understand that not dealing with unlicensed social clubs could lead to the deaths of eighty-seven people in a fire at one of those very clubs. They didn't understand that two seemingly harmless marijuana dealers could engage in a turf battle, guns blazing, at 5:30 P.M. in Bryant Park, killing a woman who was waiting for a bus to take her home after a hard day's work.

By the summer of 1977, I had spent a full eight years in the 44th Precinct and was ready for a change. I had worked very hard making hundreds of arrests while somehow managing to earn a bachelor's degree in American history from John Jay College. I then moved on to Fordham University, where I earned a master's degree, also in American history. Needless to say, I didn't get much sleep and the lines in my face were well earned. I had given serious thought to becoming a high school history teacher and, in fact, I did some per diem teaching at Pleasantville High School in Westchester County. That experience convinced me to stay in the NYPD.

Blackout

If the 1965 blackout was a romantic dream, the 1977 blackout was a nightmare.

In June 1977, I was transferred from the 44th Precinct to the Organized Crime Control Bureau, Narcotics Division, working out of the Bronx Narcotics Office located at the 50th Precinct in the Riverdale section of the Bronx. Our job was to investigate drug dealing, whether it was low level, medium level, or high level, within the borough of the Bronx. However, the fun part was that once you had initiated a case, usually with an informant, you went wherever that case took you. Early on, one of my "Bronx cases" took me to the Lower East Side of Manhattan and the Williamsburg area of Brooklyn, where I'd spend the better part of the next two years on it and other offshoot cases.

However, a month after my assignment to Bronx Narcotics Division, we had an interruption for about a week to assist in quelling the three days of rioting that surrounded the citywide blackout in July 1977. The power went off in the city around 7:00 or 7:30 P.M., while it was still daylight. As darkness descended, so did the marauding gangs who were looking to take advantage of a vulnerable city. Within hours fires were set and looting was taking place. Brand-new cars were driven through showroom windows of dealerships along Jerome Avenue in the Bronx. Similar episodes were taking place elsewhere in the city, especially in Brooklyn.

The police commissioner, Michael Codd, went on the radio that night and declared a citywide emergency and ordered all off-duty police officers to report to their precincts. This was easy for me since I both lived and worked in the Riverdale section. When we reported to our precincts, we were given little instruction, other than to go out into the streets and "help out." We were really just showing the flag, with no real clear purpose in mind. Many arrests were made, but the mayhem continued well into the morning hours.

The next day the various staffs at headquarters would coordinate much more effectively the police response the following night. Or so they thought. I, along with my partner, George Kennedy, and a group of other officers, were shipped to Brooklyn while the Brooklyn narcotics officers were shipped to the Bronx. This didn't seem very effective to me; it seemed like a waste of time. Especially when it took my partners and me almost three hours to reach the precinct to which we were to report, getting lost in Brooklyn along the way and appearing twice at the same precinct—though not the one we were supposed to report to.

On the third day of the blackout we were redirected to report to the Bronx, in my case the 44th Precinct, which would have made sense from the beginning. Slowly but surely, there was a strong and visible police presence throughout the city, and things eventually returned to normal. But there had been a lot of damage, especially to the psyche of the city. People complained about the wanton lawlessness and vandalism surrounding the blackout. Just twelve years prior, in 1965, the city had faced a similar blackout but the citizens responded en masse, volunteering to assist and direct traffic in intersections. The 1965 blackout brought the city together in ways unimaginable. Romances began the night of that blackout, and, in fact, it even inspired a movie. While the 1965 blackout was a romantic fairy tale, the 1977 blackout was a horrific nightmare, during which storeowners were shot, businesses were burned, and the police response was inadequate.

There were a lot of reasons for the poor police response in 1977. The city had not seen serious civil unrest or a riot since the late 1960s. The police officials who had mastery of tactical and personal deployment had moved on, and the quiet seven-year interlude had provided no opportunity for "practice." It was evident to me that there will always be a certain amount of chaos at the beginning of a major incident or flare-up. How long the chaos lasts largely depends upon planning and practice. The NYPD at the time had not really planned and certainly did not practice how to respond to such civil unrest. Numerous efforts were made to address these shortcomings over the next two decades. It was not until Ray Kelly became the police commissioner in 1992 that the police response to civil disorder was finally mastered.

In 1977, a young congressman by the name of Ed Koch was running for mayor. Koch had been troubled by the blackout, the uncivil way that many responded to and took advantage of the residents of New York City. He was upset with the inadequate response of the NYPD. His blunt style of confronting people who were rude, uncivil, and criminal was refreshing, and many in the city rallied behind him. Koch won the election and took office in January 1978. His wagging tongue and finger and his heavy New York accent became recognizable parts of his persona. The bluntness was charming, even endearing. Finally, it looked like someone was in charge at City Hall who was ready to restore order and civility.

Issues of civility and policing were important concerns in the early months of his administration. With the police response to the prior summer's blackout still in his mind, Koch asked a simple question: How many police officers are working in the city on any given day? The brass at One Police Plaza didn't have a clue. As a matter of fact, they didn't even have an idea of how to begin to count or account for the number of officers who were deployed on the streets of New York on a daily basis. Clearly, there were fewer police officers in 1978 than there had been before the layoffs, when five thousand officers were eliminated and another few thousand were lost as a result of attrition. Koch was committed to increasing the staffing levels at the NYPD, but he wanted some basic questions answered. How many officers were there? How many were available on a daily basis? And what, if any, would be the minimum staffing level necessary to police the city on a twenty-four-hour basis? With the assistance of academics and consultants, a new "scientific" staffing model was developed.

Narcotics Division

Once the blackout was over and the city had returned to some kind of normalcy, I was able to go back to my new job as a narcotics investigator. It was a completely different job than anything I had done before. I was required to use my brains to outsmart others who depended on their brains to make them money. It was a bit of a cat-and-mouse game. But it also opened me up to a new facet of policing—the whole idea of bringing the job home with you at night. In other words, thinking about my job while off duty. In uniform in the 44th Precinct, you worked eight hours in a police car, handled all of your assignments, maybe made an arrest—but at twelve o'clock when your shift was over, you went home, forgot everything, and then started anew the next day. No connecting dots from one day to the next. Even when I was an anti-crime officer in civilian clothes, there was no notion of "investigating" a case. We would show up at noon, patrol the streets, sometimes make an arrest, then be finished by 8:00 P.M. and home watching *Monday Night Football* by 9:00.

In the Narcotics Division it was different. I was investigating individuals and sometimes organizations. I was trying to make sense and create an organizational structure around loosely knit drug crews in the Lower East Side of Manhattan and the Williamsburg section of Brooklyn. I was investigating the Puerto Rican drug organizations on the Lower East Side, along with their Italian partners in Williamsburg and on Moore Street in Tribeca. One narcotics intelligence analyst informed me that there were more high-ranking mafioso figures in one building on Moore Street than there were in entire neighborhoods in the city. The stuff was fascinating, and it kept us thinking and rethinking and discussing and plotting on how we were going to gain entry into these organizations and bring them down.

While George Kennedy and I spent a great deal of time in the Lower East Side in Manhattan, we still had territorial responsibility in the Bronx. My team covered what was known as the Eighth Division, which included the 41st, 43rd, and 45th precincts. Technically, our team was responsible for the low-level and medium-level narcotics trafficking in that entire area. In reality, we addressed only those complaints that came to our attention. A citizen might complain about open-air drug dealing on Story Avenue in the 43rd Precinct. We would respond, make a twenty-minute observation, and sometimes, if possible, make a street-level buy followed by an arrest (a buy and bust). This would prove that the Narcotics Division had taken action. If you thought seriously about it, however, that was a poor response and did little to alleviate the drug dealing that continued once we drove off the block. This would be an important lesson for me later on in the early days of the Bratton administration, when we began to look at the effectiveness of the Narcotics Division and its contribution to crime fighting, especially in terms of homicides and drug-related shootings.

However, there were some valuable lessons to learn from my narcotics days working on the drug gangs. One was that, the more you thought outside of the box, the better your chances were of succeeding. Especially in the case of "no-knock" search warrants of apartments and houses. The question always was: How do we get inside before the bad guy flushes the drugs down the toilet? For example, in one apartment unit within a six-story walk-up in the Morrisania section of the Bronx, the drug dealer's apartment overlooked the courtyard and the main entrance. In addition, he had lookouts on every corner ready to spot the narcs as they approached in their unmarked cars.

It is interesting the drug dealers did not fear a marked police car with uniformed officers inside. They knew that uniformed officers were discouraged, and in some cases forbidden, from making narcotics arrests. What we realized was that a uniformed officer in a police car caused no suspicion. If a uniformed car went by the apartment building, the drug dealers were not worried. Uniformed cops were not involved in "inside" narcotics enforcement.

After obtaining a search warrant, signed by a judge, George Kennedy devised a plan to take down that drug dealer in Morrisania as follows: drugs were to be dropped off at the apartment at 1:00 P.M. We would hit that apartment at 2:00 P.M. At 10:00 A.M. we had had our undercover officer, a scrawny Puerto Rican policeman with long hair and a beard, go into the building carrying a battering ram wrapped up in green garbage bags. When he went into the building, he gave the appearance of being a junkie burglar bringing home the stolen loot. The undercover officer took the battering ram to the roof and left it there in the green garbage bags off to the side. Kennedy and I, dressed in full uniform, borrowed a police car from the local precinct. We also secured a city ambulance and driver to add to the show. The ambulance pulled up in front of the location, and we arrived a minute later in our marked car and entered the apartment building as if we were handling a routine sick case. We walked into the building, observed but not suspected by the drug dealer. Kennedy and I went to the roof, retrieved the battering ram, walked down two flights of stairs, and announced our presence while simultaneously knocking down the door. After two bangs, we got inside the apartment and observed the dealer scurrying around like a rat on crack. We got him and his two kilos of coke before he had a chance to flush them down the toilet.

But there was a more challenging case a month later with our undercover officer Victor Cipullo, a good-looking Italian kid with balls of steel. Victor had been an undercover for five years and could buy from the lowest junkie on the streets as well as the high-end doctors at prestigious hospitals. There was no one from whom Victor couldn't buy. Along the way Victor had proved his mettle on more than one occasion when he had had to kill the drug dealers trying to rip him off. "Victor pisses ice water," his lieutenant once noted.

The case in point was a sale of pure heroin from a house in the Soundview section of the Bronx. The house literally stood by itself on an abandoned street of mostly overgrown lots. Anybody coming onto the block was noticed immediately. Victor made the initial buy and three subsequent buys, called "B buy," "C buy," and "D buy." With each purchase, the weight and purity of the heroin increased. While ordering the fifth buy, he asked for a kilo of heroin, having proven his credibility in making the previous four buys. And so the deal was consummated. The plan was to have Victor go into the house and get a sample of the kilo, which he would take with him to have it tested for purity. If the purity was high, he would return within the hour with $80,000.

When Victor left, the plan was for us to hit the house and seize the drugs. However, upon leaving, he transmitted to us, via his hidden microphone, a very important message: "My job is done. But you guys are fucked. There are three guys in there, all armed, and they're going to fucking kill yas! One of them is wanted for shooting a cop!" We met Victor a few blocks away, and he confirmed his transmission. He was having some fun at our expense, which was not uncommon for him. Like most of the undercovers, he always argued that he had more balls than the backup teams, that his job was the really dangerous job and that the backup team merely had to go in and make the arrest. The question quickly became how would we get into the house, get the bad guys, and recover the drugs, all without getting shot in the process.

Our lieutenant, Martin O'Boyle, viewed by many to be the most knowledgeable person in the whole of the Narcotics Division in New York City, proved his mettle that day by being not only a great leader but also an even better thinker. Within five minutes he had devised a tactical plan. We would use one large van and one unmarked police car. The large van, which looked like a UPS delivery van, held eight narcotics detectives. They were all secreted in the back and were armed with rocks that they had picked up at a nearby construction site. The second car held George Kennedy and me, along with Lieutenant O'Boyle. I had the battering ram to take the door down; Kennedy and Lieutenant O'Boyle carried shotguns.

The detectives in the van were instructed to pull up in front of the house, go to all sides of the structure, and throw their rocks at the windows to distract the bad guys inside. Simultaneously, I would hit the front door with the ram; we would make our entry, seize the three individuals, and confiscate the drugs. The plan went without a hitch except for one close call: one of the three bad guys with a gun went out the back window and confronted Sergeant John Loughran, who threw his last remaining rock at the bad guy with the gun and struck him in the head. Who said cavemen can't win?

The lesson here is that when things go okay, even though unorthodox methods are used, all is forgiven and forgotten. This was not the case on my seventh wedding anniversary, when I was involved in a shootout in New York's Lower East Side. Our undercover was shot in the chest when we attempted to execute a search warrant for a half pound of heroin. We had been working the Lower East Side for quite a few months out of the Bronx Narcotics Office, something in and of itself unusual. However, my informant was familiar with all of the big players in this neighborhood and parts of Brooklyn. Most important, he had never failed me. We had been focusing on a particular drug dealer when one evening, around 4:00 P.M., I got a phone call from my informant that a delivery of heroin had just been made to the drug dealer's social club, which was located on the second floor of a tenement building on Sixth Street between Avenues C and D. We quickly got our team together and headed down to Manhattan. Four of us went directly to the club while the fifth, Robby Morales, went to the District Attorney's Office to secure a search warrant based on the information supplied by the confidential informant. The four of us headed to the location with a plan.

Our plan called for us to drop off one of our undercovers, Chago Concepcion, a veteran undercover police officer who spoke very poor English but, like most good undercovers, always got the job done somehow. The really good undercovers took pride in the challenge; the harder the challenge, the better. But this operation seemed simple. Chago would knock on the door of the club and then in Spanish ask for some fictitious name. The expectation was that someone in the club would open the door, Chago would get his foot in, keep the door open, and then my other partner, Dicky Werdan, and I, would force our way into the club and freeze the occupants until Robby's arrival with the search warrant. We dropped Chago off a half a block from the club to allow him to "walk on the set." We kept him under close observation as he approached. It was about 5:30 at night and getting dark. Snow began to fall. As Chago mounted the steps leading up to the front door of the building, some kind of conversation ensued, there was a commotion at the door, and the next thing I knew, shots rang out. Chago had his gun out and started shooting into the club. Dicky and I ran up the stoop on either side of the doorjamb. There was a flight of stairs leading up to the second floor, where a guy was holding a gun and shooting at us. We returned fire, not knowing if we hit the intended target. And then there was silence. I then heard Chago, who was now down on the sidewalk, scream, "I'm hit!" He put his hand underneath his green army jacket, and when he removed it, it was covered in blood.

We immediately got on the radio and called for assistance. "Ten-thirteen! Police officer shot!" Within less than a minute, we heard the sirens coming down Avenue B as the marked police cars made their way to us. Chago, with gun in hand, ran to meet them, with me behind him yelling, "Chago! Wait! Wait!" I knew what the respond-ing cops would be thinking. The majority of cops at the time were white guys who looked like me. The Lower East Side was a largely Puerto Rican neighborhood. The responding police officers were going to think that the cop who had been shot looked like me and that the guy who shot him looked like Chago, a dark-skinned Puerto Rican. As we were running west on Sixth toward Avenue C, the first police car came to a screeching halt; using their police car doors for cover, these officers yelled to us to drop our guns. I immediately dropped my gun. Chago, who I assume was in shock, wouldn't drop his gun. I screamed at Chago, "Drop the fucking gun!" and then yelled to the uniformed officers that we were cops. While I looked like a cop, I could have also been mistaken for a denizen of the East Village, with my long hair, green army jacket, sneakers, and jeans. Chago certainly did not look like a cop. So who could blame the responding police officers if they shot someone who refused an order to drop his weapon? Somehow I was able to convince those two uniformed officers and their backup officers that we *were* cops, and so the standoff was resolved peacefully. Within ten minutes an Emergency Service Unit (ESU—in other cities this unit is called SWAT [Special Weapons and Tactics]) was on the scene; we began an apartment-by-apartment search of the two abandoned six-story buildings on either side of the social club while Chago was rushed to the hospital. We located and arrested the shooter in a closet on the fourth floor of the abandoned building to the east of the social club. We recovered his 9-mm handgun in the snow in the back alley. The entire episode was carried on the eleven o'clock news.

I spent several hours being interviewed by a police captain regarding the discharge of my weapon. The interview was finished by midnight, and I then returned to the processing of the prisoner and drugs to answer more questions from the 9th Precinct detectives. By 8:00 A.M., all of the interviews and paperwork had been completed and I headed off to court to arraign my prisoner. Oh, and by the way, I never made my wedding anniversary dinner. This was not the first, nor the last, sacrifice made by my wife and family.

Two days later we were summoned to police headquarters to meet with the commanding officer of the Narcotics Division to review the shootout. I assumed we would get all sorts of accolades and pats on the back. Not so. The police inspector leading the discussion was Joe Flynn, a well-liked and well-respected narcotics commander. He was always kind and gracious in his dealings with us. However, this time was different. He said, "You guys will probably get a medal for bravery. And you deserve it. You also deserve a smack in the head for stupidity! Who the fuck do you think you are? Executing a search warrant without first calling Emergency Service cops? You guys are too ballsy for your own good. And what was it all for? A fucking pound of white powder? You got your partner shot for a pound of white powder? You guys are lucky to be alive, and don't ever let that happen again!"

With our tails between our legs, we left his office. The point here is that, even when cops do brave things or make an outstanding arrest, if they use poor tactics or violate policy in the process, they need to be instructed accordingly. And we were.

An interesting side note to the shootout was the impact it had on the use of bulletproof vests by police officers. Each Narcotics Office usually had a half dozen bulletproof vests available for officers to wear, at their option, while executing a search warrant. While Chago was an undercover officer on this night, he was not acting in a true undercover capacity (buying drugs), so before leaving the office, he had put on a vest underneath his bulky, green army jacket. It was a decision that saved his life. The vest stopped the copper-rounded bullet from penetrating his chest. There was a deep contusion with a lot of blood, but that was the extent of the damage. That night, the vest was held up in front of the TV cameras for all to see. This incident became the cause célèbre to rally the private sector to purchase vests for police officers.

In the early years, private individuals contributed thousands of dollars to buy vests for the officers, which eventually embarrassed the city administration into accepting that as its responsibility. In the early 1980s, vests became part of the general issue equipment for all police officers. And an ironic note: one of the early contributors to the vest campaign was John Lennon, who was reported to have donated enough money to purchase a hundred vests. Years later he would be assassinated by a delusional fan in front of his Upper West Side apartment building across the street from Central Park.

3

From Sergeant to Management

I'm in the New York Times; *I'm dead in the water.*
—*PATRICK MURPHY, CHIEF OF OPERATIONS*

I had passed the police sergeant's exam in 1973 with a decent score. However, with little seniority and no veteran's preference points, I wound up ranked between eight hundred and nine hundred on a two-thousand-person list. Historically, the NYPD would have promoted up to fifteen hundred sergeants on that list, so I was pretty certain of getting promoted. Unfortunately, with the police layoffs in 1976, there was obviously less of a need for sergeants, and so I "died" on that list.

In 1978, I took a new sergeant's exam and scored much higher. I was in the first group of sergeants to be promoted from that list two years later. The NYPD conducts a three-week orientation course that is meant to assist police officers in their transition from cop to supervisor. New sergeants are exposed to a variety of challenging situations, from conducting roll call to overseeing an internal investigation for a minor violation by a member of his or her squad. The real eye-opener of the course is a series of reality-based scenarios where a sergeant is placed in a situation in which he or she will have to make a tough decision. It is usually a confrontational situation, maybe with racial or gender overtones, maybe with a serious violation of the rules and procedures, maybe even a criminal act. Each scenario ends with the admonition phrased as a challenge: "It's your move, Sergeant." I didn't realize that I would get to play in my own real-life scenario less than a month after being assigned as a patrol sergeant to the 32nd Precinct in Central Harlem.

The 32nd Precinct is one of the most revered of the seventy-six police precincts in New York City. More police officers have been killed in that precinct than in any other. As you come through the double glass doors, you are greeted by the pictures of those officers who paid the ultimate sacrifice. The precinct commander was a deputy inspector, a tough little Italian American who had spent most of his career in Brooklyn. He was a no-nonsense commander and would remind you often: "I don't put up with that bullshit." He and I seemed to hit it off right away, and I enjoyed his fatherly advice.

Every two weeks, on payday, a supervisors' meeting was held in his office, and every sergeant and lieutenant was required to attend, even if it was their day off. At one particular meeting he informed us that the Inspections Division from headquarters had been visiting some of the hospitals throughout the city, checking on hospitalized prisoners who were guarded by police officers from the local precinct. As you might expect, the Inspections Division always found numerous violations, including situations where guarded prisoners remained uncuffed for hours on end. This was a serious breach of protocol that would not be tolerated by the fair-haired boys at One Police Plaza. The city-run Harlem Hospital was just three blocks from the precinct house and always had two or three prisoners under guard at any one time. At the supervisors' meeting the commander reminded us of our duties to check on the cops and the prisoners at least once during each shift. While doing so, we were to ensure that each and every prisoner was handcuffed, "no exceptions, no bullshit." A few days later, as part of my regular patrol duties, I visited the three police officers guarding the prisoners at Harlem Hospital. The three officers were all well groomed and fully attentive. Unfortunately, only two of the three prisoners were handcuffed. The prisoner who was not handcuffed was the most dangerous of the three by virtue of the fact that he had received his wounds in a shootout with detectives from the nearby 28th Precinct.

When I questioned the officer as to why this prisoner was not hand-cuffed, he replied, "He's not going anywhere. I have my eye on him. And besides," he added, "it's inhumane." I reminded him that he was not in the humane business, and I then directed him to handcuff the prisoner. He refused. I had an immediate flashback to the training session at the academy: "It's your move, Sarge."

The two other officers whose prisoners were handcuffed sat watching me with the obvious question on their mind: What are you gonna do, Sarge? I instructed the police officer to keep the prisoner in constant sight and I would be right back. I went downstairs, brought my driver back upstairs with me, and directed my driver to handcuff the prisoner. I indicated that he would remain guarding the prisoner for the rest of the shift. I told the original guarding officer to get the car keys and drive me back to the station, where we would address the matter. As we were driving across 135th Street to the station, the guarding police officer didn't say much except one statement, which unnerved me a little: "You know, Sarge, if I don't want you here, I can just make you disappear." That was the extent of the conversation.

At the station, I went in to see the commanding officer, told him what happened, and explained that I was taking disciplinary action against the police officer, recommending two weeks' suspension for failure to follow a direct order. The commander seemed satisfied with my actions, exclaiming, "At least somebody has got some balls around here to do what they're told." I took that as a compliment and began the paperwork process. I was soon brought to reality when two fellow sergeants confronted me, saying, "Timoney, what the fuck is wrong with you? Don't you know that cop's a psycho? That's why he's guarding prisoners!" "Oh," I replied.

A couple of weeks later, while working the late tour on a cold February night, I was reading through department directives and bulletins when I came across an announcement from the NYPD Scholarship Unit for a series of college scholarships, including one to Hunter College for a master's degree in urban planning. It seemed too good to be true: a year's leave of absence with pay to obtain a master's degree. As I look back on that cold February night, finding that scholarship announcement was probably the turning point in my career.

There was one minor problem. I had already received a master's degree five years prior on my own time. The next day I called the Scholarship Unit at the police academy to inquire if my master's degree would disqualify me from applying. The woman said, "No. That's not a problem." "But I don't have a rabbi," I replied. (In NYPD parlance, a rabbi is someone who can get favors done for you.) "You don't need a rabbi," she replied. "This is legit. It's an open, competitive process, and the winner is chosen by committee. The only thing you need to do is retake the Graduate Record Examinations." I took the GREs a few months later, scored well, and was awarded the scholarship to study urban planning at Hunter College later that year.

My first master's was in American history, as had been my bachelor's. The next year at Hunter College a whole new horizon was opened up for me. I began to mingle with professors and others who introduced me to this whole new notion of public policy. It was at Hunter where I met Donna Shalala for the first time. She had come from the U.S. Department of Housing and Urban Development to be the president of Hunter. She would later go on to become the president of the University of Wisconsin, serve for eight years in the Clinton administration, and then become the president of the University of Miami. Professor Peter Salins, a market-oriented housing expert, was affiliated with the Manhattan Institute, a think-tank policy group that would have huge influence on the so-called "new mayors" of the 1990s. Professor Eugenie Birch, a historian by training but one of the forerunners of "mapping" housing patterns—including abandoned areas and their relationship to social ills, such as crime—was working with early computer programs that examined the relationship between housing, abandonment, poverty rates, and a whole host of quality-of-life issues. It was Genie who, in 1993, shared with me a new computer program that looked at the correlation between housing abandonment, poverty, and unemployment rates. (Years later, when I became the police commissioner of Philadelphia, Genie played a critical role in providing the Philadelphia Police Department with young, talented computer mappers from the University of Pennsylvania, where she is now a professor.) And there was Professor Donald Sullivan, a great housing advocate and policy wonk who proved that he could still have fun in the sterile atmosphere of academia. Donald unfortunately died of AIDS much too young.

In September 1982, I returned to Harlem, this time to the 25th Precinct. I had my new master's degree, but I was wondering, What happens next? It was clear to me that past recipients of these scholarships were eventually brought to headquarters, usually sooner rather than later. I was ambivalent regarding working at headquarters. I wanted to return to the Narcotics Division as a sergeant. Narcotics had been so much fun the first time around.

My first day back on patrol in the 25th Precinct was a Sunday. I was the patrol sergeant on the 8:00 A.M. to 4:00 P.M. shift. My driver was a young, good-looking, six-foot-three-inch-tall Italian American named Michael Verde. Verde filled me in on his career to date. He had gone through the academy and had arrived at the 25th Precinct while I was away on leave. Most of the morning was spent visiting police officers on post and signing memo books. At one point in our conversation, Verde was talking about the precinct commander and what a good guy he was. A month earlier, Verde had gotten married, and in a very unusual step, the precinct commander had given Verde the first two weeks of August off for his wedding. The notion of a rookie getting two weeks in August off is unheard of. Recognizing that, Verde wondered out loud to me why the commander had given him the time off. He stated, "I just kind of got here, just came on; I don't know why he gave me the time. He didn't need to mollify me." I immediately directed Verde to stop the car, and I asked him, "Who are you?" He said, "Huh?" I said, "Who are you?" "I'm Michael Verde from Astoria, Queens." I said, "Not where are you from, who *are* you? Cops don't use words like *mollify*, so who are you?" "Oh," he said. "Before becoming a cop, I graduated from Columbia University." He was clearly a smart, up-and-coming young officer with the balls to match his brains. I made a conscious decision that day that, going forward, I would always keep Verde in the back of my mind.

Four months later, I received a phone call to report to the Chief of Operations Office at One Police Plaza, where I would be assigned as a research analyst for the then four-star chief of operations officer, Patrick

Murphy. I had never met Murphy but had seen him numerous times on television. With his tightly cropped silver hair and steely blue eyes, he looked like a typical Irish cop: tough. Some would say he looked nasty. It may be the first time in my life when I met someone whose personality in no way matched his looks. Pat Murphy was a kind, gentle man with self-effacing good humor, and he was always considerate of those who worked for him, including the civilian staff (which was not always the case in the NYPD). The one word that constantly comes to mind regarding Pat Murphy is *class*. It was not uncommon for him as he got his coffee in the morning to sit around for a half hour or so, talking to my fellow sergeant Bobby Nardoza and me about the department, policies, or whatever police news was in the morning headlines. He became an enormous influence in my life.

As a research analyst, it was my job to review proposed changes in policies and procedures that had been suggested or created by other entities within the NYPD, in the hope that we would improve the delivery of police services. Part of that included determining that any new policies and procedures did not conflict with any existing ones. After doing this rudimentary and boring work for three months, I was finally given an assignment I could sink my teeth into. I was assigned the task of developing the NYPD's new policy on high-speed police pursuits. My attitude toward high-speed chases was a typical cop's attitude. You blow a red light, you run from the police, you try to escape, and we'll get you, no matter how fast and how well you can drive a car. We'll get you. And most of the time we did. Clearly, there was the possibility of an accident, but with the testosterone level screaming and the pedal-to-the-metal approach, who thinks about accidents? We're gonna get the guy, even if it kills us, even if he is guilty only of running a red light.

As I began to research what was going on across the country, it became clear that most cops thought like I did. What also became clear was that an awful lot of innocent people paid with their lives so that guys like Timoney could get their guy. There needed to be some kind of balance. In the midst of my research, I discovered that the agitation for these policies was the result of lawsuits. In one particularly tragic case, a man sued a police department in the Midwest after he lost his two daughters when his car was T-boned by some knucklehead being chased by police because he had run a red light. All across the country, there was case after case with similar horrific endings. Once I began the research, it became clear that police departments needed to strike a balance. It's actually very simple. When the danger to the community outweighs the danger of allowing the person to get away, it's incumbent upon the police to terminate the vehicle pursuit. Creating the rationale for the policy is the easy part. Creating rules and procedures within the policy is what's difficult.

After numerous iterations, we created the policy that still stands today. The lesson for me was transformative. For years I had viewed the mindless memos and policies emanating from the "puzzle palace"—a derisive term for police headquarters—as an effort by the top brass to handcuff police officers, to dissuade them from doing their duty, to make their lives miserable. But as I read one tragic case after another, it became clear that there was a real need for such a policy. At the end of the day, the policy was meant to support our primary mission: *to save lives.* If by not pursuing some sixteen-year-old kid joyriding in a stolen car we save the life of an innocent pedestrian or motorist, then that's what we're all about. Ironically, I had heard this policy articulated a dozen years earlier by the informal leader of the 44th Precinct, police officer Desi Flaherty, who on more than one occasion would call off a chase that he felt was too dangerous and not worth the risk with the admonition "Don't worry. God will get him."

Congressional Hearings on Police Brutality

Not only can policy affect police shootings; so can the press. In 1983, a congressional oversight committee came to New York to investigate the issue of police brutality, including police shootings. The mayor and the police commissioner were among the many people asked to testify. The hearings were politically and racially charged, and unfortunately the committee had reached a foregone conclusion—before the hearings had even begun. They felt the NYPD was a racist organization whose cops indiscriminately shot and killed members of minority groups. I was given the task of researching police shootings over the previous fifteen years. This really piqued my interest in the issues surrounding deadly physical force, and it is an interest I still have to this day.

The research was fascinating in what it revealed. The NYPD was probably the most progressive and restrained police department in the nation, and the numbers proved it. More important for me was that the research showed that good, sound policy can have an immediate, dramatic, and lasting impact. Prior to the implementation of the shooting policy in August 1972, the records of the police shootings in the NYPD were unreliable. Police statistics for police officers discharging their weapons were kept at the police firing range. The statistics regarding those killed and wounded were pretty accurate. However, accidental discharges and "misses" were completely unreliable. So the numbers maintained at the range should be considered conservative numbers. But what they indicated was that in 1970 and 1971, the NYPD recorded around eight hundred discharges. Between ninety and a hundred people were killed, and dozens more were wounded.

The 1972 numbers showed a slight decrease. But that is deceiving. You don't appreciate the dramatic decrease until you separate the shootings from before and those from after the date the policy was implemented. Looking at police shootings for the first eight months of 1972, they appear to be quite similar to those from 1970 and 1971. However, when you look at the last four months of 1972 and prorate these numbers, there is an immediate decline in shootings of about 40 percent. There is an additional decline in 1973 and another decline in 1974. This trend continued, and a decade later, the number of all reported discharges was around 350, and the number of people killed was around twenty.

My research clearly indicated numbers that showed the NYPD had greatly improved in the area of deadly physical force. But the statistics dealt only with officers discharging their weapons. What about when officers don't discharge their weapons, even when they would be fully justified in doing so, including times when they are being shot at? Unfortunately, those statistics were not readily available. I conducted a rather laborious hand check of all Firearms Discharge and Assault Reports and was able to uncover numerous instances in which police officers could have discharged their weapons justifiably but elected not to do so. This was another indication of the restraint used by members of the NYPD. Going forward, I instituted a policy that captured these instances under the title Shot at but Did Not Return Fire.

My research put me in touch with James Fyffe. In 1977, Fyffe, a police lieutenant assigned to the police academy, completed his doctoral dissertation on police shootings in the NYPD, using the 1972 policy as the impetus for his thesis. Jim went on to become a college professor, the author of numerous books on police use of deadly physical force, and America's number one expert on the subject. Jim passed away in 2006, but his contribution to this field will live on.

Unfortunately, even with statistics on your side and a clear improvement in performance in the area of deadly physical force, opinions were set in stone. The congressional oversight committee disregarded these numbers and came to the same conclusion it had reached before the hearings began.

A few years later, while continuing to review and monitor police shootings, I noticed a disturbing trend. Not only can policy affect police shootings, so can the press. In a seven- or eight-month span, six police officers were indicted and arrested in six separate incidents involving the discharge of their weapons. One was an off-duty situation, in which the officer killed an individual and was arrested for homicide. The other five were all on-duty situations and would fall under the category "There but for the grace of God go I." The six indictments and arrests garnered inflammatory headlines in the tabloids and on television. As a result of the coverage, the number of people shot, and especially those killed, reached an all-time record low. It was clear to me that police officers had become hesitant to use their firearms even in situations where they were fully justified in doing so. It is almost impossible to prove that theory, but one anecdote may make the point.

The scene was in Brooklyn's Bushwick section. A police sergeant was signing the memo books of rookie police officers on their posts. As the sergeant was in the process of signing one rookie's book, an old man, the owner of a liquor store who had been robbed two days prior, informed the sergeant that the guy who committed the armed robbery was on the sidewalk walking toward them. The sergeant got out of his car and confronted the guy, who pulled out an automatic revolver, let some shots go at the sergeant, and then ran down the street. The sergeant pursued him on foot for about three or four blocks; along these blocks the sergeant passed no fewer than two rookies who observed the chase and his ongoing gun battle with the bad guy. The armed felon ran into an alley, climbed the fire escape, and entered a fourth-floor bedroom window.

As he entered the bedroom, he startled a man and woman as they lay in bed. The man was an off-duty NYPD officer. The woman was an off-duty transit police officer. Spotting a man with a gun coming through their window, both officers discharged their weapons, killing the felon. Good story, happy ending, except: when the sergeant began to retrace his steps and question the rookie officers he had passed during the running gun battle, they told him they weren't sure if they could shoot because they had seen a lot of police officers get arrested for discharging their weapons during the prior six or seven months. It is hard to know if this was a failure of training at the police academy or not, but clearly the negative headlines had had a negative effect on those rookie police officers.

The power of the press to influence police policy and practice is a fantastic phenomenon not often appreciated by the average citizen. The chilling effect of the negative stories regarding police officers being arrested for discharging their firearms is clear. The statistical evidence bolstered by some anecdotal evidence supports the theory. These negative stories can also have an inflammatory effect, especially in the case of prosecutors. A feeding frenzy by the press can cause some prosecutors to overreach. I have seen it time and again where police officers who did nothing wrong or who simply made a mistake were arrested or indicted.

Ben Ward

In late 1983, Police Commissioner Robert McGuire announced that he would be retiring at the end of the year, after serving six years in one of the most demanding and stressful jobs in the world. McGuire had guided the department through the turbulent years coming out of the layoffs and the blackout. He had been asked to provide the same police service even though he was about ten thousand police officers short of the 1975 staffing levels—an impossible task. Throughout this period, McGuire displayed an air of confidence and competence. By and large, the rank and file viewed him quite favorably.

Once McGuire announced his intentions, all eyes turned toward who his successor would be. Those of us who worked for Chief Pat Murphy were hoping Murphy would be chosen. However, one morning over coffee, Chief Murphy announced to us, in his typical self-effacing manner, that he would not be the choice, especially given that the *New York Times*, earlier that morning, had predicted he would be the choice. Murphy exclaimed with a rueful smile, "I'm in the *New York Times*; I'm dead in the water." He was prescient. A few days later, Mayor Koch announced that Benjamin Ward would be the first African American police commissioner in the history of the NYPD.

Speculation was rampant, as it usually is in these situations, as to why Ward was chosen. The overwhelming argument was that the racial animosity emanating from the recent congressional hearings on police brutality was largely responsible for his promotion. Mayor Koch denied this, stating that Ward had been chosen due to his police background and the fact that he had held high positions in other parts of the city government, including commissioner of the Department of Corrections. No matter what the speculation, the appointment opened old wounds regarding an incident on April 14, 1972, at a Harlem mosque on 116th Street. Officer Phillip Cardillo of the 28th Precinct was shot there after responding to a phony call for an officer needing assistance. Two other police officers were seriously injured. Hundreds of police officers responded to the location, and there were skirmishes along the streets all day and night. Tensions ran high.

Immediately after the shooting, Deputy Inspector John Haugh, the commanding officer of the 28th Precinct, arrived at the mosque and took charge. Haugh reported that when he entered the basement of the mosque, there were approximately fifteen men (suspects) facing the wall, with one other male on the floor suffering from injuries received during the skirmish with the responding officers. Haugh ordered an ambulance for the injured man and directed that the fifteen other individuals await interview by investigating detectives. Haugh then went to the street to handle a growing unruly and angry crowd.

A few higher-ranking members of the NYPD also responded to the mosque, including the chief of detectives, Al Seedman; the deputy commissioner of community affairs, Ben Ward; and the deputy commissioner for public information, Robert Daly. Also responding to the mosque was Minister Louis Farrakhan and a number of his assistants. The plan, as Haugh understood it, was to take all of the suspects to the 24th Precinct (where the borough detectives were headquartered) for further investigation to determine who shot Officer Cardillo and who assaulted Police Officer Victor Padilla.

Someone, it was not clear who, made a deal that would allow all of the suspects to leave the mosque without police escort and without handcuffs and report to the 24th Precinct for interviews. Not surprisingly, none of the suspects showed up at the 24th.

As if this was not bad enough, the top brass of the NYPD refused to issue a statement supporting Police Officer Cardillo and his fellow responding officers. Meanwhile, Minister Farrakhan held daily press conferences and made outlandish charges—including the charge that other police officers shot Officer Cardillo. Officer Cardillo succumbed to his injuries and died six days later in his hospital bed, still with no support from the top brass at headquarters. To make matters worse, if that were possible, Commissioner Murphy, who had been on a trip to England when the original incident happened, remained in England, failing to attend Officer Cardillo's funeral.

The incident at the mosque and the subsequent investigation, or lack of investigation, remained an open sore in the annals of the NYPD. There is nothing in the long history of that department that comes close to matching the killing of Officer Phillip Cardillo.

It was against this backdrop that Ben Ward was announced as the new police commissioner of the NYPD, beginning in January 1984. The allegation against Ward was that, while he had responded to the mosque to calm tensions, he had ended up striking the deal with the suspects. The bad blood that stemmed from this dogged Ward for years and resurfaced again when he was promoted to police commissioner.

Ward's position at the time—deputy commissioner of community affairs—would not have allowed him to strike a deal with the suspects in the mosque. He had no operational authority. However, Ben Ward was no shrinking violet, and it is more likely that he offered his strong opinion and recommendation to the operational commanders at the scene. Three or four years after Ward's appointment to police commissioner, Al Seedman, who had been the chief of detectives during the mosque incident, admitted he was the one who struck the bargain to allow the people involved to turn themselves in. When asked later by New York *Newsday* reporter Len Levitt why he had not come forward to admit this, Seedman responded lamely, "What difference would it have made?"

As an aside, while I was researching police shootings for the congressional hearings on police brutality, I found an old folder in the bottom of a file cabinet at headquarters that contained memos and handwritten notes regarding internal discussions about the Harlem mosque case. Though these memos and notes didn't give a full view of what happened that day, one thing was clear: Ward did get into a heated argument in front of the 24th Precinct with Haugh regarding the police response after Officer Cardillo was shot. Both Ward and Haugh were lawyers and argued with each other about the laws that were applicable to the situation. However, the finer points of the law gave way to charges by Ward that Haugh was exacerbating tensions by the way he deployed and utilized responding police personnel. Ward thought the visible display of force, particularly by the officers who carried rifles, was unnecessary. The 28th Precinct commander was highly respected by the rank and file, and his very public argument with Ward (which subsequently led to his resignation/retirement over the department's handling of the matter) added to his stature, all to the detriment of Ben Ward.

Thirty-seven years after the killing of Phillip Cardillo the case remains unsolved. In 2009, Raymond Kelly, in his second stint as police commissioner of the NYPD, ordered a reinvestigation of the incident at the mosque.

Ward hit the ground running when he became commissioner in January 1984. He chose Pat Murphy as his first deputy commissioner and Robert J. Johnston Jr., who had been the chief of patrol, as the new four-star chief of operations, and my new boss. Johnston was a silver-haired, barrel-chested man who seemed to be in perpetual motion. He was a take-charge, no-nonsense taskmaster and a great field tactician. He had a creative genius for logistics and was constantly thinking up new ways to improve police equipment and tactics. He spent endless hours over coffee with the mechanics at Fleet Maintenance, devising ways to create and build equipment. For example, he designed a fleet of trucks and cars with high-powered lighting systems that could illuminate several city blocks in the event of a blackout or civil disturbance. He also created the "Mandela mobile," similar to the Pope mobile, to facilitate African National Congress head Nelson Mandela's historic visit to New York City in 1991. Finally, Johnston was the architect and greatest proponent of overwhelming force, long before it was known as the Powell Doctrine. The bottom line was that, like most great leaders, he was both feared and loved by the troops who served under him.

By 1984, as a result of an influx in hiring over the prior four years, NYPD staffing levels were starting to rise. Though the number of police officers was nowhere near the 1973 levels, there were a few thousand more officers than existed in 1980. Ward made it clear to his executive staff that he was not just going to put the hundreds of additional officers in police cars to respond to 911 calls. His rationale was simple. The police department was already doing a decent job handling the 911 calls, and the additional officers would be able to make only marginal improvements in this area. Ward had other ideas as to how to use these new officers.

These new officers gave the police force the ability to attack crime in a serious fashion for the first time in my career in the NYPD. Until that point, the notion of fighting crime seriously had not really existed due to the focus on police corruption after the Knapp Commission hearings and the loss of nearly ten thousand officers due to layoffs and attrition.

In the early months of his administration, Ward unveiled a crime-fighting plan known as Operation Pressure Point, which dealt mainly with drugs and violence in the Lower East Side. The program was a huge success because there were extra police officers assigned to the area in both uniform and plainclothes. Imitation is the highest form of flattery, so Pressure Points 2 and 3 were unveiled later that year.

The Death of Eleanor Bumpers

While things were going well for Ward in Lower Manhattan, the same could not be said for the Bronx. In mid-1984, Emergency Service Unit police officers were dispatched to a housing project in the 44th Precinct to assist housing police officials with an eviction. ESU officers are specially trained to handle emotionally disturbed persons. The person to be evicted was Eleanor Bumpers, a sixty-seven-year-old African American grandmother. She was a large woman, over two hundred pounds, who was, at times, emotionally disturbed. Bumpers threatened to do harm to anyone who came into her apartment. Apparently, she was suffering from a paranoid delusional episode. Bumpers held a long knife in her hand as emergency service officers broke down her door down with a battering ram and entered her apartment. At the time, officers would use a T-bar (an implement about six to eight feet long that would keep the armed person at bay). The officer who was carrying the T-bar slipped upon entry into the apartment, allowing Bumpers to gain the advantage. She raised her hand, as if to plunge her knife into the back of the officer. A backup officer fired two rounds into Bumpers, killing her instantly.

This incident was a tragedy. There was no shortage of critics of the NYPD, and specifically of Officer Steve Sullivan, who had killed Bumpers. (I had worked with Steve Sullivan when I was a rookie cop in the 44th Precinct. He was an even-tempered, thoughtful police officer who was held in high regard.)

The reaction of the African American community was instant and understandable. The clear question in the air was how a sixty-seven-year-old grandmother could be evicted from a New York City Housing Authority building. In other words, this was not the action taken by a private landlord. This was the city. And how could an eviction of a grandmother ever lead to her death? Those were legitimate questions by the public. Equally legitimate were the questions, or rather feelings, of the average New York City police officer: there but for the grace of God go I. We all knew that we could find ourselves in an equally horrific situation on any given day.

The district attorney for the Bronx was Mario Merola, a person held in deep distrust by the vast majority of Bronx police officers. Merola seemed to be more of a politician than a professional district attorney. If indicting a cop could win him support or votes, a cop was not given the benefit of the doubt in close-call situations. Merola impaneled a grand jury to investigate the Bumpers case and, not surprisingly, a murder indictment was handed down against Officer Sullivan. This, in turn, brought about the largest demonstration of off-duty police officers in the history of the NYPD. Over ten thousand police officers converged at 161st Street and the Grand Concourse to express their outrage, demand Merola's resignation, and protest other assorted complaints. Needless to say, this further heightened racial tensions in the city.

Early on in the Bumpers case, Commissioner Ben Ward made an offhand but understandable comment that infuriated police officers and their union. He remarked, upon seeing a picture of Bumpers, "That could have been my grandmother." Ward was just stating a legitimate feeling that any human being would register. However, in the racially charged atmosphere, many police officers viewed Ward's words as taking a side, and not one in support of Officer Sullivan. The charges against Ward were unfair, and anyone who viewed his statement in an unemotional, detached manner would conclude that they were the statements of someone who understood the plight of Bumpers and her family. Nonetheless, Ward took an unfair beating from his police officers.

As the case moved forward, it became clear that while Ward fully empathized with the Bumpers family, he obviously understood Officer Sullivan's predicament and was quite vocal in his denouncement of Merola's indictment. When the case went to trial, there was a great deal of testimony, especially from medical personnel. A doctor testified that the first shot had struck Bumpers in the hand that was holding the knife. This immediately disabled her and brought into question the necessity of the second shot. This had an alarming impact on police officers. They began to ask themselves, Am I expected to stop after firing every single bullet to check the medical well-being of the opponent?

The issue was cleared up when the defense presented its side of the case. It turned out that officers in the Emergency Service Unit had been trained to discharge two successive blasts from their shotgun and then look to see if the opponent had been hit. Police training at the firing range is meant to instill in officers tactics and protocols that they will use in real life. The training over the years has varied, based on trends in policing. For example, when I was a rookie, we trained with bull's-eyes at twenty-five yards. The more often you hit the bull's-eye, the higher your score. There was no reality check or correlation to what actually happened on the street. Over the years, training became much more realistic. The goal of the training now is to develop what athletic coaches call "muscle memory." There is no forethought, there's no thought, there's just action. In stressful, emotional situations, the survival instincts that are embedded in police officers during training take over. In the case of Steve Sullivan, he did what he had been trained to do, and he was rightfully found not guilty.

The Eleanor Bumpers case was the beginning of a series of sometimes tragic, sometimes unfortunate, sometimes necessary police shootings that inflamed tensions during Ward's time in office. The irony was that Ward was an African American, and a lot of those who were shot were African American or another racial minority. Ward was in a no-win situation. If he supported his cops, he was seen as a traitor to his race. If he empathized with the person shot, he was viewed as not fully supportive of police. In fact, Ward supported the cops, but he also recognized that there was a better way of doing police business.

At that point, I had discharged my gun twice during my career. The first time, I killed two wild German shepherds that were running loose in a six-story apartment building and had bitten at least one tenant. The second time was during the gun battle on Sixth Street with my partner. Other than those two experiences, my dealings with police shootings had been an academic exercise. I had reviewed thousands of pages of data, conducted informal internal studies, graphed trends, and performed all of the studies a good academician would do to fully understand a topic. What I lacked was operational experience in conducting investigations of police shootings; captains had the responsibility to lead the police shooting investigations at that time. However, that was about to change, when I was promoted to captain in the summer of 1985.

4

Captain Timoney

There goes three lucky Saturdays.
—TOM WALSH, DEPUTY CHIEF

After numerous postponements of the captain's exam in 1984, the test was finally administered in January 1985. It was a good time to take the captain's exam since the Ward administration was committed to increasing the number of captains in the NYPD. My boss, Robert Johnston, was a strong proponent of this increase. He also supported tasking captains with additional responsibilities, including those that traditionally belonged to the front-line supervisors (such as sergeants and lieutenants). There were some who argued, quietly and privately, that Johnston was demeaning the rank of captain by giving them tasks sergeants and lieutenants usually performed. Others argued that by giving these tasks to captains, they were taking critical responsibilities from the front-line supervisors and, in fact, retarding their supervisory development. But Johnston was the clever silver fox. Times were changing, times were tough, the department was under siege, and there was a need for greater management control. There was also a need for greater accountability. You just can't keep blaming cops when things go wrong.

What Johnston understood and others forgot was that in the promotional system in the NYPD, the only ranks that the administration controlled were those above captain. This was a huge lesson for me, and it would come to haunt me in Philadelphia.

The NYPD's promotional system is a bifurcated system. Up to the rank of captain, there is a civil-service system based on open, competitive exams. Above the rank of captain, the promotions are at "the pleasure of the commissioner." The civil-service system means the officer controls his/her own destiny. There is nothing that anyone can do for you or against you in the promotional process. In fact, there are many jokes surrounding civil-service exams and the type of supervisors they produce. The best I have ever heard was from my immediate boss, Deputy Chief Tom Walsh, who was Chief Johnston's executive officer. He was a one-star chief who one day remarked about a captain walking by his office, a captain with whom he was not particularly impressed, "There goes three lucky Saturdays." This was a reference to the NYPD's tradition of giving the civil-service exam on Saturdays and this person's luck in passing on those days.

Above the rank of captain, promotions were controlled by Johnston, Murphy, and ultimately, Ward. They had the power to promote or not. Johnston knew that captains would be more likely to carry out new policies with the requisite understanding and enthusiasm. They wouldn't just read a series of words from some document or new policy at a roll call. Because their careers or, more correctly, their career advancement, depended upon the implementation of and adherence to these policies, captains would "buy in," which would ensure that their officers would be made to understand the rationale of the new policy. By and large, Johnston's method worked.

It was under this emerging managerial philosophy that I became a captain in 1985. I remember the new captains' orientation course, at which Ward was one of the lecturers. He was serious and funny, insightful and thoughtful. But most important, he was firm. He said, "The cops may screw up, and we'll deal with them. But I'm going to be looking to you and at you when things go wrong. You represent me out there, you represent the department, but most important, you represent the citizens of New York City. And if you think I'm bad, wait until Chief Johnston gets ahold of your ass." Nobody wanted to deal with Johnston. He was every captain's worst nightmare. However, this made the rules pretty easy to understand: this is your job, and this is how you are going to do it. Johnston was the enforcer, and everybody knew it.

Regardless of the fact that I had worked for Johnston for the previous three years, I was not exempt from critical overview. The same can be said for my old boss, First Deputy Commissioner Pat Murphy.

As I was being readied for my promotion to captain, a decision had to be made about my new assignment. Some people thought I should remain at headquarters. Others, especially Deputy Chief Tom Walsh, knew better. Chief Walsh brought me to his office one afternoon for one of those "one-on-ones" that happen every now and then. He gave me what was probably the soundest piece of advice that I had received up until that point in my career. He looked me directly in the eye and told me to resist all efforts to keep me at headquarters. "Get out of here and become a duty captain and work your way to your own command!" he strongly advised. "Otherwise, it may be held against you that you never had a command. It may not seem important now, but in the future it means everything." What he meant was, out of all of the ranks and all of the jobs in the NYPD, the most important and maybe least appreciated was a precinct commander. Running a precinct meant you had to deal with the local borough commander; the bosses in the "puzzle palace"; the politicians (either at City Hall or the local representatives); and local activists and community organizers, some who had the community's best interest at heart and others who had no heart but, rather, blind ambition. Oh, and by the way, you also had a couple of hundred cops whom you had to inspire and satisfy. To say a precinct commander had many masters was an understatement. How the precinct commander managed those masters largely determined how he fared in his career.

So I was promoted to captain. The normal route for new captains in the NYPD is an assignment as an executive officer to the commanding officer of a precinct. As the executive officer, you do a lot of the administrative paperwork, you work odd hours, and you meet with odd people. In addition, you obsess over police officer overtime. With that in mind, I was sent back to the Bronx, which I had left five years earlier. I was assigned to the 48th Precinct, which abutted the 44th Precinct on its eastern border. The 48th Precinct was based in a relatively new building. The borough headquarters was located on the second floor, having been relocated from the 46th Precinct.

The commanding officer of the 48th Precinct was a senior captain who had spent some time at headquarters as a captain and the last few years as the commanding officer at the 48th, waiting, or rather hoping, to be promoted to deputy inspector. I had met him briefly at some meetings when I was a lieutenant. He seemed like a nice enough fellow. When I reported to his office at 8:00 on a Monday morning, I found him seated at his desk. I could hear him, but I couldn't see him. He was hidden behind the mounds of paperwork waiting for his signature. He was clearly suffering from "analysis paralysis," unable to sign off on the most routine memos. What he was striving for most was to keep his name out of headquarters at all costs.

We greeted each other, and I informed him that I was there to serve and support him and that I was ready to do anything he needed. He was pleasant and cordial enough. However, he looked at me as competition. I was foe, not friend. When I asked him what he wanted me to do, he replied in a very serious monotone, "I want you to take care of the Rotation Tow Log. As you are aware, cops and tow trucks make for trouble. This is a highly corruption-prone activity, and I need you to take care of this." The Rotation Tow Log was a log in which you entered sequentially the various city-authorized tow trucks that were called by a police officer to remove a stolen or abandoned vehicle. The log was meant to prevent police officers from continually calling the same tow company, and the rotation between three or four companies on a regular basis prevented police officers from becoming too familiar with any one company.

Time and again, New York City police officers got themselves in trouble by taking five dollars from tow truck operators, and sometimes they wound up being arrested. This is what he was referencing. I understood where he was coming from, but I didn't understand why so few tasks for me. I did a quick calculation in my head. If I checked the

Rotation Tow Log every day, it would take me between sixty and seventy seconds. Without missing a beat, I responded to him: "Okay, that's fine. I'll take care of the Rotation Tow Log, but what do you want me to do with the other seven hours and fifty-nine minutes of my shift?" There was a blank stare. He didn't get it. But I did. I knew I had to get the hell out of there.

One person's misfortune becomes someone else's fortune. The commanding officer of the 77th Precinct was transferred and replaced by Captain Ralph Dumond, a good friend of mine who was the executive officer of the Midtown South Precinct. I happened to be speaking to my former boss, Deputy Chief Tom Walsh, and he suggested that I should take Ralph's spot, which would give me more exposure and put me in a better position to get my own command after some time as an executive officer. Within a week I was reassigned as the executive officer in the Midtown South Precinct. Once again I was back in Manhattan South, after a fifteen-year hiatus from my days in the 17th Precinct.

Midtown South and Quality-of-Life Crimes

When you walk into the Midtown South Precinct on Thirty-fifth Street between Eighth and Ninth avenues, in the heart of the Garment District, you are struck by the large banner hanging from the ceiling: "The Busiest Precinct in the World." I thought to myself, I wonder what the boys in the 44th Precinct would think about this as they're dodging bullets and airmail garbage from the rooftops of six-story walk-ups. Remember, I had worked for two years as a police trainee in the 17th Precinct, which bordered the Midtown South Precinct. There was no comparison between the Midtown Manhattan precincts and those of the South Bronx and Harlem. You might as well be on another planet. But here I was, and I was not going to insult my new officers with tales from the South Bronx.

The commanding officer of the Midtown South Precinct was Tosano "Tony" Simonetti, a cigar-chomping Italian American who was built like a steamroller. Tony was a yeller and screamer whose cursing made me look like a saint. But for me, Tony was the perfect commander to work for. He already was a deputy inspector and was expecting to be promoted to a full inspector. So Tony allowed me to dive in with both feet to help him run the precinct.

Immediately, I began to meet with people whom I would never have had the opportunity to meet in the Bronx. The Midtown South Precinct covered the West Side of Manhattan from Twenty-seventh Street to Forty-fifth Street. The city's three main transportation terminals—the Port Authority Bus Terminal, Penn Station, and Grand Central Station— were within the precinct boundaries, as was the Broadway Theater District and, of course, Times Square. Just to add to the fun, Madison Square Garden was exactly two blocks from the precinct station house. This precinct was busy twenty-four hours a day, seven days a week, and you could deal on a daily basis with both paupers and kings.

Prostitution and low-level drug dealing were ubiquitous. The peep shows along Forty-second Street attracted many degenerates, in addition to high school kids from the suburbs ready to spend their weekly allowance to experience "city life." I had come from a crime-fighting background from my days in the South Bronx, and I would be damned if I was going to allow a few low-life amateurs in Midtown to run roughshod over that precinct.

Every chance I had, I addressed roll calls about the duty of police officers to deal with crime and the quality of life in the Midtown South Precinct. Most of the younger cops seemed to agree with my arguments and my plea, although a small minority seemed bored and disinterested. A few appeared willing to subvert the message I was trying to get out. Rather than overlook or dismiss the malcontents or naysayers at roll call, I decided that I would challenge and confront them. My roll call message went something like this: "Gentlemen and ladies, our job is to deal with crime and the quality of life for people who live or more likely work in the Midtown South Precinct on a daily basis. I know there are a few of you, only a small minority, who don't believe in what we're trying to do. That minority is a generally negative people who don't like the job, who hate the bosses, and, in fact, some of you can't stand yourselves, your wives, and even your children. I'm not talking to you. You're a cancer in this organization. I want to speak to the hard-working dedicated officers who are looking to do the right thing day in and day out. Do me a favor, all the good people take a few steps forward and let the malcontents stand and stew in the back of the room."

It was actually humorous to watch the last police officers at the roll call formation look behind them making sure they were not the ones left standing in the "malcontent section." In fact, the known malcontents or precinct troublemakers were too embarrassed or didn't have the balls to stand by themselves in the back of the room and thus inched forward to mingle with the rest of the platoon, thinking it guaranteed them anonymity. While I agreed with the top brass that corruption was a serious problem, as far as I was concerned, the number one problem was crime and quality of life in the city, and I was committed to doing my part to address both.

A lot of the crime in the Midtown South Precinct revolved around the sex and drug trade. Horny drunks would be set up by prostitutes at the instruction of their pimps in some of the fleabag hotels surrounding Times Square. Other times, a middle-class guy from the suburbs would have his pockets picked while being sexually serviced by one of the local prostitutes. And that was bad enough. However, sometimes these guys were afraid to tell their wives that they had lost their entire paycheck to some prostitute; they would concoct fantastic stories about how three guys with guns robbed them as they entered the subway. On more than one occasion, these gentlemen would wind up being arrested for falsely reporting a crime to the police.

Another scam on Forty-second Street involved the local marijuana dealers in Bryant Park. The drug dealers sold mostly marijuana, but if they saw easy targets from the suburbs, they would sell them carpet shavings in a small brown envelope for five dollars. I would get a kick out of it when these young kids from the suburbs would complain to the police about being "ripped off." On occasion, we would ask if the young man would like us to call his parents to explain how he had lost his ten dollars. The universal reply was, "Never mind, Officer."

But even low-level marijuana dealing can be deadly. In October 1985, two marijuana dealers got involved in a turf battle at Forty-second Street and Sixth Avenue. One of the dealers pulled a gun and shot at the other dealer, missing him but striking and killing a woman who was waiting for the express bus to take her to her residence in the Bronx. As you can imagine, a woman killed at Forty-second Street and Sixth Avenue at 5:30 P.M. did not go unnoticed. Pressure from the press and the public on One Police Plaza was brought to bear on every one of us in the Midtown South Precinct.

After the shooting, four police officers were assigned to Bryant Park during every shift. This did not eliminate the drug dealing, but it did keep it to a tolerable level. Over the next few months I made numerous visits to the police officers stationed in Bryant Park, both in uniform and in plainclothes (which for me meant a three-piece suit). On two occasions I managed to catch drug dealing going on and made an arrest, much to the chagrin of the officers assigned there. Once I had a police car drive me to the station house with the prisoner just as the four o'clock roll call had assembled. I paraded the drug dealer by the officers at roll call, yelling, "Don't tell me this bullshit that there are no drug dealers left in Bryant Park!"

Once I decided to visit the police officers at the park around 1:00 A.M. As I approached one of the officers in the middle of the block, I noticed something very peculiar. Bryant Park was elevated about six feet from street level, and I thought I saw the grass moving. When I questioned the officer to see if he saw the same thing, he replied in a not-too-respectful tone, "Captain! The grass isn't moving. Those are fucking rats! Why do you think I'm out here on the sidewalk?" After that, we decided to let the officers sit in their cars in the park at night rather than walk the paths.

Because Bryant Park is located behind the main branch of the New York City Public Library, not only did you encounter drug dealers and rats, you also had the opportunity to meet some of America's greatest citizens. Many view Bryant Park as the library's enormous back garden. The head of the library at the time was Vartan Gregorian, the former provost of the University of Pennsylvania and a scholar of Byzantine history. Dr. Gregorian was about five feet eight, with salt-and-pepper hair and a goatee. And he was the scourge of the drug dealers. On more than one occasion, I ran into him as he was chasing six-foot drug dealers out of the park. He was brave beyond belief. I thought he was a mad man but a great guy. He and I quickly became good friends. I just assumed he was some regular guy who happened to be the president of the library. Later, I became acquainted with his academic achievements. He certainly did not fit the profile of a distinguished college professor. A few years later, he became the president of Brown University. I often wondered if he walked the grounds of Brown maintaining law and order the way he had done in Bryant Park.

As a result of my friendship with Dr. Gregorian, I got to meet one of New York's most distinguished citizens, Brooke Astor. The library was holding a black-tie fund-raiser one Friday night. Dr. Gregorian asked me to stop by in uniform to make sure things went all right. As I stood on the sidewalk in front of the library, a limo pulled up and an elegant elderly woman stepped out. Without missing a beat, she looked at me in my uniform and said, "Oh, you must be mine." She put out her arm; I put my hand under hers and escorted her into the gala.

The problem of the drug dealers in Bryant Park was finally solved when the park was closed for over a year for massive renovations. With the park closed, the drug dealers found other locations to ply their trade. When the park reopened in 1989, with a new restaurant and gorgeous manicured gardens, it once again became a gathering place for New Yorkers looking to enjoy sitting on a park bench, engaging in conversation, or reading a good book. This method of interrupting the drug trade became a model for the rest of the city. Soon Union Square Park in Lower Manhattan was closed for more than a year. Again, the drug dealers went elsewhere.

High Tech at the United Nations

In the fall of 1985, the United Nations celebrated its fortieth anniversary. The U.N. General Assembly held its annual meeting that October, but because it was the fortieth anniversary, it was going to be a huge event. For seven weeks I was assigned to run the day-to-day operations from a temporary police headquarters located across the street from the U.N. There were dozens upon dozens of demonstrations scheduled for the full month. It was a tremendous experience and allowed me for the first time in my career to run my own operation, including the deployment of sometimes hundreds of police officers. The protests involved issues from Castro to the Israeli/Palestinian question, the IRA and Britain's role in Northern Ireland, apartheid, Haiti, the Sandinistas in Nicaragua, and assorted others. Each demonstration had its own nuance and sensitivities. You had to be careful not to give offense when meeting with the leaders of the demonstrations to set out the ground rules in advance to prevent violence. Marching orders were quite clear. The NYPD did not take sides, no matter what the issue. Our job was to facilitate protestors getting their voices heard and their opinions aired.

By and large, all the protests and marches went off with few problems. However, there were some interesting incidents. For example, at one of the pro-Palestinian demonstrations, the angriest words came from a vociferous middle-aged white guy who didn't look Palestinian to me. Throughout the event he kept breaking my chops. Not wanting to antagonize him or the crowd, I basically humored him. In some cases I actually implemented his suggestions on how the march should proceed. A few days later, the same gentleman was leading either a pro- or anti-Nicaraguan demonstration—I can't remember which— but I knew he wasn't Nicaraguan. And he was still obnoxious. About three or four days later, a pro-Israeli demonstration was taking place at Dag Hammarskjöld Plaza on Forty-seventh Street. Here again was my non-Palestinian, non-Nicaraguan, non-Israeli demonstrator leading the charge and making demands. It finally dawned on me that this guy was a whack job and was actually disrupting things. I quietly grabbed him by the arm, took him off to the side, and told him that if he didn't get out of there, I was going to kick his ass and lock him up. He just kind of smiled and left the area. I never saw him again. But it was a lesson well learned. The squeakiest wheel shouldn't get the most oil. It is important to establish the real leaders of a demonstration or protest.

While the majority of the protests and demonstrations involved a march, the protests at the South African Mission were old-fashioned sit-ins similar to those that took place during the 1960s. The sit-ins in front of the mission would last for an hour or so and would usually result in a few symbolic arrests. One day I received a phone call letting me know that the Reverend Jesse Jackson would be arriving at the mission around 1:00 and that he would engage in symbolic civil disobedience and was hoping to be arrested by 1:15 and released shortly thereafter. The police officers covering the event were instructed, and his arrest, among others, was made. After that, a new term entered the NYPD lexicon: *arrest by arrangement.*

The most interesting part of the U.N. assignment was that, for the first time, the NYPD would be using computers and closed-circuit television (CCTV) cameras to assist in policing the demonstrations and deploying personnel throughout the month-long meetings of the General Assembly. The CCTV was crude by today's standards but basically involved installing cameras on high-rise buildings and having a point-to-point relay of images sent back to command and control. For example, the cameras along Forty-seventh Street would send pictures of demonstrators at Dag Hammarskjöld Plaza to the temporary headquarters vehicle, which was located at Forty-first Street and First Avenue, where I could observe the number and conduct of the demonstrators and make operational decisions regarding additional resources.

The combination of CCTV and computers was meant to improve the effectiveness and efficiency of police operations, with the ultimate goal of minimizing dollars spent on police over time. Prior to this event the largest amount of overtime for a General Assembly meeting had been in 1960, when Fidel Castro showed up. The cost for security from that event was the equivalent of $6 million (in 1985 dollars). Our goal was to come in under $6 million, which we did. However, I am not sure that this was the result of the CCTV or the computers. I had a small team of very smart techies who designed and implemented the programs. As word of these "technological innovations" got out, a few news organizations became interested.

I was informed by the commanding officer of Manhattan South, Assistant Chief Gerry Kerins, that a national television crew was going to come to the command post to do a piece on the technological innovations. He suggested that I show them everything we were doing and answer any questions they had. I am known as a lot of things, but most important was my nickname "Luddite." Before the camera crew came, I had my techies brief me on exactly what it was that we were doing. I did the interview, and it aired that Sunday night. After the telecast, I received numerous phone calls from friends saying how impressed they were with our U.N. operation, especially my explanation of the technology used to bring everything together. This goes to prove that even a superficial guy like me can come across as a man of substance on television. I'm not sure if that says more about television, or less about me.

Sometimes You Just Can't Win

After my seven-week stint at the U.N., I returned to my job as the executive officer of Midtown South and the mundane tasks of monitoring police overtime and answering civilian complaints against police officers. One complaint I investigated concerned a police officer who had issued a motorist a summons for "no left turn" on Thirty-fourth Street.

Complaints against police officers in the NYPD are handled either by the Civilian Complaint Review Board (CCRB) or by the local command to which the police officer is assigned. The rules are simple. The Civilian Complaint Review Board handles all complaints of FADO—that is, force, abuse of authority, discourtesy, or offensive language. All others are handled by the officer's commander or designated supervisor.

Apparently, in the "no left turn" case, the citizen didn't feel he deserved the summons (nearly every citizen feels the same way) and gave the officer a hard time. The officer in turn lost his temper and referred to the citizen as a "skell" (part of the NYPD nomenclature), and, to add insult to injury, the officer informed the citizen that this was his regular day off and that he was being paid time and a half to give citizens like him summonses. When I interviewed the officer, he denied the allegations. But I quickly shut him down with the question, "If it didn't happen, how did the driver know that it was your regular day off, that you were being paid time and a half, and who else but New York City cops use the word 'skell'?" The officer turned red, apologized, and left my office.

Unfortunately, until this time, precinct commanders had no input and sometimes no knowledge of complaints against their officers if the Civilian Complaint Review Board handled them. In fact, in all honesty, they probably didn't care since it was out of their purview. But all of that changed in December 1985.

Commissioner Ward was concerned by the increase in civilian complaints being handled by the Civilian Complaint Review Board. Ward knew that if he was going to reduce these numbers, he would have to get the precinct commanders involved in all of the complaints, including those handled by the board. While he couldn't interfere with the CCRB, he could and did create a policy that got precinct commanders involved at the back end of the complaint process.

The new policy required the director of the Civilian Complaint Review Board to provide a monthly report to each precinct commander with the names of the officers receiving complaints for the month. The precinct commanders were then directed to do two things. First, the officer receiving the complaint was brought to the commander's office and informed that an accumulation of civilian complaints would jeopardize his/her career, especially if he/she wanted to go to a choice assignment like the Detective Division or the Narcotics Division. The second direction instructed the precinct commanders to write a report to the police commissioner, through channels, which meant that at least three or four higher-ranking officers had to endorse these reports—causing them headaches and more work—anytime there was an increase in civilian complaints from one month to the next.

Ward knew that precinct commanders hated to do reports to headquarters, especially reports that had to go through channels. The bottom line is that precinct commanders and their higher-ups took an "active interest" in the complaints received by the officers they supervised. Not surprisingly, there was a significant reduction in the number of civilian complaints citywide.

Up to that point in my career, I could think of only one administrative policy that had had immediate and successful results. That was the police shooting policy issued in August 1972. The CCRB "variance report" policy had similarly immediate and dramatic results. It is rare to see a policy have an immediate effect, but it is a pleasure to experience.

If we are honest, we recognize that many policies are instituted to CYA (police parlance: cover your ass); others are required as a result of legal action. Still others are the result of a bunch of bright boys and girls getting together and trying to do the right thing. But most satisfying are those policies that actually change behavior. Sometimes they require balls. Other times they require insight into how the organization works and, more important, what makes the people inside the organization tick.

A few days before St. Patrick's Day in 1986, I had the evening duty for all of Manhattan South (the ten precincts south of Fifty-ninth Street). As often happens, the first seven hours of the shift were relatively uneventful. About an hour before going off duty, I received a call regarding a fight at Madison Square Garden involving off-duty NYPD officers, and I rushed over. As I entered one of the tunnels leading to the dressing rooms, I observed about thirty guys, whom I suspected were off-duty police officers, milling about. I was informed by the very nervous, newly promoted patrol sergeant that a fight had taken place in the stands between a group of off-duty officers and three civilians. The civilians, all African Americans, were sequestered in one dressing room; the four police officers, all of whom were white, were being held in another room. The two dozen or so officers who were in the hallway were obviously friends of the off-duty officers but, like Sergeant Schultz, they "saw nothing, knew nothing, and heard nothing."

It quickly became clear to me that to attempt to conduct an investigation amid the chaos of Madison Square Garden would be difficult. I therefore ordered all of the parties to be taken to the Midtown South Precinct building, which was two blocks away. I figured that was a better location from which to sort out the mess. As I began the interviews of the people involved, the police union delegates showed up, further complicating an already complicated situation. The investigation revealed that the police officers had gone to the Golden Gloves Tournament to watch a fellow officer compete. The officer/boxer performed very well in the first two rounds, much to the joy of the cheering and rambunctious off-duty cops in the audience. However, in the third round, the officer/boxer ran out of gas and was knocked out by his opponent, much to the delight of the three African American civilians. Yelling and finger pointing led to pushing and shoving, which then led to punches. The scuffle was broken up by cooler heads, and the main culprits, one civilian and one off-duty cop, were separated. There was some evidence that the overconsumption of beer by one of the off-duty officers may have contributed to the fight. While it may be okay for a civilian to have more beers than is wise, the same rules do not apply for New York City police officers, even when they are off duty, even when at a sporting event.

Obviously the punches thrown and landed were technically an assault, which is a crime. But as is typical in situations like this, neither party was interested in pressing criminal charges. In street parlance, it was deemed a fair fight. No harm, no foul. However, the NYPD does not govern itself by the rules of the street. Officers are held to a higher standard. They are not expected to engage in fistfights while off duty, and they are prohibited from overindulging in intoxicants.

Once the union officials became involved, they made sure that under no circumstances would I be interviewing the officer that was the "subject of the internal investigation." I was left interviewing "witness officers" and civilians in order to piece together, as best I could, what had happened. At the end of the investigation, based upon "common-sense standards," I found the police officer unfit for duty, placed him on modified assignment, and removed his badge and shield but did not remove him from the payroll (that is, I did not suspend him). I then spent the next four hours writing a report of my adventures to the Divine Trinity at One Police Plaza. I finally left work at around eight o'clock the next morning, satisfied that I had done a decent job handling the matter.

Four days later, I was assigned to work the St. Patrick's Day Parade along Fifth Avenue. As the NYPD parade contingent moved up the avenue, the first deputy commissioner, Patrick Murphy, summoned me to walk with him for a block. "John, what the hell did you do the other night? The union is pissed off. They say it was a fair fight and it should have been left at that. And I think I agree with the union!" I just kind of shrugged my shoulders and stopped marching. Within no more than a minute, the three-star chief of patrol, Robert Colangelo, summoned me to march with him. "John, what the hell happened the other night? Why didn't you lock that cop up? We can't have off-duty cops assaulting people!" Once more, I just shrugged my shoulders, stopped marching, and went back to my post at the corner of Fifty-second Street and Fifth Avenue, thinking to myself, Man, sometimes you just can't win.

I reflected back to my rookie days when I had gotten in trouble in an innocent situation, "a fair fight," to use the street parlance. I didn't think my punishment (a fine of five days' pay for not taking action when my off-duty police officer/childhood friend got into a fistfight in a restaurant over a girl) was fair, but then again, life isn't fair. As I looked back on my decision over the course of that day, I concluded that not only had I made a decision, I had probably made the correct decision, since it fit in the middle of the two polar opposite decisions that the bosses would have made. Maybe I should have started to refer to myself as Captain Solomon.

During my ten-month stint as the executive officer/duty captain of Midtown South, I managed to get involved in more than my fair share of difficult situations. Time and again my name would appear on reports going to the top brass. Most of the time I was portrayed in a favorable light, but every once in a while my decisions were questioned. This included a phone call I received one day from a very high-ranking official at police headquarters inquiring why I had suspended the Constitution to round up drug dealers at a public plaza at Forty-third Street and Sixth Avenue. Overall, I thought I had done a pretty decent job as the executive officer. More important, I had the strong backing of my commander, Assistant Chief Gerry Kerins. In June, I received a phone call from Chief Kerins letting me know that I was going to become the commanding officer of the 5th Precinct in Chinatown. This was a huge step, and exactly the type of move that Chief Walsh had encouraged a year earlier.

5

Chinatown

You are the leader. For you to be seen on television walking
around with a reporter who is viewed as very low on the
social hierarchy would demean the stature of the captain.
—SHUCK SEID, ASSISTANT TO THE COMMANDING OFFICER
OF THE 5TH PRECINCT

The 5th Precinct is just one of seventy-six precincts in New York City (strangely, the precinct numbers go up to 123, with random numbers being skipped along the way). At the time that I was named commander of the 5th Precinct, there were about thirty chiefs in the NYPD, from one-star deputy chiefs to the four-star chief of department. Of them, at least five had been prior commanders of the 5th Precinct. Clearly, the 5th Precinct was in the top tier of desirable precincts along the career path.

While the 5th Precinct has been known as the Chinatown Precinct, it also encompasses the area of Little Italy, parts of the Lower East Side, a significant portion of what is now SoHo, and, of course, the area known as the Civic Center—which includes all of the federal, state, and local courts, police headquarters, and the Brooklyn Bridge. The 5th Precinct also has the distinction of being the only police precinct that has a civilian employee who holds the title assistant to the commanding officer. This man, Shuck Seid, had been the assistant to every commanding officer since 1969. It would be virtually impossible to run that precinct efficiently and effectively without his wise counsel and vast experience. He quickly became, and still remains, my "Chinese godfather."

In my first two days as the precinct commander, Shuck Seid briefed me on a whole host of issues relating to Chinatown, including a *Reader's Digest* history going back to the turn of the twentieth century. While overall relations between police and community had gotten better, there were still some tensions. One bone of contention was an incident that had taken place prior to my arrival. A Chinese photojournalist had been arrested for taking pictures inside a polling area at a nearby school. The Chinese press consisted of a half dozen weekly newspapers, a cable television outlet, and two radio stations. It was customary to meet with the Chinese journalists once a month, and I met with them during my first week. The issue of the arrest of the Chinese photojournalist came up—in fact, it dominated the meeting. It was clear to me that I needed to address it, even if the incident had occurred before I had gotten there. I called a friend of mine, Lieutenant George Cerrone, at the NYPD's Legal Bureau. George agreed with me that it is legal to take pictures inside a polling location. (Everybody remembers seeing the local mayor or council member voting on Election Day!) The only question left for me was, Can a Chinese photographer take a picture at a polling location? Lieutenant Cerrone answered, "Of course!" We then realized that we had a bad arrest on our hands, and Lieutenant Cerrone, being a good friend, said that he would personally walk over to the courthouse and have the charges dropped.

I brought the arresting police officer into my office to let him know what I was going to do with this matter. I told him that while I support police officers in the performance of their duties, in this case he had screwed up by arresting the photographer since there had been no violation of the law. To my surprise, he agreed. I then went a step further and told the officer that I was going to assemble the Chinese press and publicly apologize to the photojournalist who had been arrested. Incredibly, the officer agreed that that was the right thing to do. I shook my head as he left my office. The next day I brought in the

Chinese press to give them an update on my first week in Chinatown and my impressions. Toward the end of the meeting, I informed the photographer about my investigation and findings regarding his arrest. I told him the arrest was not valid and that the police department's lawyer had gone to court and withdrawn the charges. I then issued a general apology on behalf of the NYPD. The assembled journalists sat there, stunned. As Shuck Seid explained to me later, losing face in Chinatown for some bad act (like being arrested) and then having that face restored publicly is vindication beyond imagination.

Shuck was right. For the remainder of my tenure in Chinatown, the members of the 5th Precinct and I had a great relationship with the members of the Chinese press. When my tenure was up and I was on my way back to headquarters, the Chinese press threw me a going-away party at which they gave me a plaque, the equivalent of their association's Man of the Year award. The gentleman who handed me the plaque said proudly, in broken English, "Captain, you are the first foreigner to ever win this award!" I replied, "I think you mean non-Chinese." We all had a good laugh.

Shuck's invaluable contribution to the department was displayed yet again in another case involving a reporter. A few months after the incident with the Chinese photographer, a television crew from a weekly news program came to the precinct to film a segment on Chinese gangs, with specific focus on the then "godfather of Chinatown," Benny Ong. After they finished filming their investigation into Ong, the reporter asked to interview me. The interview was to be conducted as we walked through the streets of Chinatown. It seemed like a good idea for the precinct commander to be seen on the streets speaking about the gang problem, including the emerging Vietnamese gangs called the BTK (Born to Kill).

When I informed Shuck Seid of the reporter's offer and my intention to accept, Shuck replied in no uncertain terms, "No, Captain, you can't do that." I wasn't quite sure where he was coming from or why he did not want me to do the interview. I thought maybe he was worried about casting Chinatown in a bad light. But his reason wasn't that obvious. He explained to me the social pecking order in Chinatown. I was the captain, he explained to me. The captain is in the top rung of officialdom in Chinatown. "You are the leader. For you to be seen on television walking around with a reporter, who is viewed as very low on the social hierarchy, would demean the stature of the captain."

Since I had promised to give an interview and couldn't back out of it, we made the decision to allow a police officer from the gang unit to walk with the reporter. But this was going to be risky because police officers are often less sophisticated and more apt to say something that is impolitic to an inquiring reporter. I then came up with a brilliant idea. I would designate a Chinese-born and Chinese-speaking police officer to accompany the reporter. This police officer was a great cop and probably our best gang fighter in the unit. However, his English was deplorable. He was difficult to understand even when speaking face-to-face. On television I knew he would be completely incomprehensible. And he was! But it did provide good footage as the officer strolled through Chinatown with the reporter in tow.

I had been in the 5th Precinct barely two weeks when my phone began to ring off the hook with calls of outrage from police headquarters. "What the hell is going on down there, Timoney?" yelled one chief. "Every time I put on my fucking television, I see young punks selling their fireworks! Now, not only do the regular fireworks buyers know where to go, but every asshole in New Jersey and Connecticut know where to buy their fireworks: Mott and Canal Street! It's like a fucking Baghdad bazaar out there, and you better stop it!" A month earlier the previous captain had put together the annual fireworks task force, which consisted of four officers who would go out daily, make arrests, and confiscate fireworks. Obviously, they were not doing enough or, more likely, their numbers were too small to deal with the huge amounts of fireworks that were available. I immediately doubled the size of the task force and paid the officers overtime to work on their days off during the lead up to the July 4 celebrations. By and large, the officers did a great job, and we made a record number of confiscations.

What made the fireworks issue so big that year was that July 4 coincided with the reopening of the refurbished Statue of Liberty and a parade of tall ships in the harbor. By the evening of July 4, after the parade and the fireworks were finished, all my other officers in Manhattan South and I had worked ten days straight, sometimes sixteen hours each day. I was exhausted. After July 4 I took off two days to rest and recuperate. I then returned to resume my normal duties as the precinct commander, only to be informed by the desk lieutenant that two people were waiting for me in my office.

When I entered my office, two men I had gotten to know over the prior three weeks greeted me. One was the local Franciscan priest, wearing his preferred attire—a Yankees hat and Yankees jacket—as opposed to his ankle-length brown robe girded with ropes and dangling rosary beads. The other was Kenny Cirillo, a local civic activist who was also the Republican district leader. (There were very few Republicans in Manhattan during this time, so he was a leader in name only.) As I walked into my office, the priest blurted out, "'Certain people' are going to kill Kenny!" Kenny was clearly distraught and unnerved. I asked why they were going to kill him. The priest replied, "Because your guys hurt their fireworks business this year with all of the confiscations. They lost tens of thousands of dollars, and they think Kenny is to blame because he was breaking your balls about the proliferation of fireworks and so you overreacted and focused extra attention on the issue. They think Kenny should've shut up."

I explained to the priest that they shouldn't blame Kenny. He wasn't the problem. The problem was all those young, indiscreet kids whom they hired this year who were granting television news interviews like they were running for office. (It appeared that there had been an insufficient number of "traditional sellers" that year. The fireworks bosses had reached out to younger and less discreet ethnic groups to augment the busy season.) When the brass at headquarters saw the kids' interviews on television about how and where to buy fireworks, they went crazy and put pressure on me.

I said, "Father, what happened in the old days when you wanted to buy fireworks? You went to see a guy who knew a guy, and that guy directed you down the street to another guy who you gave money to, and then he directed you around the corner to another guy who then sent you to an apartment building where you met someone who gave you your fireworks. Go back and tell them, Father, there's no need to kill Kenny. Just tell them to go back to their old ways of doing business. Because when you bring attention, you get attention."

As if we hadn't had enough problems with the events leading up to July 4, we were now less than two months away from the annual ten-day ritual known as the San Gennaro Festival. I had come down to the San Gennaro Festival once as a teenager and had enjoyed great Italian food, pastries, and the atmosphere of the event. Now I was about to learn the high jinks behind the scenes. Up to this point, I had been given a superficial overview of police operations for the San Gennaro Festival. It seemed simple enough: large crowds, lots of traffic, lots of drunks fighting, an occasional pickpocket. The general meat and potatoes of policing. As we got closer to the event, I began to be inundated with law enforcement agents from other agencies who were investigating the behind-the-scenes operations and moneymaking ventures by the festival organizers. Additionally, the commander of the NYPD Public Morals Division came to visit me, along with an official from the Department of Taxation and Finance. All of these people more or less made the same case: "the Mob" ran and controlled the festival, and they made hundreds of thousands, if not millions, of dollars over the course of the ten days. Suspecting it was one thing; proving it was quite another. But they all came in with their game faces on, indicating "this time it will be different."

I was then given an executive brief of how the finances of the festival worked. The event covered about ten city blocks along Mulberry Street. Both sides of the street were lined with a variety of stalls, booths, and carts with food, designer jewelry, games of chance, etc. To place a small booth or stand along the sidewalk, the "rent" was $3,000 for the ten days of the festival. For the larger stands, the "rent" was $5,000. There was also intricate financing regarding beer and food sales and gross receipts. There were even provisions for lost revenue as a result of getting rained out. Folklore surrounding the event suggested that one year it rained seven out of the ten days, but the organizers had been able to have the festival extended an additional ten days to recoup their losses due to the weather. To me, the most fascinating part of the financing of the festival was the ability of "the organizers" to charge thousands of dollars of rent for permission to use space owned by the city.

Finally, I learned that I would be meeting with "the organizers" of the event to go over the ground rules regarding the policing of the festival. The captain of the Public Morals Division, Gerry Piazza, who was a friend of mine, indicated that he wanted to sit in on that meeting. I foresaw no problems and agreed. When the meeting finally occurred, three Italian American gentlemen from the organizing committee came to my office. Also present were the Public Morals Division captain, who was Italian American, and my Italian American administrative lieutenant, John Codiglia. Within minutes the discussion between the five Italian Americans became heated, while the Irish captain just sat silently by. The organizing committee accused the captain from Public Morals of spying on them, trying to ruin their profits, and overall not being a good sport about the event.

To give this meeting some context, the crusading U.S. attorney for the Southern District of New York at the time was Rudolph "Rudy" Giuliani, also an Italian American, and he had built his reputation on his attempts to wipe out the Mob. At one point, in response to something the captain from Public Morals said, one organizer bemoaned to another, "Look, just what we need, another Italian [not the word they actually used] trying to purify the race." It was a clear reference to Rudy Giuliani.

Not wanting the meeting to degenerate any further, I jumped in and started to deal with the public-safety issues. There were certain commitments that I wanted from the committee. First, stalls or carts would not block intersections and fire hydrants. Second, beer could be sold only in plastic containers. And this was followed by a whole series of other demands and requests. The organizers said yes to my every request, which was when I realized that these boys had no intention of doing anything I asked. But I had an ace up my sleeve: Sergeant Michael Verde, another Italian American who had been my driver back in my days in Spanish Harlem and who had also worked with me at police headquarters while he was attending law school. Mike was finishing school, but I had made him my late tour sergeant in the 5th Precinct. He had the assignment of covering my back during the overnight hours when the vast majority of things that go wrong in policing normally occur.

Mike's job was to ensure that, in the week prior to the festival, none of the many tractor trailers that descended upon Mulberry Street would be allowed to drop its stalls in front of a fire hydrant, intersection, or crosswalk. Mike did a fantastic job in addressing all of these issues. But his great job clearly cost the organizers a lot of money. In prior years, about 330 stalls had been erected. With Mike's intervention, the total number of stalls was reduced to only 300 stalls, a reduction of almost ten percent, or a "loss" of more than $100,000 in "rent" and other income.

The ten days of the event went quite well, and many people re-marked that it had been the most peaceful San Gennaro Festival in recent memory. I like to think that one of the reasons it went so well is that I made it a point to walk the entire route numerous times every night, accompanied by my administrative assistant, six-foot-six body builder John Codiglia.

During my first evening walk through the festival, I noticed that something had changed from the original setup. Where there once had been a fire hydrant in plain view, now there was a sausage stand hid-ing the hydrant. The next night the crosswalk that had been left clear on Bayard and Mulberry streets sported a huge game stand that jutted out into the middle of the intersection, blocking all access to emergency vehicles. If you could throw a baseball through the hole, though, you could win a teddy bear. How satisfying. This stand-accretion process continued unabated over the next eight days, so that by the last day of the festival, there were 350 stands—twenty more than the prior year! So much for promises and Timoney's strong hand.

Occasionally, on my walks, I would meet the main organizer who had been in my office three weeks earlier, and I would inquire about the magical appearance of the new stands. He would try to change the conversation, reminding me that we were both graduates of Fordham University, as if that had anything to do with what was happening on

Mulberry Street. When I would press him, he would just smile and shrug his shoulders. I got the message: Relax. Go with the flow. Stop fighting everything.

None of this should have been a surprise to me. I really had gotten my first inkling about what was going to happen on my very first walk through the festival. As I approached a major intersection, I saw a heavyset old woman with a huge bathtub filled with ice and glass bottles of beer. She had set up directly in the middle of the intersection, blocking everything. When I discreetly inquired if she knew about the promise not to sell beverages in glass containers, she looked at me as if I was crazy and said, "No, you don't understand. I've got twelve cases, and as soon as I sell them, I'm out of here." When I asked the main organizer why the woman had been allowed to sell glass-bottled beer, he told me, "As you see, she doesn't pay rent. And Captain, she's *pazzo* [Italian for "crazy"]. Do what you have to do." I wasn't about to start a riot, escorting a seventy-year-old woman off Mulberry Street. But true to her word, when she finished selling her twelve cases of beer, she was gone. Then again, she did appear the next night and every night thereafter.

About halfway through my first year in the 5th Precinct, a few incidents occurring several weeks apart convinced me that Mulberry Street was really a Hollywood back lot. Filming was taking place, albeit covert, up and down the street. These were part of the investigations by overlapping law enforcement jurisdictions on the Mob, specifically John Gotti. A lot of the activities were in or near the Ravenite Social Club, the Gotti family headquarters.

One day, I received a phone call from a sergeant, an old friend of mine, who was working one of the organized crime task forces. He informed me that he was up the street filming by the Ravenite Social Club and had just observed a Mob guy put some guns in the trunk of a car. Rather than blow his cover and confront the individual, he called me. We sent a uniform car to the location and made the arrest.

The second incident was of much greater concern. Two of my police officers made an arrest on Mulberry Street, which resulted in bells going off in police headquarters. I received a rather frantic phone call from a deputy chief who wanted to know what was going on down there that two of my police officers had made some kind of gambling arrest—this arrest interfered with an ongoing organized crime investigation. What struck me as funny was that the officers hadn't even arrived back at the station, yet headquarters knew about this arrest long before I did. When I asked the deputy chief how he had found out about the arrest, he replied that there was a wiretap set up at the location and "Your guys obviously fucked up the ongoing investigation." What made this particularly problematic was that uniformed police officers were almost forbidden from making gambling arrests. I thought to myself, These guys better have a good story, as I waited on the precinct steps for them to return to the station house with their prisoner.

Their story seemed plausible and was something to the effect that they were summoned into a hallway in an apartment building just north of the Ravenite Social Club. As they entered the hallway, the door to an apartment was wide open and they were able to see a slot machine and other gambling paraphernalia. They made the arrest based on the items in "plain view." While the officers sold me on their story, headquarters wasn't buying any of it, and so I had my ass handed to me. The story didn't end there, however.

About three days after the arrest, the two police officers who made the arrest came into my office to see me. They seemed nervous. In fact, they seemed scared. They told me about an incident that had happened the previous night in the precinct parking lot at the base of the Manhattan Bridge just after midnight when they were going off duty. As they approached their cars, three rather thuggish individuals confronted them. One of the individuals let it be known that the arrest three days prior was not appreciated and had upset people and that if the officers didn't keep their nose out of other people's business, something bad would happen to them.

I was taken aback by this. Every police officer who's worth his salt has been threatened in the heat of the moment while making an arrest or calming a disturbance. However, I had never heard of anything as blatant, as arrogant, and as downright ballsy as what had happened to these two men. I knew I couldn't just let this sit. I couldn't have thugs threatening my police officers. As I was thinking about my response, I remembered a community meeting with the restaurant owners along Mulberry Street. Among their complaints was that my police officers were being too aggressive issuing parking summonses, which hurt the restaurants' client base. One pizza-store owner was incredulous that he could possibly get a summons on his car when he had a cardboard pizza box on the dashboard. The most outrageous complaint was from the wife of a famous mobster who had been killed a decade earlier with five shots to the head at a local restaurant. She had become a restaurateur and was complaining rather loudly that there were too many police officers on Mulberry Street, especially the young cops with the letters *NSU* on their collar (*NSU* stood for *Neighborhood Stabilization Unit*, and the unit was made up of rookie police officers who had just graduated from the police academy). She said she wanted only police officers with the number 5 on their collar, and she insisted that the *S* in NSU was for "Spying." As I left that meeting I shook my head. Every other neighborhood in New York was screaming for more cops, but these people wanted fewer cops. I kept this in the back of my mind.

Thinking back on that meeting and what to do with the three thugs who had threatened my officers, the answer was obvious. What Mulberry Street needed at this point were more cops. I called Chief Kerins at the borough office and described the incident from the night before. He, too, was upset that police officers had been threatened so blatantly. I asked the chief, "Would it be possible to get a dozen or so extra police officers from the borough task force to patrol Mulberry Street and strictly enforce all laws?" I also sent word over to Mulberry Street that if a police officer was ever threatened again, I would have a dozen police officers from the Patrol Borough Manhattan South Task Force on Mulberry Street and that their only job would be to wallpaper the street with parking tickets and enforce all other laws, big and small. We never again heard from the three thugs or their colleagues.

While I was having fun in my new assignment as the commanding officer of Chinatown, the top brass of the NYPD was not having such a grand time. A significant corruption scandal involving members of the 77th Precinct in Brooklyn had burst onto the scene and had not subsided. New allegations and discoveries were being made by two dogged reporters, Mike McAlary of *Newsday* and Michael Daly of the *New York Daily News*. The rest of the media followed their lead, and so day after day the department took a pounding on its ability to fight corruption. While I was no longer at headquarters, friends of mine who were still there filled me in on what was happening and the atmosphere on the thirteenth and fourteenth floors, the offices of the super chiefs, the chief of the department, the first deputy commissioner, and the commissioner. The pressure from the press was becoming overwhelming, and the top brass was determined to allocate the pressure equally down the management chain of command. All of the one-, two-, and three-star chiefs were summoned to headquarters for a "come to Jesus" meeting.

When I heard about the meeting, I had the feeling, to quote Yogi Berra, of "déjà vu all over again." My feelings were confirmed when Chief Kerins, my immediate boss, summoned me and other captains and inspectors from Manhattan South for a firsthand account of what was covered earlier that day with the Divine Trinity—Chief of Department Robert J. Johnston, First Deputy Commissioner Patrick J. Murphy, and Police Commissioner Ben Ward. The message was quite simple. While crime was important, increases in crime never took out a police or political administration, but a corruption problem could be fatal to both. It became clear that, once again, keeping our corruption skirts clean was going to be back on the front burner within the NYPD.

Ethnic Tensions of a Different Sort

In New York, whenever the issue of ethnic tensions arises, people most often think of the African American community's relationship with the white community or the government. Or people assume the tensions are between Hispanics and the majority community or the government. However, in the 5th Precinct I discovered a different type of ethnic tension. It was between the Italian and Chinese communities.

For most of the nineteenth century, the area known as Little Italy— bordered to the south by Canal Street, to the north by Houston Street, to the east by the Bowery, and to the west by Broadway—was dominated, obviously, by recently arrived Italian immigrants and second- or third-gencration Italians. There was also a larger area north of Houston and west of Broadway contained in the 6th Precinct, commonly referred to as the West Village.

Chinatown, on the other hand, was confined to a small geographic area south of Canal Street, squeezed between the Bowery and the Civic Center. It had remained that way for decades, but beginning in the 1970s, with an influx of Chinese immigrants from the mainland as well as from Vietnam, Chinatown began to expand. Simultaneously, many of the second- and third-generation Italian Americans in Little Italy, like other ethnic groups before them, began to head to greener pastures: the suburbs of Long Island, New Jersey, and Staten Island.

It became evident to me that the expansion of Chinatown was going to pick up speed over the next decade when a consortium of businessmen from Hong Kong came into my office one day. A very attractive English-speaking woman, the only English speaker of the group, was the liaison. Within the past month, the British had agreed to turn over the keys of Hong Kong to the mainland Chinese government. The liaison explained that these Hong Kong businessmen, as leery of the mainland Chinese communist government as that government was inimical to capitalism, had millions of dollars in cold cash ready to invest in Lower Manhattan. (I immediately wondered if they were carrying this money with them and if they were robbed what kind of headaches that would cause me. I took pride in controlling my robbery rates!)

We sat down with a map of Lower Manhattan to discuss many areas inside Little Italy, as well as the formerly Jewish area, the Lower East Side, and even some areas north of Houston Street. Their main questions revolved around the criminal activity in these areas. They seemed pleased to hear that the crime rates were relatively low, and when they left my office, it was clear to me that they would be investing heavily and quickly in local real estate.

Also clear to me was that Little Italy was quickly becoming Little, Little Italy. Stories and rumors came back to me regarding the feelings of many of the Italian American residents, especially the businessmen. It was alleged that Italian merchants along the main restaurant hub of

Mulberry Street were under orders from some unknown authority (the Mob?) not to sell any more of their businesses to anyone, especially the Chinese. These underlying tensions would manifest themselves every once in a while. I never realized that I would soon be the precipitating agent in one of these ethnic outbursts.

I received many phone calls from police headquarters and from my immediate bosses at the Manhattan South Borough Office complaining about traffic and parking in Chinatown and Little Italy. One particular afternoon, I received a phone call from Chief Kerins: "John, I was just driving from the borough office to police headquarters, and it took me forty-five minutes. [Normally, this drive would take ten minutes.] What the hell is going on down there? It's auto anarchy!" With complaints like these I put together a program that sent a team of officers out with a tow truck to ticket autos, especially those that were double parked. The autos would then be impounded. I soon began to receive complaints from members of the Italian American community to the effect that I was towing cars only in Little Italy. I also received phone calls from the Chinese community to the effect that I was towing cars only in Chinatown. To deal with these complaints, I instituted affirmative-action towing. I would tow twenty cars from Little Italy and twenty cars from Chinatown. But just like affirmative action in other walks of life, no one was satisfied.

One day, while towing one of our twenty Little Italy cars, an incident occurred in front of Gotti's Ravenite Social Club. It appeared that the car to be towed was the Mercedes belonging to Peter Gotti (John Gotti's brother). The members of the Ravenite Social Club were having none of that. Half a dozen of them appeared on the streets, blocking the tow truck operator from hooking up the car. The police officers at the scene tried to mediate the dispute, but to no avail. The patrol sergeant was requested to respond to the scene. I received a phone call in my office and indicated that I, too, would respond. Shortly thereafter, the Ravenite members, upon hearing the radio transmissions, stepped to the side and allowed the tow operator to hook up Peter's Mercedes and leave. As the tow truck pulled away, under police escort, the six gentlemen from the Ravenite Social Club stood on the sidewalk and clapped in unison, as if applauding the final scene of Verdi's *Rigoletto*.

I'm not quite sure why they allowed the tow truck to leave unchallenged. Was it because the patrol sergeant had been summoned to the scene? Or was it because the "Irish Hard-On Captain," as I was affectionately called, had been notified? We'll never know.

However, there was a great lesson learned as a result of the tow program, and it fascinated me. It helped me understand, in part, Chinese culture. On a regular basis the Chinese residents who received summonses would be irate, out of all proportion, to the issue at hand: a simple parking summons. The vast majority of New Yorkers view parking summonses as a minor irritant, and some would simply just tear up the ticket and throw it in the nearest garbage can or the gutter after taking it off their windshield.

The Chinese viewed the summons as a major offense. They really thought they had committed a bad infraction or, in Catholic parlance, a mortal sin. On some occasions the disagreement with the issuing officer over a parking summons resulted in the arrest of the citizen on such charges as disorderly conduct or interfering with an officer in the performance of his duties. In one extreme case, a police officer issued a summons to a car that was owned by a Chinese American doctor. When the tow truck arrived and began to hook up the car, the Chinese doctor, who had been pleading up to that point, mounted the bar between the tow truck and the car in protest. In the attempt to pull the doctor off of the bar, a scuffle ensued and the doctor wound up with a broken arm.

When I analyzed this, there was clearly a clash of cultures. The police officer issuing the summons, like most New Yorkers, thought it was no big deal. He couldn't understand why the Chinese doctor would get so excited. The doctor, on the other hand, felt as if he had committed a mortal sin and had "lost face."

I used these altercations and incidents as a training tool at roll call, and it went something like this: "You guys always complain that nobody respects the law, that nobody gives a shit, yet here you have a community that actually respects the law and actually gives a shit and actually thinks a summons is a serious matter! And what do you guys do? You arrest them for objecting! Think about it. We finally have friends who respect us and think what we do is important. I think we need to find some other way to resolve our minor disagreements!" The cops got the irony and the humor of the situation.

During my time in Chinatown, I learned a lot about Chinese culture: the understanding of numbers and gambling and the roles that luck and the color red play in their world; the realization that the biggest gambling day in Chinatown was Monday, when the businesses were closed; the importance of male children within the family; and the importance of family itself. Shuck Seid would regularly provide me with Chinese proverbs neatly typed on small pink or red pads. One saying had to do with worrying about the snow in front of your own door and not concerning yourself with the snow on another man's roof. Loosely translated, it referred to an individual's loyalty and where that loyalty should be concentrated. In some respects, this is counter to many of our Western notions. For example, the great hero in Western culture is the Good Samaritan, someone who is willing to endanger his own life to help others. This notion permeates our literature and, in modern times, our movies—Gary Cooper, in the movie *High Noon*, epitomizes the Good Samaritan. Chinese culture does not view the Good Samaritan as favorably. Their rationale is that a man's first obligation is to his family, and that the Good Samaritan, by getting involved in other people's business, risks his own existence and therefore that of his family unit and his role within it.

The highlight of Chinatown is the Chinese New Year. In addition to the magnificent parades and fireworks displays are the family-association dinners. These dinners, usually involving well over a thousand attendees, feature a ten-course feast. After a while, you are able to tell where you are within the feast by which dish is served. Fish comes at a specific point, as does duck or chicken. Like anything else in life, there are gradations—some feasts are fabulous, while others are not so fabulous. Within the police family the menus were rated from A to D. I made sure I attended all of the A- and B-menu feasts, but I would try to delegate the responsibility of attending the D feasts. Unfortunately, one night my luck ran out.

In addition to my role as commanding officer of the 5th Precinct, one Sunday evening I was the acting borough duty captain, which meant that I was not only responsible for the 5th Precinct but also for any major incident that occurred anywhere in Manhattan South. When I attended a dinner that night, I realized too late that it was a D menu. I sat down at the table, prepared for a long night of eating D-menu food while dreaming of A-menu entrées. As luck would have it, I was summoned on the radio to respond to an emotionally disturbed person. A naked man armed with a sword inside the Holland Tunnel had brought all New Jersey–bound traffic to a complete halt. I left the feast and headed toward the Holland Tunnel, happy to have escaped the D-grade dinner. Traffic was horrible, and it appeared that I would never get to my destination. This was fine by me. All of a sudden the traffic opened up, and I found myself at the foot of the tunnel with a group of cops, two of whom were handcuffing and putting a blanket around the naked, crazy man. As I approached, one of the cops yelled to me, "We're okay, boss. Everything's resolved!" It may have been resolved for him, but not for me. I had lost only a half hour, which meant that I would too soon be back at the banquet. On the good side, I would have missed five or six courses of the ten-course meal. When I got back to the dinner and once again sat at the table, the kind, thoughtful hosts let me know that they had kept a plate of each of the six courses I had missed. I then had to gulp those dishes down in order to catch up with the rest of the guests. Not only did I have D-menu food, I had *cold* D-menu food. Lesson: I should have told the waiter to skip my seat when serving the last six courses!

Larry Davis

The worst of my days in Chinatown had nothing to do with Chinatown but with my childhood friend, Tommy McCarren. I had grown up in Washington Heights with Tommy, although he was two years my senior. He was a fantastic athlete, especially at hockey, and was viewed by most as the toughest guy in the neighborhood. He was also one of the nicest and most mild-tempered human beings you could encounter. While I was assigned to the 44th Precinct with Peter Dunne and

Tommy Hyland, Tom McCarren was assigned to the 48th Precinct on the eastern border of the 44th. Tommy's partner in the 48th was Patrick Harnett, who was also actually a resident of the 44th.

In the early 1970s, the Black Liberation Army had declared war on America and was dedicated to killing police officers as a means of overthrowing the U.S. government. The police commissioner had made a public promise to immediately promote, to the rank of detective, any uniformed officer who arrested members of the Black Liberation Army.

On June 5, 1971, early in the morning, two young police officers of the 48th Precinct responded to a robbery in progress at a South Bronx social club. After a few hours of excellent police work, they arrested a group of Black Liberation Army members who were in the process of robbing the dozens of patrons in the club. Within days, the two officers were promoted, as promised, to the rank of detective. The new detectives, Tom McCarren and Patrick "Buddy" Harnett, were now members of a select, world-renowned group: NYPD detectives. Over the next eight years, they would solve many of the great robbery and homicide cases in the Bronx. In 1981, they would part ways when Pat Harnett became a sergeant, choosing the career stepladder to chief, while Tom McCarren remained in the trenches, fighting the good fight for all of the unknowns in the South Bronx.

On November 19, 1986, Tommy McCarren, who was assigned to the Homicide Squad, went to an apartment in the South Bronx accompanied by six other officers with the intent to arrest Larry Davis, a well-known felon and local drug dealer in the Bronx, for the homicides of four local drug dealers. Larry Davis was known to be armed and extremely dangerous. When the police officers entered the apartment, there were two women and children in the living room and two infants in the back bedroom. Fearing for the safety of the women and children, police officers withheld fire. Davis, on the other hand, had no such compunction as he blasted away using a sawed-off shotgun and a .45-caliber pistol. Six of the seven police officers were struck, the most seriously injured of whom was Tommy McCarren, who was shot through the mouth. The bullet exited through the back of his neck. Amid the chaos, Larry Davis escaped.

The lieutenant leading the raid, Jack Seebring, told me the story of what happened, focusing on Tommy McCarren. As Seebring entered the apartment building, he observed McCarren at the top of the stairs, bleeding profusely from the mouth. He fully expected McCarren to fall forward down the stairs; it was a scene out of a movie. But he soon learned just how tough McCarren was. McCarren walked down the stairs, passed Seebring, and walked across the street to the local hospital. Seebring concluded the story with what I already knew: "Tommy McCarren is the toughest son of a gun I've ever seen."

Needless to say, the event grabbed the headlines for the next several days. At the same time, the NYPD conducted a citywide search for Davis. Normally, a search of this type would have been conducted out of the Bronx Borough Detectives Office. However, in this case, the search was organized out of the Chief of Department's Office at headquarters, an extraordinarily unusual operational decision. Some veteran detectives speculated that the top brass was fearful that a local apprehension team would shoot first and ask questions later—that is, they were afraid the team would execute "street justice" and take out Larry Davis. Others opined that there was no confidence in the local detective commanders to locate and arrest Davis without further bloodshed. The bottom line was that there was huge resentment among the Bronx detectives toward the seemingly heavy-handed tactics coming from police headquarters. They also complained that the bureaucratic system, which required notification and approval for each decision, actually hampered the quick location and arrest of Davis.

Seventeen days later, Davis was finally located, holed up in an apartment in the South Bronx. Hostage negotiations were set up, and Davis was eventually convinced to surrender by one of the NYPD's main hostage negotiators, Peter Martin, who had grown up with McCarren and me in Washington Heights. Since the hostage negotiations took so many hours, top police brass responded to the scene. The arrest of Davis was captured on television and in the papers, with the four-star chief, Robert Johnston, leading Davis from the apartment complex. Seeing these pictures could lead one to conclude that justice had been done.

But not so fast. When Davis came to trial in the Bronx, his defense attorney was well-known civil rights attorney William Kunstler, famed lawyer for the Chicago Seven. Kunstler argued that while Davis admitted to shooting the police officers, he had done so in self-defense. Incredibly, but not surprising to any cop who worked the Bronx, the jury found Davis not guilty. He was found guilty, however, of possession of an illegal weapon, for which he was sent to jail. Later, he was also convicted of a separate murder of a drug dealer and was sentenced to twenty-five years to life. In February 2008, while he was still in prison, Davis was stabbed and killed by a fellow inmate, the jailhouse equivalent of "street justice."

The Davis case is discussed in police circles even today. Detectives argue that politics, especially racial politics, was allowed to influence police operational decisions. While it is hard to know the thinking behind Chief Johnston's decision, it is indisputable that Davis was captured and that no other police officers were injured. Johnston probably knew, and factored into his decision, the notion that, had local detectives become involved in a shootout with Davis, and had they shot and wounded, or even killed, him, there would have been a public outcry that Davis had been summarily executed by the NYPD.

Unfortunately, immediately after the shooting of the police officers, Davis became a bit of a folk hero in the South Bronx because he had wounded six police officers and made good his escape. Had he been shot and killed in an exchange of gunfire with the NYPD, he would have become a folk hero *and* a martyr. Instead, Larry Davis was just another thug who died at the hands of some other thug. In the end, justice, no matter how imperfect, prevailed.

For Chief Johnston it had been a no-win situation. Police chiefs sometimes find themselves in situations in which they know ahead of time that no one will be satisfied with the outcome. It's why they pay us the little bucks. When faced with a situation like this, a chief must weigh all of the facts and trust his gut. If he has been a good decision maker in the past, he will probably make the right decision in a no-win situation. If he has not been a good decision maker in the past, his no-win decision will probably cost him his job.

Remarkably, Tommy McCarren survived his injuries and trained with me a few years later for the New York City marathon. Though still suffering from the effects of the bullet wound and a severe case of asthma, which further complicated his training regimen, he completed the marathon and even beat me in the process. As many have said, Tommy McCarren is one tough guy.

In July 1987, I received a phone call from Deputy Chief Tom Walsh asking me to stop in to see him. Chief Walsh informed me that he was reorganizing his office to make it more efficient and effective, and he thought it would be a good idea if I came back to headquarters. I had mixed emotions regarding the offer because I hadn't completed my two years as commanding officer of the 5th Precinct, which was generally the accepted tour of duty. When I decided to take him up on the opportunity, I asked him if he could wait two months until I had completed my second San Gennaro Festival. I thought it would be unfair to throw a new captain into the responsibilities of the festival so soon after his taking office. Also, I would then have under my belt two Chinese New Years, two July 4 celebrations, and two San Gennaro Festivals—the three big-ticket items for someone commanding the 5th Precinct.

Walsh concurred with my request. The added benefit of this two-month delay in transfer was that I had the opportunity to lobby for my successor. My choice coincided with the borough chief's choice: Gerry Frey. Gerry was a young, smart commander, a great athlete, and in possession of the appropriate temperament for Chinatown. Gerry was named my successor three weeks before I left. We had an invaluable two-week transition period during which Gerry worked with me on a daily basis, which normally does not happen in the NYPD. Gerry and I worked the ten days of the San Gennaro Festival together, and it went flawlessly. However, our combined strength could not reduce the number of stands along Mulberry Street.

6

Back to Headquarters Under Dinkins

"Dave, Do Something!"
—NEW YORK POST *HEADLINE*

My new assignment at police headquarters was as commanding officer of the Chief of the Department's Office, which meant running the office's day-to-day operations. This would allow Deputy Chief Walsh to concentrate on the bigger issues facing the department, ranging from focusing on critical policy development to assisting operations in staffing a series of protests known as "Days of Outrage." It also allowed me to be the understudy of Chief Walsh, who had a major skill that I lacked: attention to detail. Working under him made me understand how the department was organized, how to deploy thousands of officers to police a certain event, and how the budget was created. In other words, when you're out in the field calling in various numbers and requests, you don't necessarily understand the big picture. The NYPD is an organization of thirty thousand to forty thousand people, so it is quite possible to work in one area of the city and fail to recognize how that area relates to another precinct or, in fact, to the overall picture.

In addition to working closely with Chief Walsh, I also was able to work next to the four-star chief, Robert Johnston. I had worked for Chief Johnston for about a year before I became captain. But now I was working with him, in the same office, and could see him in action on a daily basis. By this point in his career, he had become an NYPD legend, one who was both feared and loved. To me, he was just a good guy, even if, at times, he was too demanding. Working with these two gentlemen provided me with a solid knowledge base that I used when I began to move into the upper ranks.

The following summer, my education on how to handle catastrophic events involving the department grew as a result of an incident in Tompkins Square Park. Located in the East Village in Manhattan, the park has been the site of intermittent protests and riots going back more than a hundred years. The event that took place there in 1988 was no different, except the police commissioner himself described it as a police riot. Throughout the summer, there had been numerous events, including concerts, in the park. These would often require police intervention either to stop some nonsense or to reduce the volume of music. But one night, and it is still unclear who is to blame, all hell broke loose, and the police officers assigned to the park found themselves in a pitched battle with homeless people, radicals, and assorted other individuals. Because the police officers at the scene were outnumbered, a citywide assistance call went out. Police officers from as far away as the Bronx and Brooklyn responded. In addition, the captain at the scene called for air support—a helicopter to fly over and illuminate the park.

The low-flying helicopter whipped up a lot of debris and created a lot of noise, which enhanced the sense of chaos. For those citizens who couldn't see the chaos on the ground or hear the engines of the chopper, they could see the bright lights over the scene from two or three blocks away. Hundreds of curious onlookers went to the park to see what the excitement was all about. These innocent citizens confronted the dozens of running protesters leaving the park as they were chased by baton-wielding police officers. In the melee, there were clashes throughout the area around the park, and some curious onlookers were injured and, in some cases, arrested. Responding police officers from the outer boroughs came in with no supervision and little direction. This further added to the chaos. A lot of the police conduct that night was captured on home video cameras and displayed on the evening news on nearly every channel night after night over the next few weeks. Commissioner

Ward ordered an internal investigation of the officers who used unnecessary force and simultaneously created a panel to review police response and tactics at the event. The three-person panel was made up of the deputy commissioner of Public Information, Alice McGillian; the chief of the Organized Crime Bureau, Anthony Volker; and the commanding officer of the Office of Management Analysis and Planning (OMAP), Raymond Kelly, who was a two-star chief.

While the panel's report was a short twenty pages, it was sweeping in its indictment and recommendations regarding police response to civil disturbances. It dealt with poor decision making, poor response, and poor tactics at the scene of a specific incident. It did not deal with the larger issue of police mobilization, tactics, logistics, and incident command for major civil disturbances (a few years later, Ray Kelly would fix once and for all how police would mobilize and respond to major civil disturbances). In typical NYPD fashion, the Tompkins Square Park incident resulted in a few police officers being fired but also in the reassignment of high-ranking police officials, including the precinct commander. Ben Ward was determined to address the many complex issues within the 9th Precinct stemming from anarchists and squatters, communists and homeless people, artists and con artists. He chose the bright and eclectic Deputy Inspector Mike Julian as commander. Julian was a commander from central casting, the future chief of big ideas, and my best friend.

The late 1980s were a particularly tough time in New York City. Racial tensions were at the boiling point. Reverend Al Sharpton led a series of "Days of Outrage" protests in response to the killing of Yusuf Hawkins, a young black man who was shot to death in 1989 by a group of whites in the Bensonhurst neighborhood of Brooklyn. (Sharpton had burst onto the New York scene after the acquittal of Bernhard Goetz, a white man who in 1984 had shot four black teenagers on a New York City subway who, he maintained, had tried to rob him.) A year later Sharpton led a series of protests through Howard Beach, Queens, after the death of Michael Griffen, a black man who had been chased by a group of white youths into a traffic lane where he was struck by a car and killed. Often the subject of Sharpton's protests was the NYPD.

Other times, it was whites. Still other times, it was Mayor Ed Koch, who was in the last two years of his third term. And as if the racial tensions were not enough, there were also many protests, some of which turned violent, by gay activist groups such as Act Up and Queer Nation to call attention to the ineffective and insufficient response on the part of the government to the AIDS epidemic. By the late 1980s, it seemed as if no one was happy or satisfied, and there was a clamor for change. Breaking corruption scandals involving some of the city's leading Democratic politicians—most notably Donald Manes of Queens, who committed suicide, and Stanley Friedman of the Bronx, who went to jail—added to the mix.

In the September 1989 Democratic primary, David Dinkins, the Manhattan borough president, defeated Mayor Ed Koch for the mayoral nomination. Two months later, Dinkins defeated Republican nominee Rudy Giuliani to become the first African American mayor in the city's history. It was assumed that there would be a big change not only at City Hall but also at police headquarters. Finally, there was also a feeling throughout most of the city that with an African American mayor, at least we would have racial calm.

Mayor Dinkins chose Dr. Lee Patrick Brown as his new police commissioner. Brown had been the chief of the Houston and Atlanta police departments and had served in a number of other police departments throughout the country. Commissioner Brown was also the incoming president of the International Association of Chiefs of Police, which required some of his attention and led to derisive commentary by the New York media because of the travel commitments of that role.

While there was the expectation of change and rumors of great change, there was, in fact, very little change. Immediately, Commissioner Brown let it be known that Chief Johnston would be staying in his position as the four-star chief of the department. In a dinner conversation years later, Commissioner Brown told me that he had been convinced to keep Chief Johnston in his position as the number three man in the NYPD as a result of his numerous conversations with former police commissioner Ben Ward and others. Ward believed that Chief Johnston had a strong hold on the department and that the men and women of the NYPD would always respond to his strong leadership. While the prior five years had been tumultuous, the NYPD avoided any major conflagrations as a result of Johnston's strong leadership.

When Commissioner Brown was appointed, Raymond Kelly was a two-star assistant chief and the commanding officer of the Office of Management Analysis and Planning. In that position, Kelly was the go-to person for the department during the Brown transition. Upon taking office, Commissioner Brown chose Chief Kelly as his first deputy commissioner, the number two person in the NYPD. There were some rumors and grumbling about the minimal changes. Many of the one-star and two-star chiefs had been hoping for massive change at the three- and four-star level, which did not happen. Some of them argued among themselves, self-servingly, that to have radical change within the department, you needed to have radical change at the top—not just the commissioner, but also the positions of the super chiefs, including the chief of the department.

Kelly's appointment caused a separate problem. He was now in a position to supervise those who had supervised him, specifically the four-star chief of the department, Robert Johnston. Somehow Commissioner Brown was convinced to change the organizational structure so that the four-star chief of the department reported directly to the police commissioner. Johnston would report directly to the police commissioner, or, in other words, number three would report directly to number one, thus bypassing number two. This meant Kelly would have no say in day-to-day police operations. The move was unprecedented and untenable, as would become evident a year later during the Crown Heights Riots.

Police Commissioner Brown was the single biggest advocate in America of community policing, a philosophy of policing that had emerged in the mid-1980s. Commissioner Ward first introduced it into the NYPD in the middle of that decade. Under his program, approximately ten officers in every precinct were assigned as problem-solving officers for a given geographical area. These officers were meant to deal with the root causes of crimes, involving quality-of-life issues. There were some successes with the community-policing program, but by and large these officers did little to improve crime rates or the quality of life. For example, when I became the commander of the 5th Precinct, I had ten Community Patrol Officer Program (CPOP) cops. One of these officers was assigned to the Mulberry Street beat. He worked steady shifts from ten in the morning to six in the evening and had Saturdays and Sundays off. The restaurants on Mulberry Street didn't open until 6:00 P.M. and were generally very busy on weekends, exactly when this officer was not around. This was not an uncommon situation for CPOP cops throughout the city. Quite simply, they were working opposite the problems they were meant to address.

When Brown took office, his number one goal was to transform CPOP, which he correctly viewed as a program, into a department-wide operating philosophy. He wanted every single police officer and detective, no matter what his assignment, to be imbued with the community-policing philosophy. He gave numerous talks and speeches on how community policing would deal with the problems of the city. It all sounded too good, if somewhat nebulous.

But there was a problem. Crime, in both perception and reality, was out of control. The murder rate was unprecedented throughout Brown's first year in office, with a total of 2,245 people killed. The New York tabloid headlines created an even more damning picture. In September 1990, Brian Watkins, a young tourist from Utah who was visiting New York City for the U.S. Open Tennis Tournament, was stabbed to death in front of his parents by a gang of youths at a New York City subway station. A few weeks later, after three youths were killed by gunfire, the *New York Post* ran the headline "Dave, Do Something!" The resulting uproar over crime led the mayor to ask a simple question of the police department: What resources did the department need to deal with the crime epidemic?

As a result of Dinkins's question, First Deputy Commissioner Kelly began a massive study to determine what staffing level the NYPD needed in order to deal adequately with crime and the fear of crime. The study took the better part of six months. When it was finished, Kelly produced a comprehensive document covering every single unit within the department; it concluded the NYPD needed around 33,500 officers, an increase of 6,000 or 7,000 cops. This plan was presented to, City Council, whose members reduced the overall figure by a thousand cops—just to be able to say that they had had input and were not pissing away the taxpayers' money. While it is easy to allocate and authorize a higher police number, it is a whole other matter to achieve that goal. But the bottom line is that there was a plan, and it helped to quell the public outcry. (The irony of ironies was that the main beneficiary of this increase in staffing was Rudy Giuliani, who had run against the mayor and the NYPD on the issue of crime. But more on that later.)

A second rationale for the increase in staffing levels was to provide enough police officers not only to fill precinct sector cars but also to fill foot beats, which were an integral part of the community-policing initiative. Throughout Commissioner Brown's first two years in office, a tremendous amount of time was spent on training police officers, especially supervisors and precinct commanders, on the philosophy of community policing. By and large, there was a great deal of skepticism on the part of many and some resistance on the part of a few. Whether the skepticism and resistance were the result of internal assassins or whether the overall policy lacked structure and substance was anybody's guess. It was my sense at the time that it was too ethereal; ultimately, it was too difficult to wrap your head around. The resistance and skepticism were more a result of frustration than anything else.

The issue of operational control of the department surfaced early in the first year of the Brown administration. The operational structure of all police services in Staten Island was completely different than the rest of the city, in that the patrol borough commander controlled not just uniformed services but also the detectives. As a result of a staffing shortage in Staten Island, detective supervision was light on the overnight shift, meaning that a detective captain did not work those hours. Noticing this clear lack of supervision, First Deputy Commissioner Kelly issued a memorandum directing the detective chief from Patrol Borough Brooklyn South Detectives to provide staff supervision for Staten Island detectives on the overnight shift.

The matter appeared minor, but Kelly's memo seemed to violate the agreement that the first deputy commissioner would have no role in day-to-day operations. The chief of detectives, Joe Borelli, resented the memo and the interference of Kelly in police operations, and he brought the memo to the attention of Chief Johnston. Johnston saw the memo as a clear violation of the prior agreement. I accompanied him to the commissioner's office with the memo, and I felt very uncomfortable. Kelly was summoned to Brown's office to discuss the matter. Brown concluded that the memo had, in fact, violated Kelly's noninterference agreement. It was an awkward moment, to say the least. But it was clear that Brown backed Johnston in this case. While the disagreement was minor, the message was powerful: Kelly was to stay out of day-to-day operations.

In the spring of 1991, the Site Selection Committee of the Democratic National Convention came to New York City as part of its multicity tour to determine the location of the 1992 convention. Chief Johnston, with me in tow, visited the committee at a Midtown hotel and gave members a presentation on how the NYPD would provide security for the event. New York had hosted two conventions in recent memory, in 1976 and in 1980.

A few months later, New York was selected as the site for the 1992 convention, and Chief Johnston designated me the security coordinator. I began planning for the event on a part-time basis while continuing my regular job as Chief Johnston's executive officer. The understanding was that, at some point, I would leave my regular duties and do the security planning on a full-time basis. In July, Chief Johnston announced that he would be retiring by mid-August. That was fortuitous since it meant that a new chief of department with a new executive officer would be coming in and I could be taken off line to work full-time on the security for the convention.

The Crown Heights Riots

Chief David Scott, the three-star chief of patrol, was chosen to succeed Chief Johnston as the four-star chief of department. Scott was a highly regarded, respected, well-liked, and telegenic chief who was a natural fit for the job. He was also the first African American to hold the four-star position. His first week in office, the week of August 19, coincided with his annual vacation, which he had committed to and paid for months earlier. There was also a new chief of patrol, Mario Selvaggi. While Scott was on vacation for the week, the chief of detectives, Joe Borelli, was the acting chief of department. Monday, August 19, the first day of Scott's administration, was uneventful, and I spent most of my time bringing my replacement, Deputy Chief Kevin Farrell, up to speed on issues facing the office.

That evening was hot and muggy, with people on the streets escaping the stuffiness of their apartment buildings. In the Brooklyn neighborhood of Crown Heights, a station wagon carrying four Lubavitch Jews struck and killed a seven-year-old black child, Gavin Cato. The station wagon's occupants were the security detail for the Grand Rebbe Menachem Schneerson, who was in the car ahead of them. An unmarked police car with lights and siren had been escorting the two-car motorcade. To complicate matters further, the responding private Jewish ambulance service, Hatzolah, appeared to treat the occupants of the station wagon but not the child. As you can imagine, rumors and outrage spread quickly. Local youths took to the streets. Officers were called into the area. All hell broke loose. And so began what came to be known as the Crown Heights Riots. That evening a young rabbinical student, Yankel Rosenbaum, was stabbed and later died at a local hospital.

Complaints mounted over the first few days regarding the lack of police presence. On the third day of the riots, the mayor's car was attacked, as was Police Commissioner Brown's car. Accusations flew regarding police response and the culpability of City Hall—that is, the mayor. Later that night, the top brass, the mayor, and his aides met at a local hospital to determine how best to put an end to the civil unrest. At 2:00 A.M., I received a phone call from a sergeant at the Operations Unit (the police command center) to report to the first deputy police commissioner's office by 7:00 the next morning. While I knew nothing of the cause of that phone call, I surmised that Commissioner Kelly was taking control of police operations.

I arrived at his conference room early that Thursday morning and was joined by the two-star chief from Brooklyn, Tom Gallagher, and another one-star chief. Also in the conference room were the other super chiefs. Chief Borelli briefed everyone on the situation of the night before and said that Commissioner Kelly was livid and aimed to take control of the matter. A short time later, Kelly arrived; in a no-nonsense fashion he began to query us all on the best plan to end the riots. I had worked for Chief Johnston for the prior four years and, as a result, had an intimate knowledge of the mechanics of organizing and deploying thousands of police officers to any given situation. I suggested that we throw the chart out and go to two twelve-hour shifts, that we cancel all days off, and that we put the plainclothes narcotics detectives in uniform, similar to the way I had been deployed in the 1977 blackout riots.

As a result of the meeting, a few things were put into play. In a highly unusual step, a deputy chief from Patrol Borough Manhattan South, Jim McCabe, was assigned to Brooklyn North to assist in the coordination and deployment of police resources. Jim had wide experience from Manhattan South, which often dealt with the deployment of thousands of police officers on a regular basis, whether at the United Nations or other high-profile locations. Kelly made the decision to handpick the field commanders who would handle operations at the ground level. He chose proven performers such as Louis Anemone, Mike Julian, and Mike Tiffany. By late Thursday afternoon, the plan was in effect. Later that evening, hundreds had been arrested and the civil unrest brought under control. The next week or two remained tense, but for all intents and purposes, the riot had been squelched within twenty-four hours of Ray Kelly's taking control.

At least three lessons came out of the Crown Heights Riots. For me, the most obvious was that a void had been created by the retirement of Bob Johnston. For seven years, Johnston had handled all of the major events in the city, including the "Days of Outrage," and he had, as I noted earlier, given the NYPD its own Powell Doctrine regarding the use of overwhelming force to crush any incident. I can remember people opining behind Johnston's back that he used too many resources when dealing with these incidents, but I think Johnston was proved right in the long run. The second lesson was not to designate the chief of detectives as the acting chief of department. The primary function of the chief of detectives is to investigate serious crimes. To have that same individual attempt to oversee all police operations is unrealistic, at least in a department the size of the NYPD. The third and most important lesson was that the department did not have an up-to-date plan for rapid mobilization and deployment, nor had the department trained its officers, supervisors, and, just as important, high-ranking bosses on how and when to respond and what resources to use.

As the tensions subsided, the recriminations and finger pointing only increased. The pressure became such that the governor of New York intervened and established a blue ribbon commission, under the leadership of Richard Girgenti, to look into what happened and who was responsible. The conclusions and recommendations of the report were appropriate. However, one finding was, in my opinion, unfair, and it had to do with Ray Kelly and his responsibility. "Given the seriousness of the disturbance," the report stated, "it is unfortunate that the First Deputy Commissioner did not assume a role in coordinating the development and implementation of a different strategy sooner."

Kelly maintained—correctly, I believe—that he was out of the operational loop on this event. Many people found this argument not to be credible. However, had they understood the agreement in January 1990, which removed Kelly from all operational responsibilities, or had they known of Commissioner Brown's reiteration of that agreement during the meeting regarding the memo about detective supervision in Staten Island, they may have understood Kelly's point of view. Years later, in a dinner conversation with one of the Girgenti Commission members, I discussed the agreement to have Chief Johnston report directly to the police commissioner as well as the fact that the agreement had been reinforced as a result of the Staten Island detective memo. Clearly, Kelly had been ordered to stay out of day-to-day operations. The commission member said that, had the commission known this background, they would have been less harsh with Ray Kelly.

The 1992 Democratic National Convention

For the remainder of 1991 and into the spring of 1992, I devoted my full attention to the planning for the security of the convention that would take place at the end of that July. Rather than reinvent the wheel, I used the plans for the 1976 and 1980 Democratic conventions as my starting point. Of course, there had been changes, over the preceding dozen years, in what we needed to be prepared for. The concern was not just violent protestors and demonstrators: What if there was a terrorist attack? During the year I spent planning for the convention, I trained for and ran two marathons. During my long training runs, I would think of nothing but the planning of the convention so I would not have to acknowledge the pain I was in. I found that I would have good ideas about what needed to be done between miles ten and fifteen. But when I finished my run, I could remember nothing. So I took to carrying a small tape recorder to record my thoughts.

As a result of my ideas during those training runs, we put a total containment vessel (a bomb disposal unit) within the hall. That way, if a bomb or some other device were found, it could be rendered safe within the bowl of the convention hall, rather than our having to send in the robots (part of the Bomb Squad's equipment is a remote-control robot that carries a suspected bomb to a total containment vessel). We also created a light-coding system along the roof of Madison Square Garden, which would alert security personnel within the bowl of an emerging incident. And we created a temporary morgue complete with twenty thousand body bags at the general post office at Thirty-first Street and Eighth Avenue.

The overall policing of the convention was broken down into nine sectors or zones. It included the inner perimeter, the outer perimeter, the transportation detail, and the dignitary protection detail. The most important zone as far as I was concerned was the one that handled protests and demonstrations. We were not looking for a replica of Chicago 1968. The person I chose as the demonstration commander was Michael Julian. Mike was tough and agile but also had a sense of humor and great interpersonal skills, plus he was not easily intimidated. He was a lawyer by training who had great respect for the Constitution and the notions of freedom of assembly and freedom of speech.

During one of my training runs, I thought about implementing a stand-alone Command and Control Center and Office of Emergency Management modeled on the one at police headquarters. This was quite an undertaking in terms of available space and duplicative resources, not just from the NYPD but also from other city agencies. The difficult part was creating a stand-alone communications system, which would require its own radio repeater systems—rather large objects that weighed several tons. We managed to secure sufficient space at the Fashion Institute of Technology, just four blocks south of Madison Square Garden. There were some who thought that this part of the operation could have been run quite easily from police headquarters. I maintained that if an incident requiring a citywide response occurred, thus demanding the full attention of the Command and Control Center and Office of Emergency Management at police headquarters, we would need a base from which to run the convention. This part of the overall security plan continued to have its detractors, who thought it was expensive, duplicative, and unnecessary.

Another thought that occurred to me on one of my runs was to bring back the retired commanders from the 1976 and 1980 conventions. We brought them in for a full-day session at the Operations Unit at police headquarters. Breakfast and lunch were provided, and there were great photo ops as we paired past commanders with their present counterparts. There was a good exchange of information, a sharing of old cop stories, and it seemed to be a beneficial session.

Shortly thereafter, I was summoned to Chief Scott's office and was informed that a higher-ranking officer, a two-star chief, Dennis Ryan, was being placed as the overall commander of the convention. I would now effectively be his executive officer. This was less than three months before the start of the convention. Apparently, one of the old-timers let it be known that while I was probably a very nice guy and even talented and intelligent, I was way too young and too junior to be put in charge of an event of this magnitude. The argument was that if something went dangerously or desperately wrong, the four-star chief, David Scott, would be faulted for allowing such a junior officer to run such a large event. Needless to say, my pride and ego were badly damaged. My first reaction was to request a transfer, but First Deputy Commissioner Kelly dissuaded me from such action. Later, I would understand the need to have the two-star chief running the operation. It was a tough lesson in not letting your ego get the better of you. It was also a reality check on how big events must be policed and the command structure that must be involved. It was a hard pill to swallow, but in the end, it was the correct decision.

While we were doing the planning for the Democratic convention, I was also given the task of coordinating the security for the Christopher Columbus quincentenary celebration—the five hundredth anniversary of Columbus's discovering America. It involved a parade of tall ships, fireworks displays, and other festivities. It was in many ways similar to the July 4, 1986, unveiling of the refurbished Statue of Liberty. The celebration went off without a hitch. Not only did the public have a good time, but the police officers also enjoyed the event.

At the end of the celebration, a few of my colleagues and I, although exhausted after having worked eighty hours that week, went across the street from police headquarters to have a burger and a few beers and to celebrate the success of the event. We had just ordered our burgers and were sipping our first beers when everyone's beepers went off simultaneously: a drug dealer, Kiko Garcia, had just been killed in the 34th Precinct in northern Manhattan by a plainclothes officer. This precipitated what became known as the Washington Heights Riots, with only a week left before the beginning of the Democratic convention. The timing could not have been worse.

The riots lasted three days but the situation remained tense throughout the remainder of the summer. While there was some property damage and some assaults on police officers, the overall damage was relatively minor compared to some past riots. The way in which the Washington Heights Riots were handled politically would later become fodder for the 1993 mayoral elections between David Dinkins and Rudy Giuliani.

For the week leading up to the convention, there was clear concern as to what impact the riots would have on the convention attendees and their overall perception of the city. However, for the police department, these were two completely separate events. While earlier it had looked like not such a good idea to set up the Command and Control Center at the Fashion Institute of Technology, it now looked like a genius move in light of the fact that the policing of the Washington Heights Riots was being coordinated by the Command and Control Center out of police headquarters. Only in New York could you have thirty-five hundred police officers assigned to a political convention in Midtown Manhattan, another four or five thousand handling a riot and its aftermath in northern Manhattan, plus another fifteen thousand police officers handling day-to-day operations throughout the remainder of the city. Size matters. And so do cops.

As the Democratic convention approached, it became increasingly clear why choosing Mike Julian as the demonstration/protestor commander was such a good idea, even if he was my best friend! There were dozens of groups, with hundreds of grievances, that wanted to be heard at the same time, on the same night, at the same location. To make matters worse, there were some groups who thought that they were much more important than others—animal rights activists do not take second seat to those concerned with the issue of homelessness. There is no meeting of the minds between anti-abortionists and pro-choice protestors. Certainly pro-Israeli and pro-Palestinian protestors can't be too close together. Finally, the ACLU demands to be within sight and sound (the sight-and-sound provision from the Supreme Court means it has to be within sight and sound of the object of its protest), and their sight may not be what you see, and their sound may not be what you hear.

Julian handled all of this masterfully. Fortunately, he had a prior relationship with the head of the ACLU from his days as a lawyer in the department's Legal Bureau. Mike created a lottery system under which each protest group would be allocated a certain amount of time, usually two hours, to demonstrate in the "free speech zone" on Eighth Avenue, to the back of the Madison Square Garden. The ACLU raised the point that since the delegates entered on Seventh Avenue, the protestors would be out of sight. Mike worked out a deal with the ACLU whereby he provided a table with a handful of protestors handing out leaflets to the delegates arriving at the Seventh Avenue entrance. This entrance was a "frozen zone" created by the Secret Service. The Secret Service initially objected to the leaflet table, but Julian was able to convince them that it was in keeping with the spirit of the Court's decision and satisfied the demands of the ACLU.

How Mike handled the day-to-day demonstrations became legend overnight. To the homeless protestors, he not only gave them prime-time viewing, he also fed them. With other protest groups he reduced the tension between the cops and the protestors with good humor. When the police officers assigned to the demonstration zone showed up for duty, they usually brought their required equipment, helmets and batons (or, in police parlance, "hats and bats"). Mike had assembled a couple of dozen large plastic containers that he used to demarcate the protest zone. He used these empty containers to store the hats and bats so they would be accessible in the event things got out of hand. Mike's theory was that the open display of the hats and bats when there was no immediate threat was unnecessarily provocative. In short, if you looked like you were dressed for a battle, you would usually wind up in a battle.

The first three days of the convention went very smoothly, and there was praise on all sides from both the police and protestors. But we were not out of the woods yet, and we knew it. Mike and I had studied the two prior conventions, and we had found that for both of those events, the last night, when the candidate gave his speech, had been the most problematic, resulting in violent protests and property damage. The 1992 convention turned out to be no different. How it was handled, however, was *entirely* different. At around 8:00 P.M., as the evening session of the convention got under way, about five hundred protestors appeared on the scene, some walking in, some coming from the subway. All of them, it seemed, were coming from Julian's old precinct, the East Village. These were the so-called anarchists: the denizens of the East Village and frequent protestors from Tompkins Square Park.

Julian was prepared and confronted the leaders of the protest at

Thirty-third and Eighth. One was in possession of the equivalent of a quarter stick of dynamite. Julian confronted the guy, got into a fight with him, rolled around on the ground with him, and secured the explosives. A few arrests were made, and then there was a standoff. The protestors demanded that they had the right to march. Julian assembled hundreds of cops to accompany the march, which ended up going east on Thirty-fourth Street and continued to Third Avenue, where it turned north. By this point, it was apparent that the group had degenerated into a leaderless pack with no clear objective in mind. They disassembled on the East Side and took the subway back to Lower Manhattan. Violence had been avoided, a few arrests had been made, and the rest of the night was uneventful. The cops were pleasantly surprised to see Julian roll around on the ground and get the guy with the explosives under control. He had proved me right in that, when he needed to be a tough guy, Julian was as tough as they come. But he had a heart and he had brains, which some tough guys don't have.

The financial commitment on the part of the city to host the Democratic convention was approximately $20 million, which included in-kind services. Six million dollars of that was set aside for security costs, specifically police overtime. Because I was planning the security for this event, I was also aware that of all the city services, the one that dealt most closely with the delegates, the press, the protestors, and other interested parties, was the police. The vast majority of these people were from out of town, and their impression of New York would in some respect be based on their encounters and interactions with the members of the NYPD. I felt strongly about this issue and convinced myself early on that every police officer would have a smile and be dressed in clean, well-pressed uniforms. Easier said than done. I had handled enough demonstrations and protests to know that some of the police officers arriving from the tougher police stations in the Bronx and Brooklyn often viewed the condition and cleanliness of their uniform as number five or six on their priority list; their first priority was always staying alive.

In the year leading up to the convention, the NYPD had begun the process of hiring hundreds of police officers. Some of them had just graduated from the academy, while others were scheduled to graduate that summer. We determined that the officers covering the outer perimeter and other noncritical assignments would be made up entirely of rookies; they would smile when ordered and were guaranteed to have brand-new uniforms, clean and fully pressed. But that plan did not go without a hitch. The head of the police union, with whom I was friendly, broke my chops and said I was using rookies so I could save on the overtime costs; a veteran police officer is much more expensive than a rookie, who basically gets paid slave wages.

I tried to convince the union head that this move was all about style and not about substance, but I failed to convince him, even though I was telling the truth. The bottom line is that when the convention was over, we had spent only $3 million of the $6 million allocated for security costs. I am not sure whether it was because I saved the city $3 million or because I did a good job, or perhaps because I was the best-looking guy available, but two weeks after the convention concluded, I was promoted to deputy chief.

At the end of the promotion ceremony, Ray Kelly pulled me off to the side and said that while he knew I would be busy over the next month writing an after-action report on the convention, he wanted me to look into the police response in the Washington Heights Riots. Clearly, Kelly was convinced that the department's response was less than stellar. He also intimated that I should include a look at the response to the Crown Heights Riots of the year before.

My review was not to evaluate the performance of individual ranking officers, but rather the mechanics and the logistics of how we as a department respond to situations of civil unrest. However, I knew opinions regarding the leaders would bleed over into any evaluation. In addition to looking at the logistics and mechanics of the response, Kelly asked me to focus on the front-line supervisors, the sergeants, and the responding officers to get their opinion on how the response had unfolded and how they viewed the department's structure, including the leadership. I was a little surprised by Kelly's request since nothing had changed about the command structure: Kelly was still out of the operational loop, with the four-star chief of department reporting directly to the police commissioner. I also understood, though it was not stated, that this review was to be kept confidential, with only one copy of the report produced and delivered directly to the first deputy commissioner himself.

Over the next month, I conducted a series of interviews with police officers and sergeants and some lieutenants who had responded to the riots. I promised them anonymity since I needed to know their opinions no matter how critical they were of the department. In some cases, they were blistering in their assessment of the top leadership at the scene. At the same time, their observations were profound in their simplicity. For example, they talked about hundreds of police officers responding to a mobilization point, such as under the West Side Highway at 125th Street. Once they arrived there, they encountered hundreds of other police officers all asking the same questions: "Who do I report to, and where do I report?" One officer made the suggestion that, for simplicity's sake, the mobilization point should be divided up according to the patrol borough or the division from which the officers came, and that these boroughs or divisions should be clearly marked either by placards or simply by chalk markings on the ground.

Another bone of contention for the police officers was the issue of what happened to the police cars that they drove to the mobilization point. Police officers from the Bronx would be designated to respond to the mobilization point with three other officers from their precinct. Once they reached the mobilization point, the drivers would turn over their car keys to the supervisor in charge so the cars could be used as part of the mobile field force. After those officers who had driven finished their twelve-hour shift and attempted to retrieve their vehicles to drive back to the Bronx, they ran into all sorts of obstacles and excuses, and the bottom line was that they were told to fend for themselves at 2:00 in the morning. Officers from the Bronx or Brooklyn would end up having to take the subway back to their local command. Naturally, the subways do not run frequently during those early-morning hours, so it could take officers two to two and half hours to get back to their command. Once they arrived, an irate sergeant or lieutenant confronted them about where their cars were. Word quickly got around regarding this problem, and soon police officers were parking their police vehicles two blocks away from the mobilization point, then walking over and indicating that they had taken the subway because there were no available cars from their precinct.

There were other suggestions that I included in the report to the first deputy commissioner. I expected to hear back from Kelly regarding his reaction to the report. When I didn't hear from him, I assumed that the report was probably in some desk drawer in his office. I was wrong. Kelly had read the report in its entirety but had a different plan in mind on how to use the information within and how to revamp the police department's response to civil unrest. The next time I saw the report was in February of the following year, when Louis Anemone was promoted to deputy chief and given the task of creating a whole new response plan for civil unrest—something I'll come back to later.

Patrol Borough Manhattan South

In late August 1992, after completing the review for Commissioner Kelly and also the after-action report for the convention, I was transferred to Patrol Borough Manhattan South as one of two executive officers. On Labor Day weekend, I was the citywide duty chief, with instructions to work out of the mobilization point that had been set up a month and a half earlier to deal with the Washington Heights Riots. The police commitment was much reduced there, but a significant presence would still exist throughout Washington Heights until we got past the Labor Day weekend, the official end of summer. I patrolled the streets of my old neighborhood and never had the sense that just six weeks earlier the place had been engulfed in community tensions, burning cars, and looting. It was now almost serene. Conversing with some of the police officers during that weekend, I was informed that the police union, the Patrolmen's Benevolent Association (PBA), was planning a major protest at City Hall regarding Mayor Dinkins's plan to introduce legislation to create an all-civilian form of the Civilian Complaint Review Board—something that that had been soundly defeated back in 1966 in a citywide referendum.

I had two opinions regarding the proposal and law. First, I felt strongly that the law would not pass because I did not think the mayor had enough support; the existing Civilian Complaint Review Board worked effectively; therefore, there was no need to fix what was not broken. My second opinion was that if the law did pass, it was no big deal and, in fact, would be beneficial to police officers in that the history of these review boards throughout the nation has been (1) they are not very effective, and (2) they are more sympathetic to police officers than to the top brass. So to me, this planned demonstration seemed like a huge waste of time.

About two weeks later, the day of the demonstration arrived. The responsibility for policing this event fell to Patrol Borough Manhattan South. The overall commander for the event was two-star Assistant Chief Charles Reuther, and his two deputy chiefs—Alan Hoehl and yours truly. While there were predictions of thousands of police officers showing up, I was not convinced that the response would be that big. How wrong I was. At about 8:30 in the morning, hundreds of police officers began to appear around City Hall Plaza. Within an hour, there were a few thousand police officers at City Hall. Many of them had just completed the overnight shift. They had that pallor that suggested their skin had never seen sun and their eyes appeared never to have had more than three hours of sleep.

Initially, they were well behaved. While there were a significant number of supervisors assigned to the detail (that is, sergeants and above) there was not nearly enough. Dozens of uniformed cops were also assigned, but in my experience with police demonstrations, it is unrealistic to expect police officers to police other police officers. Instead, you need bosses and plenty of them. Especially in the emotionally charged atmosphere surrounding an issue that directly affects not only the protestors but also those charged with policing the protestors. I know this is not a satisfactory observation regarding the policing of these events, but it is true nonetheless. I have been, in my career, on both sides of the barricades. It's not something I relish or am proud of, but it is a fact of life.

About an hour into the demonstration, the demonstrating officers began to march in a circular fashion around City Hall Park. As the group rounded for the second or third time, it became clear that there were breakaway groups within the large group, hell-bent on getting inside the heavily fortified City Hall parking lot. Once a small group penetrated the fortress, others followed. Before we knew it, thousands of police officers occupied the lot in front of City Hall. I've handled many demonstrations in my career, most of which have been very peaceful. You can sense a peaceful crowd, no matter how big. Similarly, you can sense the ugliness of a disorderly crowd, even before the disorder begins. I remember, in college, discussing the criminologist Gustave Le Bon's theory on crowd mentality and the notion of the individual disappearing in the crowd and a different mind-set emerging. I knew we were in for a long day. One thing was clear from the outset: even with the uniformed police officers assigned to the demonstration, we were clearly outnumbered.

At some point during the demonstration, another group broke off and walked toward the Brooklyn Bridge. Initially, it was just a few dozen officers whom I assumed were heading home. But soon dozens more joined them, then hundreds more. I could see that there was a problem brewing on the bridge. When I looked at the huge crowd heading across to Brooklyn, it was obvious that there was no uniform presence. Traffic had come to a complete standstill on the inbound ramps. I was convinced that in no time there would be a confrontation between the protesting police officers crossing the bridge and the motorists who were trying to come into Manhattan but were stuck.

I had witnessed such confrontations back in the police demonstrations of 1975, and they were ugly and embarrassing. Rather than leave the Brooklyn-bound protesting police officers by themselves, I grabbed a uniformed sergeant and a police officer to come with me in order to "escort" the crowd across the bridge. I felt that if they saw a "white shirt"—that is, a "big boss"—with them on the bridge, it might dissuade them from engaging in altercations with the motorists. The Brooklyn Bridge spans more than a mile, and I initially thought that the officers would go up on the bridge span and then turn around and come back to City Hall. As I walked with them and tried to talk to some of the informal leaders at the head of the line, they just kept walking.

When we passed the midpoint of the bridge, I contacted my Brooklyn counterparts to make sure we had sufficient police resources to meet the protesting police officers and escort them to their desired location. Once it became clear that the officers were, in fact, going to go into Brooklyn and were not going to physically interact with any of the motorists, I turned around and headed back to Manhattan. Some of the protesting police officers followed me, but most stayed in Brooklyn. As I came down off the bridge on the Manhattan side, there were fewer protesting officers than there had been before I headed to the bridge. There was some damage to city vehicles in the City Hall parking lot, but the vast majority of the police officers had gone to the west side of City Hall on Duane Street, where a makeshift stage had been set up and the Republican candidate for mayor, Rudy Giuliani, was addressing the crowd. Giuliani's appearance had been advertised, but his rally had been relocated one block west of City Hall as a result of the demonstration chaos.

By midday the demonstration was over, and things returned to a state of relative normalcy. However, the public outrage over the police demonstration and its aftermath was anything but normal. Especially troublesome were the racist signs some of the protesting police officers had held, criticizing Mayor Dinkins, the city's first African American mayor. One of the most despicable signs referred to the mayor as a "washroom attendant." By late afternoon, it was clear that the department's reputation had been badly damaged and that the careers of senior police officials, including mine, were in great jeopardy. Most important, speculation was rampant regarding the impact of the demonstration on the future of First Deputy Commissioner Ray Kelly. At this point, Kelly was the acting police commissioner. Lee Brown had resigned a few weeks earlier to spend time with his wife, who was suffering from terminal cancer. Would the demonstration derail Ray Kelly's chances of becoming the police commissioner?

I, along with the senior officers assigned to the demonstration, spent the rest of that night answering questions and writing and rewriting reports regarding the day's events and, specifically, what each individual ranking officer did or didn't do. I felt that I had done the right thing in going up on the Brooklyn Bridge to at least establish some semblance of order and authority. But there were others who maintained I should not have left the main contingent at City Hall. My feeling was that, since there had never been sufficient supervisory presence at City Hall, one fewer was not going to make much of a difference. On the other hand, to leave about a thousand mobile protesting police officers alone, unsupervised and with no semblance of authority anywhere in sight, was a recipe for disaster.

While I felt I had done the right thing, I must admit that I continued to second-guess myself throughout the night. The next day's papers were scathing in their assessment of the policing of the event. But there was one paragraph that gave me solace in my decision to go up on the bridge. In an article in *Newsday*, the author, who was very critical of the event, wrote of the unruly mob that had gone onto the Brooklyn Bridge and mentioned the lone white shirt, the only obvious symbol of authority, who was escorting them across. It wasn't much comfort, but it was something.

Looking back, I am not so sure I would do anything differently. I was not the senior commander at the scene. Chief Reuther deployed his resources the best he could. It is clear that a thousand unruly police officers were headed to Brooklyn and that someone needed to confront them and at least show the flag. I have always prided myself on the fact that I know police officers intimately and that I understand how they think, that I can predict their actions and reactions. What I envisioned happening on the Brooklyn Bridge didn't happen. I don't know if my presence there prevented a serious confrontation with a motorist, but I do know that police officers saw me, knew I saw them, and my presence may have dissuaded them from doing something untoward. Just like with crime, it is always impossible to measure what you prevent.

The tradition in the NYPD is that when something goes wrong, heads will roll—even if those heads are only tangentially involved in the issue at hand. At the protest at City Hall, clearly the top three bosses—Chief Reuther, Chief Hoehl, and I—were more than tangentially involved. With anybody else in charge, we would have been either demoted or offered the opportunity to retire. But Ray Kelly, the acting police commissioner, looked at all of the facts and evidently concluded we had done as well as could have been expected under the circumstances. About three weeks after the incident, on October 16, 1992, Ray Kelly, deservedly, was appointed commissioner. He was held in high esteem by the bosses and also by the average cop on the street. There was a real feeling that we had one of our own in charge, someone who had come up through the ranks.

The Think Tank

In late December 1992, I received a call from Commissioner Kelly asking me to come see him. When I met him in his office, he informed me that, at the beginning of the New Year, I would come to work for him as the commanding officer of the Office of Management Analysis and Planning, the department's think tank. I was obviously filled with pride: it was a great honor to work directly for Ray Kelly, a guy who had it all, including a great sense of humor. From a strictly selfish and ego-gratifying perspective, this was the cat's meow. Almost every person who had held this position previously, including Ray Kelly, had advanced to a two- or three-star position and, in the case of Kelly, to the first deputy commissioner. There were approximately twenty deputy chiefs in the NYPD at the time, but by far the most prestigious was the person who commanded OMAP, because that person developed department policy, created new pilot programs, and kept the department ahead of the curve in best practices for the profession. Most important, he had the ear of the commissioner.

The Office of Management Analysis and Planning consisted of dozens of uniformed and civilian personnel whose job it was to create policy, do research, and complete statistical analysis. To say that the personnel assigned there thought highly of themselves would be an understatement; the department boasted a crew that included lawyers and a PhD in statistics. My predecessor at OMAP had a policy of denying requests from his staff to transfer to other units; his theory was that no one really wanted to work for this office. At my first staff meeting I announced that anybody who wanted to leave OMAP was free to do so and that, as a matter of fact, I would assist them in obtaining their desired next assignment. I also made it clear that there were some people who did not want to leave OMAP but would have to do so anyway and that I would also assist them in obtaining their desired next assignment. This meeting sent the message that, going forward, things would not be quite the same at the office.

I was committed to bringing some patrol and operational experience to OMAP. I felt strongly that while OMAP had extraordinarily bright people, it lacked what is known today as "street cred." To give OMAP its much-needed street cred, I reached out to Michael Tiffany, the commanding officer of the 40th Precinct in the South Bronx. Mike and I had been sergeants in the 25th Precinct in Harlem a decade earlier. He had spent his entire twenty-plus years in uniform patrol, mostly in the Bronx and Harlem. Mike was unusual for the NYPD. He had earned a B.A. and a master's in philosophy before entering the NYPD. His colleagues admiringly referred to him as the "philosopher cop." The most unusual thing about Mike was that he wore no police department medals or ribbons, opting instead for the plain blue uniform with his shield attached, even though he had earned dozens of medals for outstanding arrests and bravery over course of his career. I, on the other hand, wore every medal I had ever been awarded. I maintained that they matched my blue eyes. Mike was an instant hit, and morale in OMAP skyrocketed. *His* street cred gave *them* street cred. But it was really the way he managed people and got them to do their work that made Mike so effective.

While Mike Tiffany handled the research arm of OMAP, the special projects arm was just as impressive. Mike Julian, who had brains to spare, handled the department's implementation of the community-policing philosophy. Louis Anemone was every cop's idea of what General Patton would have been had he been a cop. Having just been promoted to deputy chief, he had one job and one job only: to create the department's response to civil disobedience. All of a sudden OMAP, which heretofore had been viewed as a wishy-washy, left-leaning, quiche-eating, NPR-listening-unit within the NYPD, was now being viewed as the cutting edge of police operations and best practices, whether it was handling an emotionally disturbed person or responding to the next potential riot or disturbance.

Louis Anemone spent the entire year creating, developing, and implementing the department's plan for handling civil disturbances. It is the plan that still exists today, and it is a model for other departments throughout the country. Mike Julian and I now had the opportunity to propose and implement policies and procedures that we had merely talked about in the past.

For example, we were both big proponents of putting police officers out on bikes, and we implemented a pilot project to begin bike patrols—much to the chagrin of higher-ups in the department. One of the objectives of community policing was to get police officers out of their cars and walking a foot beat. This made sense along the commercial corridors and in some of the congested neighborhoods of the city. However, there were other residential areas that were spread out over a large distance. Putting a foot officer in those areas was less than efficient. A bike, though, would allow an officer to cover a large territory without the isolation of a radio car. From such a perch, the officer could then touch, smell, and feel the neighborhood. Obviously, we had the backing of Commissioner Kelly, and so the program went forward. Now, bike patrols have become a staple in policing—not just in New York but around the country as well.

Guns and Squeegees

Probably the most important policy change in 1993 was the NYPD's decision to transition from six-shot .38-caliber revolvers to 9-mm semi-automatic pistols. The debate surrounding this transition had been going on for almost a decade. Police officers maintained that, quite simply, they were outgunned on the streets. It was hard to disagree with them. Yet, Mike Julian and I held to the view that the revolver provided the proper balance in terms of public safety in a congested city like New York. Julian had conducted a short study showing that, on average, police officers hit their target 20 percent of the time, which meant that for every five rounds shot, four missed their target and could strike or kill innocent civilians. A sixteen-shot 9-mm pistol meant more bullets, more misses, and a greater probability that an innocent civilian would be struck.

It was not that Julian and I were unsympathetic to the police officers' concerns. We were. In fact, I had had an experience that brought home, in dramatic fashion, what officers were facing on the street. In late 1992, as the citywide duty chief, I had responded to a scene in Spanish Harlem in which officers had exchanged gunfire with a group of eight local drug dealers. No one was injured, and the drug dealers had made good their escape but had left behind their weapons. When I arrived at the scene, a detective walked me through it, pointing out the eight 9-mm pistols left behind. It was quite an eye-opener but not really a surprise. Just three years before, in 1989, the NYPD, for the first time in its history, confiscated more pistols than revolvers. Other departments across the country saw the same phenomenon. There really was an arms race between the thugs and the cops, and people like Mike Julian and me were losing the argument.

There were many in the department, including top bosses, who were arguing for the switch to 9-mm pistols. One of my best friends, Pat Harnett, felt strongly that the cops were outgunned and that we had to make the transition. At the time, Pat was the commanding officer of the Emergency Service Unit. One day he had to appear at City Hall to brief a deputy mayor on a police-related matter. While there, Pat got into a discussion, which may have become heated, about why he felt it was necessary to make the switch. Pat's position was clearly at odds with the official position of the police department and that of City Hall. A few days later, Pat was transferred from the prestigious assignment as commanding officer of the elite Emergency Service Unit to commanding officer of the Seventh Division Uniform Patrol in the South Bronx. Where he had been one of one, he was now one of eighteen division inspectors. It was never made clear to Pat why he had been transferred, but many of us suspected that his conversation regarding the use of 9-mm pistols was the reason. When Pat inquired why he was being transferred, he was assured that it was in no way a demotion and that the Seventh Division was the most important division in the city. Pat replied sardonically, "Yeah, that's why the position's been vacant for the last six months."

Several months later, Commissioner Kelly brought Julian and me into his office to let us know that the department was going to begin transitioning from revolvers to 9-mm pistols. Kelly had made it a practice of going out at night and jumping in the backseat of a radio car to patrol with random police officers. He indicated to us that every single time he rode with officers, they brought up the issue of the 9-mm pistol. They never complained about pay or conditions, just their desire to carry a 9-mm pistol. The final straw occurred when Governor Mario Cuomo allocated a few million dollars from the state budget to purchase 9-mm pistols for NYPD officers, thus removing any financial excuse not to make the transition. (Cuomo was running for reelection that year and wanted the support of the police union.) While I still had my misgivings regarding the transition, we immediately began to implement a pilot program for the use of the 9-mm guns.

Figuring out how to deal with the intractable squeegee pests also occupied our time during 1993. These were individuals, usually young men, who greeted commuters coming into New York at the major intersections and thoroughfares branching off from the bridges, tunnels, and highways that led into the city. They often appeared threatening, although most of the time they were harmless beggars. Once in a while, however, they might reach inside the car of an unsuspecting woman and steal her purse off of the front seat. The squeegee pests had become the symbol of crime and incivility for most New Yorkers and for those who did business in New York. Episodic enforcement by the NYPD did little to solve the problem. Enter Michael Julian.

Under Police Commissioner Kelly's direction, Mike Julian was given the task of dealing with the squeegee pests once and for all. Mike, being a lawyer, an academic, and a street cop, knew he had to come up with a system that would withstand court challenge, would withstand pressure from homeless advocates, and, most of all, would deal effectively with the issue.

Mike's first step was simple yet profound: measure the extent of the problem and the number of people involved in the squeegee trade. If you asked the average New Yorker how many squeegee men were in the city, specifically Manhattan, they would have answered in unison, "Thousands!" When Mike and a cadre of police officers began to conduct an actual count of the number of these individuals at the critical locations throughout Manhattan, he determined that the overall number was somewhere between ninety and one hundred. A manageable figure.

Mike created a three-phase program, beginning with the offer of social services and employment and ending with arrest; everything imaginable was in between. The result was the effective elimination of the squeegee pests. (The elaborate program was chronicled and documented by Professor George Kelling from Rutgers University, who, along with James Q. Wilson and Catherine Coles, developed the "broken windows" theory—which we will come back to.) The bottom line was that the squeegee pest problem was eliminated under the administration of Ray Kelly, contrary to those revisionist historians of the Giuliani administration.

The Election of Rudy Guiliani

In 1993, Rudy Giuliani ran once again against David Dinkins for the position of the mayor of New York City. This time, during his campaign, Giuliani ran against the NYPD. He used the Crown Heights Riots, the Washington Heights Riots, and the black community's boycott of a Korean grocery store in Brooklyn (conducted by community activists because, they maintained, the store owner disrespected his black customers) as proof of the ineffectiveness of the NYPD in enforcing the law and protecting citizens. In addition, he constantly reminded people that the NYPD had made forty thousand fewer narcotic arrests under Mayor Dinkins as compared to the last four years of Mayor Koch's term. It was a job of OMAP, specifically me, to provide the data to refute the arrest-reduction numbers. Unfortunately, at least as far as narcotics arrests were concerned, Giuliani had the winning hand. We did, in fact, make forty thousand fewer arrests. However, in trying to put the arrest reduction in context, we explained that the quality of the narcotics arrests being made now was much higher, since the purity of the heroin and the cocaine confiscated was much greater. These arguments, understandably, fell on deaf ears.

Rudy Giuliani won the election by nearly the same margin he had lost it four years earlier. The vast majority of the top command within the police department, especially me, hoped that Ray Kelly would stay on as the police commissioner. By all accounts, he had done a great job over the prior seventeen months and deserved to be retained. However, Giuliani had dedicated much of his campaign running against the NYPD and, thus, against Ray Kelly. So while I hoped that Kelly would be retained, in my heart of hearts I knew it wasn't likely. A few years later, I had a conversation over lunch at the Harvard Club with Herman Badillo, the former congressman and Bronx borough president, also a key adviser to Rudy Giuliani. He confirmed what I had suspected back in 1993. He said, "How could we have kept Ray Kelly on when we ran against the NYPD and therefore against Ray Kelly?"

In early December, Bill Bratton was announced as the new police commissioner.

7

The Bratton Era Begins

Your friend Julian says you're the best guy for the job.
—BILL BRATTON, NEW YORK CITY POLICE COMMISSIONER DESIGNATE

I did not know Bill Bratton before he was hired as police commissioner. I had met him only once, when he stopped by to meet with a group of NYPD runners prior to the 1993 Boston Marathon. At that time, Bratton was the number two guy at the Boston Police Department, having returned to that city after a two-year stint as the head of the New York City Transit Police. Bratton had done a great job with the Transit Police and, in the process, had received a great deal of attention from the press. This was highly unusual for the Transit Police, which usually played second fiddle to the big, bad NYPD. The only time you saw a transit official on television was when he was defending a blunder or explaining a mistake. Bratton, on the other hand, would be on television extolling the good work of the Transit Police and the reduction of crime the agency had seen during his tenure. He also began producing radio ads, on which he would announce to some recently released parolee, in his thick Boston accent, "Hello, Joe. We're the Transit Police and we're here to welcome you back to society. We want you to do well, but we also want you to know that while you're here, the Transit Police are going to keep an eye on you." So for the first time in my recollection, the Transit Police were getting press coverage for all the things that were going right and not because of some mistake or blunder. Naturally, the vast majority of the credit went to Bratton. It was largely his success as Transit Police chief that propelled him to the office of the police commissioner in the city of New York.

Bratton set up his transition team in an old city office building about three blocks from police headquarters. He surrounded himself with a small group of advisers, most notably Jack Maple, who had been a transit lieutenant and close adviser to Bratton during his days with the Transit Police. He also had a few civilian advisers, some of whom had done work with the NYPD during the first two years of Lee Brown's tenure as police commissioner. The guessing game within police headquarters and throughout the department was who would be the select few to join the Bratton team and how big this "few" would be. Was it going to be just two or three individuals getting new jobs, similar to what had happened under Ben Ward and Lee Brown? Or was there going to be massive change and bloodletting similar to what had happened more than twenty years earlier, when Pat Murphy became the police commissioner after the Knapp Commission hearings?

I was pretty sure that Mike Julian and I would at least have access to the new administration because, in any police transition, OMAP plays a significant role in briefing the incoming police commissioner. This was the role Ray Kelly had played back in 1990 when Lee Brown took office. Ray Kelly jumped from a two-star assistant chief to the number two person, the first deputy commissioner, in the organization. As an aside, Julian had already had access to the new police commissioner because of his relationship with a local television reporter, John Miller. Julian and Miller traveled in the same social circles and vied for the title of New York City's most eligible bachelor. Miller was a close confidante of Bill Bratton.

About two weeks after Bratton had been announced, Julian and I were asked to go to the transition office to meet with him and brief him on some of the critical issues facing the department. Mike went into Bratton's office by himself, and I stayed in the outer office to talk with Jack Maple, whom I was meeting for the first time. A short while later, Julian emerged and took my spot with Maple while I went in to meet with Bratton. It was immediately clear that this wasn't a typical brief-ing on the major issues facing the department. Instead, Bratton talked to me about crime and asked what I thought the police department should do about it. At the end of our conversation, Bratton informed me that this was the first time in his career when he had interviewed two individuals for a position and each individual said the other was the best man for the job. Bratton, with a somewhat bemused smile on his face, said, "Your friend Julian says you're the best guy for the job." I just smiled and nodded, not knowing what job he was talking about.

When I spoke to Julian afterward about what job he thought we were being considered for, Mike indicated that he thought it was for the chief of department, the highest ranking for a uniformed member of the department. The chief of department was in charge of all day-to-day operations, both uniformed and detectives. Overall, the position was the number three spot in the NYPD. Speculation was running high as to who would get the chief of department job, especially after Dave Scott, the then chief of department, was elevated to first deputy com-missioner. A few names were being mentioned, but they did not include Mike Julian's or mine.

About two weeks after my initial meeting with Bratton, I was asked to come to his office for a formal interview. He was very gracious, and we talked about numerous subjects, primarily crime. A short time after that, I was approached by one of Bratton's civilian advisers, who said that the meeting with Bratton had not gone all that well. Bratton was unsure and wanted to have a follow-up interview. At the second meet-ing we spoke more about crime, and we also discussed specific person-alities within the NYPD. I made the point that, if I were to get the job as the chief of department, changes would be made and more than a few chiefs would be asked to leave. I felt strongly that the department needed to be shaken up. When Ben Ward became the police commis-sioner there had been minimal change, likewise with Commissioner Lee Brown. At any rate, I left the meeting with a good feeling.

In the interim I had a series of meetings with Jack Maple. He was going to be the crime czar in the Bratton administration. Not only had Jack been a transit lieutenant, he had also been the commanding officer of transit's decoy unit and other anticrime and investigations units within the New York City Transit Police. However, there was a limit to Maple's experience in that his police life largely revolved around crimes committed on the transit system. While he knew a tremendous amount about robberies and the mind-set of robbers, he had little experience in the area of narcotics enforcement and narcotics-related homicides, and understandably so. Maple spent the entire transition period studying crime statistics and the workings of the hundreds of units within the NYPD. He was like a sponge soaking up information. During one of our conversations, Maple offered his opinion regarding the Narcotics Division, how it should be run and who should run it. I looked at Maple and said, "The most knowledgeable person in the NYPD when it comes to narcotics is Deputy Chief Marty O'Boyle." Maple looked at me, slack-jawed, and said, "Who's Marty O'Boyle? How come I haven't met him? How come no one else has mentioned him?" I just smiled at him and said, "Jack, you've been traveling in the wrong circles." Maple asked if he could meet him. I said, "When?" He said, "Now." Within minutes O'Boyle joined us in the office, and we spent the next two hours going over narcotics strategies. After Marty left, Maple exclaimed, "That's the smartest son of a bitch I've ever met."

A couple of days after my final interview with Bill Bratton, he called me, told me I was going to be his new chief of department, and asked if I would drive over to Staten Island, where he and Mayor Giuliani were going to be attending a community forum that afternoon. I hooked up with Bratton, and we went to meet Giuliani and his first deputy mayor, Peter Powers, Giuliani's childhood friend—and best friend. We exchanged pleasantries, and there was a clear understanding that things were going to be different going forward, and not just within the police department. I left that meeting feeling that these two guys, Giuliani and Powers, were pretty confident and, more important, pretty competent.

When I got back to headquarters, the place was abuzz. While I have always had lots of friends, I now had a lot more. Driving home that night, I began to think of what the new NYPD would look like. Just then, my phone rang, and one of the guys I had been thinking about, Louie Anemone, was calling to congratulate me. I had known Anemone since the early 1980s when he was a captain in Manhattan North narcotics with my childhood best friend, John Condon, the number one sergeant in Manhattan North narcotics and maybe in the entire Narcotics Division. While I had gotten to know Anemone personally in the early 1980s, I had known his reputation as a hard charger years before that. I wasn't quite sure how much discretion I would have in selecting the new team, but I told him I would make sure that he was a key player.

A day or two later, while in a conversation with Bratton, he asked me if I had given any thought to the new team. I told him that I had and that there were some individuals whom I thought had to play a role. I mentioned, quite innocently, that we should promote Marty O'Boyle to the position of two-star chief of the Narcotics Division. I said, "He's a good guy, and he's from Mayo." Bratton seemed a little taken aback, and said, "The entire team isn't going to be from Ireland, are they?" I replied, "No, Marty's great. He just happens to be from Ireland." With that, Bratton asked me to take a few days and present him with the new team by the end of the week. This is the part of the story where you learn to be careful what you wish for. Being a braggart, an egomaniac, and sometimes a loudmouth, I had often said, "Boy, if I ever get to the top . . . !" This was an "It's your move, Timoney" moment.

I had a restless night and got no sleep, tossing and turning and thinking about the new team: who should go, who should stay, and what the rationale was behind it all. It wasn't a good feeling because some of these guys had been my bosses, and some, as in the case of Mario Selvaggi, the chief of patrol, I had become quite friendly with. I knew Bratton had in mind certain individuals who he thought should go, but our mental lists did not necessarily coincide. The second night was another sleepless one. At about two o'clock in the morning, I concluded that if we were really going to shake up the department, we had to have an entirely new team at the top. This would be revolutionary in that the entire leadership was changing, from police commissioner to first deputy commissioner to chief of department, and on down. Everyone above the rank of two-star chief would be new. This would also create a trickle-down effect in that there would be many new openings in the one- and two-star chief positions, and of course the inspector and deputy inspector positions.

The next day the plan was for me to see First Deputy Commissioner David Scott and tell him my recommendations. Then he and I would go see Bratton. I wasn't quite sure how Scott would take my recommendations since they would affect at least two people who were considered to be close to him. When I briefed Scott of the plan, he said, "Great, let's go see the boss." And that was that. When we met with Bratton and told him of our recommendations, he showed no emotion and said, "Good. Let's do it."

The super chiefs were given the equivalent of a thirty-day notice—that is, in thirty days someone else would be taking their spot. Although that sounds reasonable and desirable and the right thing to do, it provided for some awkward moments. While the super chiefs of the prior administration were still in place, the new team was assembled and announced. The hard-charging Louie Anemone was going to become the chief of patrol. The chief of big ideas, Mike Julian, would become the chief of personnel. Charlie Reuther, who had headed the Narcotics Division years earlier, would become chief of the Organized Crime Control Bureau. Marty O'Boyle was named as chief of the Narcotics Division. Joe Borelli, the chief of detectives, was to remain in his position for the next six months, until he reached his mandatory retirement age of sixty-three. As expected, these changes at the top had an impact on every other rank in the organization, from the two-star chief down to the first level of supervisor, the sergeants. There was a palpable feeling of change, and there was a clear surge of confidence within the NYPD.

The first of many awkward moments happened when I responded to an emergency incident in Queens, as did the then chief of patrol, Mario Selvaggi, and the newly named chief of patrol, Louie Anemone. When I got to the scene, Chief Selvaggi briefed me on what was happening and asked me if there was anything else he should do. It was a little awkward since Selvaggi had been one of my bosses just two weeks earlier. The awkwardness increased when Anemone showed up, wanting to take charge but recognizing that he was not yet officially the chief of patrol and thus felt he should defer to Selvaggi, with whom he was very friendly. In fact, Selvaggi used to look upon Louie as his son.

It was awkward for all involved. We could have avoided these moments had we not granted the thirty days' notice and had we made the personnel changes effective immediately. But that plan would have made the Bratton administration appear only more heartless than it already did. Bratton took a lot of criticism for cleaning out the entire top brass, and many people maintained that our handling of the situation was not the right way to treat professionals who had an average of thirty years each within the NYPD. At the retirement party for these super chiefs two months later, the former commissioner, Ray Kelly, reiterated that charge as I sat uncomfortably in the front row, accepting the slings and arrows.

As time has passed, I have had the opportunity to think about the decision regarding the three-star chiefs. Was it the right decision? Could it have been done better? I have concluded that not only was it the right decision, it was the only decision I could have made at the time. We were looking to change an organization radically, and to do so we had to have radical change. It was no different than when Pat Murphy cleaned house on the heels of the Knapp Commission. The issue then was police corruption, which had been tolerated, or at least given a wink and a nod. The issue now was crime.

For the past decade, the crime rate in New York had gone off the charts, especially that of violent crime. In fact, one could argue that the crime rate had been on a continuous upward trend from the time of the Knapp Commission and certainly from the time of the layoffs in 1975. Over that period, two strong competing themes had emerged. First was the notion that police could do little to reduce crime. Second, a post-Knapp attitude that corruption was the number one issue that had to be dealt with permeated the department. On more than one occasion a risky new crime initiative had run headlong into the reality of the corruption paradigm, and in each situation it was the corruption paradigm that survived.

What was necessary now in the NYPD was a paradigm shift. To

do that, we needed believers. We needed people who felt and were committed to the notion that police officers, properly supervised and directed, could reduce crime. The corruption paradigm crushed any belief and creativity as individuals moved up the chain of command. By the time a person became captain, it was clear that in order to get ahead his corruption skirts had to be clean. This attitude created a risk-averse cadre of bosses who suppressed any inclinations to fight crime in a serious fashion. There was, however, a small minority of bosses whom I would refer to as "true believers"; they thought police officers could have an impact on crime. Anemone was certainly a believer, as was Marty O'Boyle. Jack Maple was a true believer, and Julian and I were true believers.

The Pat Murphy model in the post-Knapp NYPD was a good model to follow—that is, complete and total change in the upper ranks of the department. Murphy had needed to change an attitude that had existed within the NYPD for decades: that police corruption was a part of police work and that little could be done about it. Up to this period, police corruption was systemic.

Systemic corruption is characterized by the notion of pads and lists, of sharing the corruption profits with your immediate supervisor or commanders. The most invidious aspect of systemic corruption is that while it's known to exist, little effort is made to do away with it. Non-systemic corruption is corruption committed by individual police officers, with the proceeds kept secret by those offending officers, except in those cases where it is shared with the officers' partner. The term of art used to describe nonsystemic acts of corruption is *score*. It is not tolerated by the top command, nor is it a part of the culture of the department.

Pat Murphy did not succumb to the notion that police corruption, particularly systemic corruption, was impossible to deal with. But he felt you had to deal with it from the top down and put systems in place, including training, to imbue the organization with a different culture and attitude regarding corruption. These changes did not guarantee there would be no corruption in the future, but they did ensure that the endemic systemic corruption would no longer exist. What he recognized was that if you put forth a strong plan to deal with systemic police corruption—a plan powerful enough to advance careers or end them—you could eliminate it.

The issue that came out of the Murphy years was the failure to transition the police department from focusing on dealing with systemic corruption to accepting the idea that some nonsystemic corruption is a fact of life. Once the framework for dealing with systemic corruption is in place, it should not remain the number one priority for police administrators year after year. The focus should then naturally shift to some other area of law enforcement, for example, fighting crime.

Similar to Murphy, Bratton had to radically change the top command in order to radically change the organization. After more than twenty years, we were finally in the position to make the transition from a corruption-centric department to a crime-centric department. There were plenty of naysayers. For example, the former head of Internal Affairs during the 1980s, John Guido, was one of them. Regarding our plans to have uniformed police officers return to making drug arrests, he told a reporter, "With cops, you always have to watch them. You'll have officers on roofs, in apartments, loose for two, three hours with no supervision. This is a tremendous corruption hazard. Bratton is more optimistic about cops than I am." There were even some corruption prosecutors reported to be licking their chops in anticipation of more corruption arrests as a result of Bratton's crime-fighting initiatives.

Bratton's house cleaning was even more radical than it appeared. Not only were the top chiefs let go, their replacements were unusual. Mike Julian, Louie Anemone, and I had all worked directly for Ray Kelly. We were considered "Kelly's guys," and therefore loyal to Kelly. Often, when a new commissioner takes office, the senior staff members who have been closest to the outgoing police commissioner are sent to the NYPD's equivalent of Siberia, or effectively taken out and shot by way of forced retirement. People often make the mistake of thinking that senior police officials are loyal to the individual in charge. What Bratton realized was that although senior police officials will have some loyalty to their commissioner, their ultimate loyalty is to the organization. Choosing the three of us might have been risky on Bratton's part, but you can't make a radical change unless you are willing to take risks.

As we were creating the new top team to run the department, I needed to create a separate team to run my office and, in some cases, to run my life. The gatekeeper who would determine who got to see or didn't get to see the chief of department was Sergeant Jimmy Cambria. Jimmy had worked for me when I was the commanding officer in the Chief of Department's Office and also at OMAP. He was a tough, smart guy from Staten Island who I believe would literally have taken a bullet for me. He was the type of confidential aide all chiefs need: loyal, strong, and discreet.

To run the Chief of Department's Office, I chose Lieutenant Brian Nicholson. It was Brian who had convinced me to take the police test way back in 1967. He was one of my dearest and closest friends growing up in Washington Heights. He was also a cop in the South Bronx's famous 41st Precinct, also known as Fort Apache. Brian had spent fifteen years there pushing a radio car and performing the duties of the precinct's union rep. When Brian made sergeant, he was assigned to the 42nd Precinct in the South Bronx. In the late 1980s, it took all of my persuasive powers to convince Brian to come to headquarters to work for Chief Johnston. Chief Johnston's reaction to Brian was the same as that of everyone else who had met Brian: He loved him. Brian was the person I needed to run the office efficiently and effectively, someone who took pride in his final work product. He had no equal.

Whom I would select as my driver was a no-brainer. Detective Bobby Muldoon, whom I had known since the time I had arrived in the United States, would be the man. I had gone to grammar school with his sister, and Bobby was six years younger than we were. I had helped convince Bobby to join the NYPD a dozen years earlier. He was extremely loyal and smart to boot. And best of all, he knew the city inside out because he had been a part-time cabdriver while in school.

I needed a second driver and asked Bobby to make a recommendation. He suggested his old radio car partner, Don McCallen, from the Midtown North Precinct. Donny, in many respects, was much like

Bobby: smart and discreet. He was also a great driver. One really cool thing about these picks was that all three of us were Ranger fans. There was a downside, however. While Bobby knew the city inside out, he couldn't drive to save himself. Donny, on the other hand, could drive like the dickens, but he didn't know where he was going. On more than one occasion, while trying to get to some shooting scene in Brooklyn at 2:00 in the morning, I would say to Donny, "Why are you asking me where we are? Call your partner and he'll tell you." It became a standing joke at headquarters.

Probably the easiest appointment Bratton made was the person he chose as the deputy commissioner for public information—John Miller, local TV reporter, Emmy Award–winning journalist, and one of New York's leading jet-setters. Many of the top brass couldn't understand why Miller, considered to be the best reporter in town, would take a half-million-dollar pay cut just to join the ranks of the NYPD. But if they had known Miller, they would have understood immediately the old adage that "money isn't everything." From the time Miller had been a teenager, he had hung around with many detectives and Emergency Service Unit bosses. They had basically taken Miller under their wing. Miller had benefited professionally from these relationships, but that was not his motivation in cultivating them. There was a genuine fondness on both sides.

Miller would make huge contributions throughout the first year, none more important than convincing recalcitrant detective bosses that pushing out information quickly on a crime could reap immediate benefits through phone calls and tips. In the first few months, numerous high-profile cases were solved as a result of Miller's getting the information out to the media. But sometimes getting that information to release wasn't so easy.

One night, Miller called me regarding a police shooting. As expected, the press was all over the story. Miller explained that he needed the basic information to give to the press people, who were hounding him. I told John to call the lieutenant at the Operations Unit, knowing that the lieutenant would have the most up-to-date information on what had occurred. About an hour later, Miller called me back and said, "The lieutenant is having trouble getting the information." I replied, "Johnny boy, if he's having trouble getting the information, it usually means there's trouble with the information." I then told him, "By the way, the corollary to that rule is: 'The first information you get is always wrong.' You can bet on it."

John did a great job getting critical information out to the media; sometimes in his enthusiasm, he would go to the scene directly. He and Jack Maple had a habit of riding around the city in the wee hours of the morning chasing police calls and showing up at crime scenes uninvited. One particular morning I received a phone call from an irate commander. "Chief, Maple and Miller showed up at that shooting last night. Miller went on the air, panicked, and fucked everything up." I told the commander that I would have a talk with my two wayward boys.

An hour later they appeared in my office, joking and grab assing. When they saw that I was serious, they became serious. I said, in my derisive Irish tone, "Commissioner Miller, one of the commanders said you showed up to the shooting scene last night, got on the radio, panicked, and fucked the whole thing up. What do you have to say for yourself?" Miller responded, "I may have fucked everything up, but I did not panic."

Neither John nor Jack had screwed anything up. It was just that the detective bosses were not used to having "civilians" show up at their crime scenes and look over their shoulders.

Strategies for Fighting Crime

Immediately upon taking office, we made dealing with crime in a strategic fashion our goal. For the first time in my career as a police officer, we were no longer going to be a reactive organization waiting for crime to happen. We were going to be proactive by predicting where and when crime might occur, and we were going to respond quickly, making immediate arrests, so that we might prevent other crimes from being committed by the same perpetrators. For example, if we responded quickly to a narcotics-related shooting and made an immediate arrest, we would likely prevent a retaliation shooting from happening later that day.

We created in written form six operational strategies for various crimes and quality-of-life issues. To make sure that everyone knew the strategies and understood their intent and rationale, a short booklet on each strategy was printed and distributed to every member of the department. This ensured that everyone was on the same page regarding how the strategies would be operationalized, and it removed the typical excuse offered by an officer or detective: "Oh, I'm sorry, I didn't know."

In robberies and burglaries we worked to spot patterns early, deploy resources quickly, and make an arrest before another burglary was committed. Traditionally, if two robbers were on a spree, committing a robbery a day, it might have gone unnoticed in the department for a month or two. When it was noticed, efforts would be undertaken to capture the suspects. That might take another month. Doing a quick calculation, you could assume that the robbers would commit ninety robberies over a three-month period. The new NYPD, with its crime strategies, focused on the early detection of patterns. Now the robbery pattern would be detected after two or three weeks, and resources would be devoted to actively arrest the robbers within a week or two. Thus, you suffered robberies for just one month, effectively preventing the additional thirty to sixty robberies that the pair could have otherwise committed. This notion of "prevention through apprehension" was a novel one.

It was clear to everyone that the most critical issue facing the city was violent crime, especially the crime surrounding the drug trade and the easy availability of guns. We needed a proper analysis to measure the scope of the problem in order to determine our approach. Mike Farrell, a civilian employee who had taken over OMAP after I left, conducted the research. Mike was assisted—we would laughingly say persecuted—by Jack Maple. They made a great team. Mike had brains to spare, and Maple was only too happy to relieve him of those extra brain cells.

Mike and Maple focused their attention on Police Strategy #1: Getting Guns Off the Streets and Police Strategy #3: Driving Drug Dealers Out of New York. (I helped write Police Strategy #2: Dealing with Youth

Violence.) Maple in particular was obsessed with the easy availability of illegal guns and was absolutely determined to have an impact. For example, when we looked at the statistics in 1960, there were seventy-five homicides committed in the city with handguns. By 1992, there were fifteen hundred homicides committed with handguns. We knew for a fact that upward of 95 percent of all guns confiscated in New York City came from states outside of New York, most notably Pennsylvania, Virginia, Georgia, and Florida. So the gun issue for the city was not a homegrown one, but rather an imported one. The gun strategy involved nearly everyone in the criminal justice system—from the police officer on the beat and the detectives in the Career Criminal Investigations Unit to detectives assigned to the Organized Crime Control Bureau and their counterparts at ATF. The overall aims of the strategy were to confiscate more guns, to debrief all prisoners regarding their knowledge of how they came into possession of any illegal guns, to enhance the prosecution of those in possession of illegal guns, and to pressure judges to take the gun cases seriously.

The next strategy tackled was Driving Drug Dealers Out of New York. Drugs had ravaged many neighborhoods in the city over the past three decades. The police department had responded with some successful programs, such as Ben Ward's Operation Pressure Point in 1984, but also with a lot of less successful strategies, including the antidrug program during Mayor John Lindsay's reelection campaign in 1969.

The drug strategy was going to use every available asset within the criminal justice system. This included a revitalized Civil Enforcement Unit, under the leadership of the deputy commissioner for legal matters, Jeremy Travis, with fourteen new lawyers whose only job would be to close drug locations and seize assets used or gained in illegal activity. There was also to be greater cooperation and coordination with our federal partners in the DEA and the FBI in handling the high-level drug dealers.

The unusual part of the strategy called for the average patrol officer to get involved in the enforcement of drug laws. Heretofore, uniformed officers were discouraged, and in some cases forbidden, from making narcotics arrests because of the fear of corruption. Now that fighting crime was our number one priority, all uniformed patrol personnel were "being directed to act on narcotics violations occurring in their presence." As a side note, many precincts that had disbanded their Street Narcotics Enforcement Unit (SNEU) in the early 1990s, due to their fear of police corruption, were directed by me to reinstitute them. Quite literally, it became an "all hands on deck" effort. Narcotics enforcement was no longer the purview of the specialized plainclothes officers of the Narcotics Division.

Youth violence had also become a serious crime over the prior decade in New York City, and in reality, across the entire nation. For example, the number of gun cases handled by the city's five family courts had increased by more than 600 percent over the past ten years. Homicide had become the leading cause of death for those between the ages of fifteen and twenty-four. According to the Census Bureau, New York City's youth population (ages nineteen and younger) declined by 25 percent between 1970 and 1992. Yet arrests for felonies, particularly those of a violent nature, rose dramatically. Youth arrests per capita of youths accused of murder quadrupled. Youths arrested for robbery doubled. The statistics were similar for other criminal offenses.

The youth statistic that caught my eye was that during school hours, victims of robberies, in 30 percent of the cases, described their perpetrator as being a youth under sixteen. It didn't take a genius to figure out that if kids were committing robberies during school hours, it meant that they were not in school. An integral part of Police Strategy #2: Dealing with Youth Violence, was an enhanced and expanded truancy program for all patrol boroughs based on the model used by Patrol Borough Manhattan South. As a deputy chief in that borough I had witnessed firsthand how effective the Borough Truancy Unit was, and I was committed to expanding it to other parts of the city. In Patrol Borough Manhattan South, one sergeant and five police officers were assigned to the truancy unit. This was the basic model we used for other boroughs, although the actual number of police officers could vary depending on the number of high schools in each borough.

The first of the six strategies to be completed was Police Strategy #4: Breaking the Cycle of Domestic Violence. Ironically, the majority of the research into the recommended best practices for developing this strategy had actually been conducted in 1993, during Ray Kelly's last year as police commissioner. Kelly had appointed me, as the head of OMAP, to co-chair a domestic violence task force with Susan Herman, the former legal counsel for Ben Ward and then president of a victims' services agency. Throughout 1993, we had numerous executive meetings with experts from all over the country, on both the police and advocate sides, who shared their recommended best practices. At the end of the yearlong study, the committee produced a substantial report to Commissioner Kelly on what the NYPD needed to do to be at the national forefront on the issue of domestic violence. The report to Commissioner Kelly, which provided the basis for Police Strategy #4, was ready for publication within the first month of the Bratton administration. However, for reasons known only to City Hall, the strategy was not published until the end of April 1994. (Some light was shed on the reason for the delay a few years later, after I had left the NYPD. Governor George Pataki had appointed me to a state commission whose goal was to hold hearings on how domestic violence cases were handled by police and prosecutors throughout the state. The Giuliani administration objected to the creation of this commission and to my serving on it. Incredibly, Giuliani's health czar, Maria Mitchell, told the press that, back in 1994, Timoney had been the biggest obstacle in getting the domestic violence strategy out sooner.)

Strategy #5: Reclaiming the Public Spaces of New York has received the most notoriety, even if it hasn't been deserved. Known as the quality-of-life strategy, Strategy #5 was meant to clean the city of the most annoying signs of urban decay and incivility. These included peddling, panhandling, prostitution, underage drinking, and a whole host of other quality-of-life offenses. It also dealt with noise, whether coming from a handheld boom box, a car radio, or a loud nightclub down the block. The strategy was all encompassing in that it left no quality-of-life issue, regardless of size, untouched. It was quite successful, but ironically, it became famous when it got the credit for one thing it actually didn't achieve: removing the squeegee pests from the streets of New York. This, as I noted earlier, had already occurred under Police Commissioner Ray Kelly.

Quality-of-life initiatives were nothing new to the NYPD. Going back to the early 1970s, Neighborhood Police Teams (NPTs) were established throughout the city. The NPTs went by the wayside as a result of the 1975 layoffs. By 1980, it had become apparent that the layoffs of those five thousand officers, plus the attrition of another five thousand officers, had caused both a marked decrease in the quality of life throughout the city and a significant increase in overall crime. In the spring of 1981, the NYPD created division-wide Quality-of-Life Units to deal with these issues. Because of the shortage of personnel, it was impossible for each precinct to staff its own Quality-of-Life Unit, thus the problem was handled on a division level. Each unit consisted of one sergeant and four to six officers, and they were tasked with covering a division that consisted of three to four precincts—basically an impossible job. Nonetheless, it was an attempt to deal with the matter.

In March 1982, George Kelling—who had chronicled the squeegee pest problem—and James Q. Wilson wrote their seminal article for the *The Atlantic* entitled "Broken Windows." They theorized that a broken window in a neighborhood, if left unattended, encouraged the breaking of more windows. The message was simple: quality-of-life violations that are left unaddressed encourage more quality-of-life violations and, ultimately, an environment in which crime flourishes. In other words, higher crime rates occur in neighborhoods with dilapidated housing, open-air drug dealing, and garbage-spewing vacant lots. The article addressed what the average citizen in most neighborhoods felt deeply. Even in the toughest of neighborhoods, the number one complaint at a community meeting isn't about the rash of shootings or the occasional homicide, but rather about the police department's failure to address adequately the low-level quality-of-life violations that take place. The thought was that if an alien were dropped into the city, he would immediately know which neighborhood was safe, and which was not, based on the signs of urban decay.

In 1984, during a visit to Harvard's Kennedy School of Government, Police Commissioner Ben Ward was exposed to Kelling and Wilson's article. It quickly became required reading within the NYPD and was sure to come up in any promotional interview with Ward.

Community Policing Front and Center

It was also in the mid-1980s when the community-policing philosophy began to emerge. Community policing or "problem-solving" policing, as it was also known, was the notion that cops and the community could work together to deal with quality-of-life infractions. Ben Ward was committed to the idea but did not have the personnel to deploy this philosophy on a department-wide basis, and so he developed the Community Patrol Officer Program. CPOP consisted of a sergeant and ten police officers, per precinct, who dealt with quality-of-life issues.

Many of the prior quality-of-life initiatives within CPOP came up short, in part, because they relied on the sophistication and initiative of individual police officers in a given area. It was unrealistic to expect every officer to have the requisite initiative, let alone the sophistication, to deal with many of these intractable problems. For example, should we expect a twenty-two-year-old rookie, just out of the academy, to have the wherewithal to deal with a decade-old problem on a street in Washington Heights, especially when that rookie grew up in some suburban enclave on Long Island?

Under Police Strategy #5, the central character in implementing a quality-of-life strategy would be precinct commander, not the police officer. We had, in fact, made a conscious decision after much debate to designate precinct commanders as the central actors in all of our strategies. Much like Chief Johnston in the mid-1980s, we recognized that captains and precinct commanders were motivated when they had the power to shape and control their own careers. In the Bratton administration, we developed a meritocracy based on performance, which created incentive for captains and commanders to make a real difference.

It is always difficult to prove a nexus between low-level quality-of-life violations and major crimes. However, there are some very convincing arguments that support the theory. When the Transit Police, under Bill Bratton, began to deal seriously with fare beaters, a low-level crime deemed unworthy of enforcement by most police officers, a strange but predictable thing happened: robberies on the subway system decreased dramatically. If you took a second to think about it, it made perfect sense. If you are enforcing the law against all fare beaters, certainly you are going to arrest potential robbers before they even enter the subway system. In one Brooklyn subway station, 70 percent of the patrons were not paying their fare. One of the thugs arrested there remarked, "Only chumps pay."

The other benefit of cracking down on fare beaters: a significant number of them were wanted on outstanding warrants or were carrying illegal weapons or other contraband. Thus, while Jack Maple and his decoy squad had a great impact on the robbery rates in the subway, the effectiveness of enforcing the law against fare beaters, as a preventative measure for other types of crime, should not be underestimated.

In the early 1990s, the 6th Precinct, which included the West Village, had a problem with weekend robberies and assaults. Some of these crimes were committed by normally law-abiding teens from the suburbs who had come into the Village to drink and have a good time. Once drunk, however, they would sometimes engage in thuggish behavior such as beating up gays or robbing people in general. To deal with this problem, the precinct commander began aggressively enforcing a policy against open beer containers, which meant that young people possessing open beer containers would be cited and their beers would be confiscated. The citations and confiscations at seven and eight in the evening ensured that these youths would not be drunk at ten and eleven, which, in turn, prevented their thuggish behavior as the evening wore on. Not surprisingly, the weekend robberies and assaults declined dramatically.

There are dozens of other examples of how enforcing low-level quality-of-life laws had a positive impact on reducing the amount of more serious crime. But even if we hadn't seen such an impact, enforcing quality-of-life laws is absolutely the right thing to do. These issues are important to community members and come up at every community meeting. The best reason for a strong, aggressive quality-of-life initiative was a sentiment issued by a woman from Overtown (a low-income neighborhood in Miami) whom I met in my office upon first becoming the police chief in Miami: "Just because we live in Overtown doesn't mean we don't deserve a good quality of life."

New Policies and a New Look

Developing crime strategies was not the only concern that captured the attention of the Bratton administration during its first six months: the men and women of the NYPD also got a new and dramatic look. Actually, in some cases, it was a return to the past. The light blue shirts police officers had worn for the past twenty-five years were replaced with the dark blue color that I had worn as a rookie. The beauty of the darker color was that it didn't highlight the last meal the police officer had eaten. Second, and more important, the officers appeared more slender, and their overall appearance was more distinguished and professional. NYPD cops no longer looked like rent-a-cops.

On the policy front, we began to develop and implement guidelines that would facilitate and sustain our crime-fighting efforts. When I was appointed chief of department, I chose as my executive officer Pat Harnett. Pat was uniquely qualified for the position. Not only did he have vast patrol and detective experience, but he was also, believe it or not, a "techie." Even more important, he was a very deep thinker. Finally, if you wanted to get a difficult job done, you gave it to Pat Harnett. He was tenacious beyond all reasonable expectation.

Immediately upon assuming his new position, Pat began to look at ways of improving police officers' performance during their day-to-day activities. In the NYPD, police officers prepare a Monthly Activity Report to document their productivity, or rather their activity, for the preceding month. This report had been changed several years earlier to reflect activities congruent with and supportive of the community-policing philosophy. Harnett was incredulous that police officers were actually getting "credit" on their activity reports for attending community meetings.

While it may have been necessary sometimes for a police officer to attend a community meeting, the precinct commander or one of his lieutenants and a community-relations officer generally attended those meetings. To encourage and "credit" police officers for attending these meetings bordered on the insane. "We want them out on the street," Harnett said, "taking enforcement actions and dealing with quality-of-life issues, not in some air-conditioned room glad-handing or hand-holding this or that 'community leader.'" I agreed with Pat. "You are just the man to redesign the form," I told him. Pat went about the task of redesign, and in no time, police officers were filling out Monthly Activity Reports that reflected real productive activity as opposed to make-believe activity. They were now measured on the number of criminals they met rather than the number of meetings they attended.

Harnett's next idea was one of the most radical reforms of the Bratton administration. Over the course of my career, police consultants and law enforcement carpetbaggers would come in and out of the NYPD with ideas of how to improve efficiency and effectiveness, how to streamline the organization—or whatever was the latest buzzword to come out of the Harvard Business School or the Kennedy School of Government. After these consultants left, there was never any discernable improvement. However, the department was a lot lighter in the pocketbook after paying the extravagant consultant fees, which could reach into the hundreds of thousands of dollars. The credo of police consultants in the early 1990s was to "reduce the layers of the multilayered wedding cake." Or, as Jack Maple mockingly referred to it, as he put together his two palms and squinted his eyes, "We have to crush the organization!"

One day, Pat Harnett came to my office and said he believed that we actually could reduce at least one layer within the NYPD—that of division commander. I looked at him like he was crazy. "You can't just eliminate the division commanders! They're too important to the organizational structure, particularly at the patrol borough level. Pat, they're just too important, and they've been around over a hundred years!" Pat was adamant. He said, "I couldn't disagree with you more. I was a division commander in the 7th Division in the Bronx, supposedly the busiest and most prestigious division in the city, and I know what a division commander does: nothing! It's a useless position. By the way, the position was vacant for six months prior to my getting there, and the division seemed to function just fine without me." The more I thought about it and thought back to the division commanders I had worked for, I realized Pat was right. They really didn't do too much.

Doing away with the division commanders, who all held the rank of inspector, was the easy part. What to do with the inspectors was a little more complex. From my days in OMAP I knew that eliminating the division commanders would be music to the ears of the widget counters at the city budget office. They would view it as "savings." But I also knew that in any police department the promotion process is sometimes the greatest motivational force in getting the mission accomplished. So eliminating the division commanders would have a huge negative impact on moral. Eliminating the division office was one thing, reducing the upper ranks by eighteen inspectors and thirty-six deputy inspectors was a whole other matter. A year earlier, I had discussed an idea with Captains Mike Tiffany and Eddie Young while we were at OMAP. Eliminating the divisions gave me the opportunity I needed to test this idea.

There is a saying within the NYPD: "Patrol is the backbone of the job." By and large this was mere lip service. But now, for the first time in the NYPD, we were going to make that slogan a reality.

There are seventy-six precincts in the NYPD. If you asked most police officials which ten precincts were the busiest and which ten were the quietest, most would guess eight or nine of the precincts correctly in each category. We decided to rate the seventy-six precincts in numerical order of activity, using a regression analysis model with a dozen or so independent variables. We categorized the busiest ten precincts as "A" precincts, which would be commanded by a full inspector. The next thirty precincts were categorized as "B" precincts; they would be commanded by a deputy inspector. The remaining thirty-six precincts would be "C" precincts, and they would be commanded by captains. The rationale was that captains could command a "C" precinct. If they did a good job, they would be promoted to the position of deputy inspector and be moved to a "B" precinct. If they did a good job there, they would be promoted to the rank of inspector and moved to an "A" precinct.

This made the reallocation of inspectors and deputy inspectors from the divisions more palatable. Each patrol borough office would keep one full inspector as the borough adjutant (as opposed to the three they had had before) and two deputy inspectors (as opposed to the four to six they had had before) to handle administration and special projects. The elimination of the division layer and the reallocation of the inspectors and deputy inspectors was a win-win move across the board. We had reduced a significant layer from the hierarchy while at the same time setting up a career path within the Patrol Services Borough. Finally, there was truth to the adage that patrol was the backbone of the department. The commanders who labored in patrol precincts would now be rewarded.

While there were many major changes in policies and procedures, smaller changes were also significant. For example, since our days at OMAP, Mike Julian and I had often discussed the Rodney King incident, which had occurred in Los Angeles on March 3, 1991. King was a motorist who led police on a wild chase. At the end of the chase, King was assaulted by some of the responding police officers, and the assault was caught on videotape that became familiar to millions of viewers around the world. King was struck fifty-six times by baton-wielding officers. He was in a supine position and appeared to be offering little, if any, resistance. The beating looked awful and was certainly unnecessary.

What shocked the conscience of the average citizen viewing the videotape was the fifty-six baton blows to King's body. While I, too, was disturbed by the video, what upset me even more was the failure of any officer present to intercede and stop the behavior. Almost every officer has been in a highly charged situation where emotions are running high and there's maybe an added punch that was probably unnecessary. But usually, cooler heads prevail. Other officers will intercede to stop the extra punch and take control of the situation. (The failure to control the King situation resulted in four officers being indicted for assault. Thirteen months later, on April 29, 1992, those four officers were acquitted. The city's mounting racial tension boiled over. The riots that followed ultimately resulted in the deaths of more than fifty people and property damage in the hundreds of thousands of dollars.)

In the conversations Mike Julian and I had about the failure of any officers to take control of the King situation, we crafted a paragraph, to be inserted into the preamble section of the Patrol Guide, dealing with force and deadly physical force. It stated that responding officers, though not the primary officers, had the affirmative obligation to intercede and stop the behavior in a situation where the primary officer may have become overemotional and was engaging in excessive force.

This notion of the affirmative obligation to intercede in highly emotional and charged situations was drilled into police officers' heads during training, in the classroom, and at roll call. While the expectation was that all police officers had an affirmative obligation to act, it was the duty—part of the job description—for every sergeant to do so at the scene of such an incident. It had been the failure of the sergeant the night of the Thomas Ryan incident in June 1975 in the 44th Precinct that allowed that situation to get completely out of hand, damaging the careers of good police officers and hurting the reputation of an entire precinct.

The central irony of the Rodney King incident was that one of the main culprits was one of the sergeants at the scene. Instead of stopping the behavior of the other officers that night, Sergeant Stacey Koon basically encouraged it as he led the assault on King.

These few policy changes were among the many during Bratton's first year. In the NYPD, new policies and procedures are issued as Interim Orders and then later incorporated into the Patrol Guide and the Administrative Guide. In an average year, you can expect between 90 and 100 Interim Orders to be issued. In Bratton's two years at the helm, there were between 160 to 170 Interim Orders issued *each year*, the signal of a dynamic and radically changing organization. The year after he left, the number of Interim Orders issued dropped to between 60 and 70.

8

CompStat, Crowd Control, and the "Dirty Thirty"

Look at how well we're doing, and we haven't even broken a sweat.

—JACK MAPLE

Probably the best-known—but least-understood—management technique in the Bratton administration was CompStat: a weekly crime meeting held at police headquarters by the top police brass and all of the local commanders, including specialized units such as detectives and those who dealt with narcotics, gangs, and warrants. *CompStat* is short for *comparative statistics* or *computerized statistics*. (I prefer *comparative statistics* since computers had very little to do with the initial creation and development of the crime meetings.) Many people in the Bratton administration have their own opinion on how the CompStat process first began. It all depends on where you sat at the time.

In the early months, Jack Maple, Bratton's crime czar, spent a great deal of time in my office sharing war stories, but we also had many serious conversations about how we were going to deal with crime. Jack seemed particularly frustrated with the inability to get meaningful crime statistics in a timely fashion. There was absolutely no problem in finding out what happened in certain parts of the city six months or a year earlier, but finding out what happened last month or last week was an entirely different matter. My background in OMAP was particularly helpful in explaining to Maple how the system worked. However, my explanations didn't satisfy Jack and, in fact, frustrated him even more. He thought that the Management Information Systems Division (MISD) should have the crime information readily available in a timely manner. I just laughed, having had years of experiences with MISD, whose operating credo was "It can't be done" and whose favorite answer to any question was "No."

While timely crime information was not available at headquarters, the local borough commanders did keep up-to-date crime details regarding certain crimes that plagued their communities, most notably robberies. So the best way to get any type of updated information was to ask the borough commanders. Rather than visit each of the seven borough commanders, we decided that we would have the borough commanders come to headquarters with their staff to brief the top brass about what was going on in their individual boroughs regarding crime.

The early meetings with the borough commanders, their staffs in tow, were held in my conference room. We viewed a series of charts and maps with acetate overlays depicting certain crimes and hot spots. The initial meetings consisted of a presentation by the borough commander, with some follow-up questions asked mainly by Jack Maple and Louie Anemone. It quickly occurred to everyone present that the borough commanders could not answer certain questions since they dealt with what the detectives were doing and how many times the Narcotics Division had been in certain precincts during the course of the prior week. More people, especially from the specialized units, needed to be at these meetings. More important, we needed a bigger room. My conference room (which could comfortably accommodate forty to forty-five people) had become inadequate.

The new CompStat meetings were then held in the pressroom on the second floor of headquarters. As attendance at these meetings grew, setting up the pressroom for CompStat meetings and then breaking it down for a press conference or other such meeting became a logistical nightmare. So CompStat made its third and final move to the

Operations Unit on the eighth floor of police headquarters, a large room that generally went unused, except during occasional citywide emergencies when every city agency and its staff would report. This new room had more technology and better access to communications than any other room in headquarters, by virtue of the fact that it was adjacent to the Operations Unit's twenty-four-hour desk and also to the 911 call center. Over the next two years, constant improvements were made. As CompStat evolved, so, too, did the CompStat room and its equipment.

While the CompStat meetings began as a very rudimentary process of presentations by the borough commanders, they evolved into full-blown crime meetings, attended by every crime-fighting unit within the department, including the nonpolice crime-fighting apparatus within the criminal justice system—parole, probation, and the local district attorney, just to name a few.

The downside of the CompStat meetings became evident early on: an undeserved reputation for nonprofessionalism, demeaning behavior, and undue pressure on precinct commanders, detective commanders, and narcotics commanders. While there was an occasional incident of poor behavior on the part of some of the questioners, by and large the CompStat sessions were conducted professionally. Regarding the pressure, the vast majority of the precinct commanders rose to the challenge and embraced the questions. The pressure was not intolerable: it was fair and pointed and held the commander accountable. If simply asking a precinct commander what he was doing regarding a series of robberies in his precinct was viewed as too much pressure, then that precinct commander should step aside and allow another individual to take over the job.

What I will acknowledge, however, is that the nature of the Comp-Stat process may have appeared, to those outsiders just visiting and observing, as totally foreign and anathema to good management philosophy. As the CompStat process became better known and written and talked about, people from all over the United States and other parts of the world came to visit and sit in on the sessions. The rough-and-tumble world of the CompStat meetings was shocking to some visitors, amusing to others, and completely misunderstood by the vast majority.

What the visitors were observing was New York culture in full bloom. New Yorkers have a reputation for being obnoxious and aggressive. So for us in the NYPD, the behavior in a typical CompStat meeting was just another day at the office. For the outside visitor, though, it may have appeared sometimes as if the Christians were being thrown to the lions. The really critical mistake was in believing that the aggressive, obnoxious, loud behavior frequently seen in a New York meeting was a requisite part of any CompStat process. After leaving New York, I sometimes visited a newly established CompStat meeting at which the main inquisitor yelled and screamed at the top of his lungs—life imitating art, I suppose, but it was a poor imitation.

Outside visitors to CompStat meetings seemed to respond in one of two ways. First, some police departments across America established their own CompStat units, with the head inquisitor yelling with no apparent method to the madness. Or the response was similar to what happened in a certain American city where the CompStat process had already been established: after viewing the New York model, the chief returned home on the next plane and immediately dismantled his CompStat division because he viewed the one in New York as unprofessional and demeaning. I guess the thought never occurred to that chief that he could have created his own CompStat model, much in his own image and likeness, but then again, such a CompStat process would have reflected his personality: dull.

The upsides to CompStat were innumerable. For the first time, the NYPD was dealing with crime as a front-burner issue; it was clearly the department's top priority. The results were immediate and dramatic. "Expect what you inspect" is the old adage from the police-management books. Even before CompStat became the whiz-bang, dramatic, computerized meetings it has now become famous for, there were decreases in crime.

I can still remember Maple in my office, smiling like a Cheshire cat and saying, "Look how well we're doing, and we haven't even broken a sweat! We're just warming up. Wait till we get this bad boy up and running." And Maple was right—it only got better. For me, personally, the most impressive part of the CompStat process was how it released and encouraged the creative genius of the precinct commanders. I would sit in total amazement at the ideas these individuals came up with to fight crime. The main benefit of CompStat was that it highlighted and rewarded productive performers. Young captains, who prior to this never would have had the opportunity to talk with the chief of department or even to meet or see the police commissioner or the first deputy commissioner, now could interact with these individuals on a weekly basis. In an organization as large as the NYPD, this was revolutionary. And while this revolution was going on, we were creating, for the first time, a meritocracy. By and large, going forward, promotions were based on how you performed rather than whom you knew.

The classic example was Patrick Brennan. Pat was a captain when the Bratton administration began. Although he was much older than his contemporaries, Pat performed better than all of them. (Who says you can't teach an old dog new tricks?) Pat had the brains of an academic, the command presence of a Broadway actor, and a smile that went from New York to his home county of Mayo. He was promoted to deputy inspector and then a year later to inspector, largely as a result of his performance in driving down crime.

In February 1996, we had a meeting of the Promotion Advisory Board to make promotional recommendations to Commissioner Bratton. The board consisted of me (I had at that point been promoted to first deputy commissioner) along with the chief of department, Louie Anemone, and the then chief of personnel, Michael Markman. As we were discussing the rank of deputy chief, Louie Anemone said he had a problem. It turned out that Louie, at one of his commander meetings, said he would promote whatever precinct commander had the highest decrease in crime for 1995. It turned out that Pat Brennan had led the city, with a decline in crime of about 15 percent in the rough-and-tumble 70th Precinct in Brooklyn. Louie said, "I feel awful because I made the promise, but unfortunately we promoted Pat about eight months ago." I looked at Louie and said, "A promise is a promise, and a deal is a deal. If you want to promote Pat Brennan, you have my support." With a huge grin, Louie said, "Thanks. This is going to send a great message." And so, in two short years, Pat Brennan went from captain to deputy chief, all on his own merit, thanks to the CompStat process.

The little-noticed and least-appreciated benefit of CompStat was how its process informed top management about crime in a city. While the precinct commanders and their detective counterparts were expected to be intimate with crime and quality-of-life issues in their area, no such expectations were held for the top brass, who were seven layers removed from the street—besides, how could a chief of department be expected to know about crime in every neighborhood of the city? The CompStat process changed all of that. After a few months of attending CompStat meetings, the top brass became intimate with the nature of crime in all areas throughout the entire city. The chief of patrol was made aware of the car break-in problem in Bensonhurst. The chief of detectives was made aware of the nagging burglary problem at the Bronx Terminal Market. The police commissioner himself was made aware of "Bam Bam," the leader of a drug gang who was selling crack at 141st Street and Bradhurst.

Much has been written about the CompStat process and how it holds the local commanders accountable. What is often not noticed, and certainly not written about, is how the CompStat process holds the top brass accountable, too. The top brass now know where the crimes are happening, and they have an obligation to deal with it. The bottom line is that CompStat is the most accountability-driven mechanism in the history of policing.

Avoiding Another Stonewall

The Stonewall Riots occurred on June 27, 1969, when a group of NYPD officers pushed and shoved several gay patrons at the Stonewall Club in the West Village during a raid. The protests that followed that event marked the beginning of the gay pride movement. In June 1994, a huge march commemorating the twenty-fifth anniversary of the Stonewall incident was planned. People from all over the United

States were expected to attend, and crowd estimates reached a quarter million.

We had begun planning for this event several months earlier. What we had not planned for was the New York Rangers winning the Stanley Cup Championship for the first time since 1942. The Rangers' opponent, the Calgary Flames, had won game six, which meant game seven would be held in Madison Square Garden. After game six, Calgary fans rioted and performed a variety of illegal acts that had become all too frequent after major sporting events. When the Rangers won game seven, which I attended as a lifelong Ranger fan, a spontaneous eruption of joy spread throughout the city, but there were no incidents of misconduct. Two days later, I led the Rangers' victory parade up the Canyon of Heroes, a celebration watched by more than a million spectators. Thousands of police officers were assigned along the parade route, and there were no incidents of violence. This was an important victory for the NYPD in that it signaled, once again, that the force could handle large-scale events without allowing them to get out of control. Had there been trouble during the Rangers' celebration, it would have been a bad omen for the upcoming Stonewall commemoration.

The Stonewall anniversary march was scheduled to take place a week later. A quarter of a million people, in support of gay rights and in commemoration of the riots, were expected to march, beginning in the Village, going across town and then up First Avenue, passing the United Nations. Unfortunately, there was a breakaway group whose object of hostility was the Catholic Church, represented by St. Patrick's Cathedral, which is located at Fifth Avenue and Fifty-first Street. The breakaway group was determined to march up Fifth Avenue and conduct a symbolic protest in front of the cathedral, then continue north on Fifth Avenue into Central Park, where it would then rejoin the main group.

Clearly, the second march was going to be a huge drain on police and other city services. More important, it was going to create an issue of public safety: with marches on First and Fifth avenues, crosstown traffic in Manhattan would be brought to a standstill, and gridlock would occur, thus preventing access for emergency vehicles, especially ambulances. The breakaway group had applied for a separate parade permit, but the permit was denied on the grounds of public safety. The group, with legal representation, fought that decision in federal court. Three days before the event was to take place, I was called to testify at the federal courthouse and asked why the permit had been denied. After making my case, the plaintiff's lawyer cross-examined me.

"Chief Timoney, isn't it a fact that every time you all in the NYPD want to deny somebody their civil rights, their right to protest, or their right to parade, you conveniently use the public safety argument? And isn't it a fact, Chief Timoney, that public safety will not be jeopardized if both parades are allowed?"

I reiterated my prior public safety arguments and closed with the following observation: "We in the NYPD believe we are the best at handling parades, demonstrations, and protests. We do so with the intent of allowing those protesting or marching to exercise their constitutionally guaranteed rights. But we also have an obligation to ensure public safety. And it is that obligation that I'm talking about today. You know, there is a saying, 'If you want to handle a presidential visit, you can use the Dallas model or the NYPD model. If you want to handle a political convention, you can use the Chicago model or the NYPD model.' And lately, they are saying that if you want to handle a sporting celebration, you can use the Calgary model or the NYPD model." The judge, the city's lawyer, and the plaintiff's attorney all broke out in simultaneous laughter. The judge quipped, "He got you there."

At the end of the day, the judge ruled in the city's favor, upholding the denial of the permit. But it was a Pyrrhic victory. And I knew it. It was clear to me that although members of the breakaway group had lost in court, they were still hell-bent on following through with their initial plans. Neither Timoney nor any of his "boyos" in the NYPD were going to stop them.

On Saturday, the day before the march, I had a long conversation with Mike Julian on how to deal with the breakaway group the next day. I didn't have a good feel for the tensions surrounding the march. Mike and I decided to go to the Village that night and walk around to gauge the temperature of the crowds. It was a warm night, and we were both dressed in shorts and T-shirts, quite unusual for big-shot NYPD chiefs. The streets were teeming with visitors from all across the country who had come to the city to participate in the march. The mood was one of celebration and joy, and there appeared to be no hostility or tension in the air. We stopped in the Lion's Head for a beer, and I kidded Mike about the facial reactions of some of the uniformed police officers we had passed as we strolled through the Village—but not hand in hand!

The next morning Bobby Muldoon drove to the start of the parade with Jack Maple and me. I felt a lot more comfortable after my previous night's visit to the Village with Julian. I sensed we would have no problems, even with the breakaway group. I had made the decision in my mind to allow the breakaway group to march up Fifth Avenue. I was not looking to create Stonewall 2. I sincerely felt that we could move the group along expeditiously and with as little fanfare as possible. I had also made the decision that I would stay with the breakaway group in case something untoward happened. That way I wouldn't have, nor did I want, plausible deniability.

About ten minutes before the parade was to begin, I received a call from Mayor Rudy Giuliani. "So what have you decided, John?" he asked. I told him my decision and the reasons behind it, and he fully concurred. The breakaway group consisted of between ten and twenty thousand highly agitated individuals, of all shapes and sizes and lots of different styles of clothing, from full body cover to little body cover. Very little. The march was basically uneventful until we arrived at St. Patrick's Cathedral, where there were some ugly and obscene protests against the Church. The protests didn't last too long, and we were able to keep the members of the group moving on toward Central Park, where they met up with the marchers from the sanctioned parade.

I immediately jumped into a waiting helicopter with Maple to get a bird's-eye view of those still on First Avenue in order to see how it was progressing. By and large, things looked pretty orderly. When the helicopter landed, I was greeted by a group of reporters asking typical questions about how things went and whether or not I was satisfied with the event. I said a lot of things in response, but the summation was, "All things considered, I thought it went pretty well."

The next day I was battered with those words by the *New York Post* as its photos focused almost entirely on the exhibitionist protestors in front of St. Patrick's. Sometimes when you win, you still lose. The bottom line was that I had had to make a decision about the breakaway group. My decision was to allow them to offend certain sensibilities and to commit technical violations of the law as a trade-off to avoiding the alternative: violence or a repeat of the Stonewall incident.

The irony of the feigned outrage on the part of some of the media was that every year during the annual gay pride parade, similar exhibitions had occurred in front of St. Patrick's and no one had ever paid too much attention. In the end, you have to make decisions based on your experience, and sometimes based on your gut instinct, but always with public safety in mind. You also need to recognize that some people will be okay with your decision, and others will hate it and you for making it. But cops are in the decision-making business, and if I had to choose a profession with the best decision makers, it would be cops. From the time a rookie comes out of the academy, he begins making life-and-death decisions. The more decisions a cop makes over his career, the better decision maker he becomes.

The Dirty Thirty

While things were going well throughout the first year on the crime front, not all was right on the corruption side. When Bratton came into office, he walked in on an extensive corruption investigation that had begun in the early 1990s in northern Manhattan. Throughout 1993, rumors swirled through the department regarding corrupt cops and drugs and multiple investigations from multiple law enforcement agencies. It was known that at least three separate investigations were ongoing. The Manhattan D.A.'s Office was conducting its investigation, the U.S. attorney for the Southern District was conducting her investigation, and the Mollen Commission, which had been established by Mayor Dinkins, was, as I noted earlier, in the midst of its own investigation. At one point in 1993, I received a phone call from one of the lead investigators from the Mollen Commission who was looking to talk. We met in an isolated spot in Battery Park one morning, with the Statue of Liberty in the background and the sun coming up over the horizon. After listening to this investigator and his request for me to take a message to the police commissioner, I concluded that he had seen one too many movies.

In early 1994, three arrests were made for corruption-related activities by police officers in the 30th Precinct. The Manhattan D.A. requested that we come to his office to hold a press conference announcing these arrests. Commissioner Bratton, Jack Maple, and I went over for the press conference. The D.A. and Bratton both spoke. I had a nonspeaking role: I was the blue potted plant at the end of the table. When the conference was over, the lead investigator for the D.A.'s Office asked me if I wanted to see the video of the officers who had stolen the drugs and the money. The first video clearly showed a uniformed officer entering a one-room apartment occupied by an undercover cop posing as a drug dealer. The officer conducted a search for drugs, in the process finding $2,000 in cash. He put the money in his pocket and then left the apartment.

The second video showed two police officers entering the same apartment. One officer, a rookie right out of the academy, is clearly unsure of himself, while the other, an eight-year veteran, runs the show and does most of the questioning. After inquiring about the location of the drugs and not receiving a satisfactory answer from the undercover, the police officer is seen searching a side closet. You clearly see the veteran police officer take out the $2,000, look at it, and put it back. He then asks the undercover posing as the dealer, "Where are the drugs?" When he doesn't get an answer, the officer picks up a scale used for weighing drugs and flings it in the direction of the drug dealer, intentionally missing him. When the scale hits the wall, the drug dealer flinches, but the rookie flinches even more. The veteran cop confronts the drug dealer and knees him in the groin. It is clear on the video that the rookie cop is scared. Both officers then leave the apartment. The veteran cop is charged with felonious assault, and the rookie cop is charged with altering an official government document, in that he did not properly record the incident in his memo book. At a meeting back at headquarters I let my feelings be known regarding the rookie police officer. I thought the idea of arresting and charging him was ludicrous, and I said so.

Walter Mack, a former federal prosecutor, was head of Internal Affairs at the time; he had been hired under the previous administration by Commissioner Kelly. Mack agreed that the rookie should not have been charged, but he maintained that there was little we could do to prevent the arrest. I disagreed and made my feelings known to all present.

Over the next few months, more arrests were made. However, there didn't appear to be any sense of urgency on the part of the prosecutors to bring these investigations to a conclusion. Tensions in the 30th Precinct were running high. Officers were openly accusing other officers of being snitches, and there was warranted suspicion by some that the officers sitting next to them at roll call or in the police car were "dirty" cops—wearing wires, trying to entrap them in a crime.

One Sunday morning, I received a phone call from one of the lead investigators from District Attorney Robert Morgenthau's office informing me that one of my police officers had just shot and wounded another officer in front of the desk lieutenant at the 30th Precinct. I found it shocking that I was first hearing about this incident from an individual outside of the department. Why hadn't the officer in charge of the Operations Division notified me, as would have been normal protocol? The investigator informed me that the officer who did the shooting was a dirty cop who had been arrested but then had been put back out on the street with a gun and a shield to snare other dirty cops. I was incredulous. It turned out that the police officer who had been shot had accused—correctly—the other officer of being a dirty cop working for the outside investigators. As if to add insult to injury, a suggestion was made that since everyone thought that the shooting was accidental, maybe the dirty cop could be allowed to continue to work with his gun and badge in hopes of turning over more dirty cops. Needless to say, I went nuts.

In July 1994, the cost of these corruption investigations became very personal when Captain Terrence Tunnock committed suicide. Tunnock was the executive officer in the 30th Precinct, and his integrity was beyond reproach. The year before, Tunnock had suspected a sergeant of committing a corrupt act and had voluntarily reported the incident to Internal Affairs. Terry was a very sensitive man who was loved by every cop who ever worked for him. While I didn't know him that well, I had worked a few details with him, including the West Indian Day Parade in 1985 when I was a captain and he was a lieutenant.

The West Indian Day Parade is held every Labor Day as a celebration of West Indian heritage. It easily attracts up to 2 million participants and attendees. At the time, it was one of the more difficult policing events in the city (over the last two decades, the parade organizers have exerted greater control and have worked closely with the police department so that now there are few if any problems). In the early 1980s, however, the parade was plagued with a host of problems, including shootings.

At the 1985 parade, Tunnock was my aide. After checking the troops at around 3:00 P.M., we went into the temporary police headquarters, which was located inside a local public school. While I was checking the staffing rosters, Terry went to the rest room. A short time later, a police officer informed me that Tunnock was in the bathroom bleeding profusely from his lower left leg. When I went into the bathroom, there was as much blood as I had ever seen at any crime scene. When I asked Terry what had happened, he indicated that a severe laceration on his leg had ruptured. Terry thought that our long walk along the parade route had aggravated his prior injury. Nearby medical personnel attended to Terry and quickly bandaged his open wound. Terry refused to go to the hospital and insisted on going back out on patrol with me. While I appreciated his dedication, I told him that I was giving him a direct order—he should get into his car and go back to his home in the Bronx. Terry responded that he didn't have a car and had taken three different subway lines to get to the parade detail that morning in Brooklyn. I shook my head in amazement: Terry was clearly old school and tough as nails. I ordered two police officers who had brought their police car from the Bronx (against regulations) to take Terry home. I reminded the police officers that if they got Terry home safely, I would overlook their minor violation of taking a marked police car to the parade.

Terry struck me as the sincerest of men. When he committed suicide, it certainly was not because he was the subject of any investigation— all investigators agreed that he was never a suspect. It was clear to me and to Louie Anemone that the pressure and chaos surrounding the 30th Precinct that year had disturbed Terry so much that he wound up taking his life. Anemone, who had known Terry intimately, was visibly shaken, and Anemone was one tough guy. If Anemone could be so shaken, what about the cops working the 30th Precinct? The answer came soon enough.

On a Friday afternoon in early October, I received a telephone call from the desk officer of the 30th Precinct, Lieutenant Steve Rubino, whom I had supervised a dozen years earlier when I was a sergeant in the 32nd Precinct. Steve said, "Chief, you've got to get up here. We've got a cop in the bathroom with a gun in his mouth, threatening suicide, and he won't come out." I grabbed Jack Maple and got my driver, Don, to drive as fast as he possibly could, with lights and siren, up the FDR Drive through heavy rush-hour traffic. When I got to the station house, there were dozens of press people already there. I spoke to Lieutenant Rubino, and he informed me that a detective had been able to convince the young officer to put down his gun. We then made a decision to sneak the officer out the back gate away from the waiting press and take him to Bellevue Hospital for psychiatric evaluation. To say that the men and women of the 30th Precinct were in a state of shock would be putting it mildly.

Walking around the station house, I could see that police officers were both unnerved and fiercely angry. I grabbed one of the union delegates and began to engage him in a conversation. He didn't hold back for a second. Other cops in uniform and in plainclothes began to mill around and also voice their opinions. I made a decision to create a more formal atmosphere in the muster room and told Lieutenant Rubino to direct all of the police cars that were working the 30th Precinct to come into the station house. I told him to notify the borough office to ask the

Patrol Borough Manhattan North Task Force officers to patrol the precinct until midnight and to answer all calls for service.

The session with the police officers was a free-flowing and frank exchange of opinions. I let the police officers know they could say anything that they wanted to say. I was particularly moved by a plainclothes female police officer who asked me, rather naively, if all of the police officers present were willing to accept a full month's suspension, would we be satisfied and leave them alone?

The most emotional moment of the night was when a very sharp ten-year veteran, who looked like he was out of central casting, took the floor. He looked me straight in the eye and said, "How can you guys do this? How can you guys allow these prosecutors to arrest dirty cops and then give them back their guns and their shields so that they can wear a wire and catch cops for lesser crimes or violations while at the same time endangering every police officer's life in the process?" Jack Maple stood up and began to try to explain that, in order to get a dirty cop, you sometimes have to use dirty cops. I knew Jack's heart wasn't in the explanation. I just tugged his coat and told him to sit down, saying, "They're right. What's going on here is wrong."

The next day I called Paul Shechtman, assistant U.S. attorney, top corruption prosecutor, and a good friend. I pleaded with him to do all he could to bring these investigations to an end. Paul promised that he would do what he could. Over the next few months, efforts were made to wrap up the investigations, with one exception: Louis Manetta. Louis Manetta was the new commanding officer of the 33rd Precinct and prior to that had been the executive officer of the 30th Precinct. During the Mollen Commission hearings, the star witness, known as Officer Otto, had testified with a black hood over his head about corrupt activities within the 30th Precinct. One of the allegations made by Otto concerned Captain Manetta. The allegation was that Captain Manetta warned police officers about Internal Affairs investigations and condoned and even witnessed police officers "booming doors" (entering illegally) of drug-infested apartments without an authorized search warrant. Over the next two years, prosecutors were foaming at the mouth in anticipation of getting Manetta.

I had worked with Manetta when I was a sergeant in the 32nd Precinct and he was an anticrime cop. I always found him to be tough but honest and one of the best cops assigned to that Harlem precinct. I had always been always skeptical of Officer Otto's assertions. Nonetheless, these allegations dogged Manetta unfairly for two years—they prevented him from being promoted to deputy inspector even though he was rated the top captain, out of more than three hundred, in the NYPD by his colleagues and supervisors. In early 1995, Otto was proved to be a phony and a fraud; in fact, he had been a corrupt cop himself, along with his partner George Nova, one of the "Dirty Thirty" cops who had been arrested. When Otto was exposed, his credibility was shot, and some of the corruption cases against other police officers were tainted. As for Louis Manetta, he retired in frustration but with his head held high, knowing that his accuser was a boldfaced liar. This ended one of the most horrific corruption episodes in the history of the NYPD.

The Queens Boulevard Shooting

There are big cases and then there are *really* big cases, with many complexities and many lessons. On a Sunday evening in December, a Chinese immigrant, Hsu Wen-Ping, after a dispute with his landlord, went on a shooting spree at three separate locations. The first location was his residence, where he shot and killed his landlord. He then proceeded to a Chinese restaurant on Queens Boulevard, where he shot and killed the landlord's wife. Another bullet struck the pregnant woman who was working the register. A number of calls were made to 911, which resulted in a heavy police response, including personnel from the Emergency Service Unit. The man fled the restaurant and engaged responding police personnel in numerous exchanges of gunfire as he moved down Queens Boulevard. He ran down the ramp of an underground garage, where he again engaged police in a gun battle. He was eventually cornered and killed in a final exchange of gunfire. At the bottom of the parking garage ramp an innocent man, Laakhraj Dalipram, an immigrant from Trinidad, was shot and killed as he attempted to drive out of the garage to pick up his family, which was waiting for him at a nearby restaurant.

A preliminary investigation revealed that the shooter had discharged over a hundred rounds at NYPD personnel. In return, they had discharged over two hundred fifty rounds at him. This was the largest number of rounds fired in one case in the recent history of the NYPD. Before the dust had settled, there were accusations and recriminations regarding the police response at the Chinese restaurant and especially regarding the killing of the driver who had been caught in the crossfire. It was unclear whose bullet had killed Dalipram, but we suspected it had come from a cop's gun. We just needed confirmation from our ballistic experts.

Normally, a captain investigates police gun discharges. This case cried out for a more in-depth investigation, not only because of the number of bullets fired but also because of the police response at the Chinese restaurant and the killing of the innocent civilian. I asked Pat Harnett, my executive officer, with his vast investigative experience, to put together a small team to look into the entire matter.

Shortly after the shooting, the ballistic experts confirmed that the bullet that had killed Dalipram had come from a police officer's gun. Unfortunately, this information was leaked to a local TV reporter, who then announced to the world that the NYPD had killed an innocent man. Although Bratton and I had been fully prepared to announce that it was a police bullet that had killed the innocent driver, the leak gave the appearance that we were trying to withhold the information to spare embarrassment and that we were a callous and uncaring police department. Nothing could have been further from the truth. But once a story gets out ahead of an official announcement, it becomes open to interpretation and manipulation, which further unnecessarily complicates an already complicated situation.

The next morning, I discussed the case with Bratton to determine what our response should be regarding the innocent civilian. He was heading to Boston, so we agreed that I would apologize to the civilian's family on behalf of the NYPD. That evening Jack Maple and I drove up to the funeral home in the North Bronx, where the family was having a private viewing. To avoid any press, we got there an hour early and waited for the family to arrive to say their prayers. Then, in a very emotional moment, we expressed our sincerest apologies.

As we left the funeral parlor, there was a throng of media on the sidewalk looking for comment. Maple and I brushed past the TV cameras, got in our car, and drove off. I called John Miller, as had been previously arranged. Miller was with the mayor, and both of them were curious as to how things had gone. Mayor Giuliani got on the phone and said, "How'd it go, John?" I said, "It was highly emotional. The family was more gracious to me than I would have been to them had the situation been reversed." The mayor then asked if he should pay the family a visit and apologize on behalf of the city. I replied that I thought that was an excellent idea. That night, the mayor apologized to the family and then held a small press conference afterward. A few days later, an editorial in the *New York Daily News* suggested that the NYPD could learn about class and humility from Rudy Giuliani's visit and apology.

Within a couple of weeks, Harnett finished his investigation and wrote an extensive report on his findings. One troubling part of the investigation had been an allegation that when the police officers initially responded to calls from the Chinese restaurant and encountered the pregnant female, they failed to render first aid. In fact, it was alleged that they left the scene in a hurry to join their fellow officers in pursuit of the gun-wielding madman. Harnett had made it clear in his interviews with the police officers that he was not looking to assign blame but rather to understand the thinking behind their actions. When Harnett pressed them as to why the officers did not take the time to render first aid to the injured pregnant woman, the police officers seemed surprised. They responded to the effect, "My partners were in trouble, and my primary job is to protect my partners." In a paternal tone, Harnett replied, "I assume you're always going to protect your partners. But your primary duty is to protect the public."

We discussed Harnett's findings at great length. Even the recently retired Mike Julian concluded that something had changed over the years. We felt that if the same question had been asked of any of us, we would have responded that our primary job was to protect the public. When did protecting your partner become an officer's number one priority? When did this paradigm shift occur? Had something happened over the past twenty-five years in how we trained our police officers, or were we just a bunch of grousing old-timers?

New York City Police Department guidelines prohibit police officers from discharging their weapons when such discharge will "unnecessarily endanger the lives of innocent people." In this situation that prohibition did not apply. This was a running gun battle with an armed and dangerous madman who had already committed murder. The police officers had no other choice but to return fire as they pursued him into the underground garage. Unfortunately, Dalipram was killed. But horrible things happen in policing every day. The ballistics exam revealed that the bullet came from a police weapon. Though it could have come from any one of the officers' guns, we made the decision that the department would take the responsibility for the driver's death. There was no point in assigning that responsibility to a specific officer. To single out the officer whose gun discharged the bullet would only ruin yet another life.

Among the people shot by Hsu Wen-Ping that night on Queens Boulevard was Detective Tommy Koehler, who was hit in the left thigh, with the bullet severing his femoral artery. Detective Koehler almost bled out at the scene, but his partner managed to secure a tourniquet around his leg to stop the bleeding. Unfortunately, even after a series of operations, Detective Koehler lost his left leg below the knee. Tommy was a world-class athlete, and this was a devastating blow. However, he never stopped competing: he set a new record for an American below-knee amputee in the 2006 New York City Marathon.

Bratton and the Press

Most police officers I have encountered throughout my career, including chiefs, despise the press. They view the media as the enemy, whose sole purpose is to embarrass the police, or so they will tell you. The fact that the NYPD titles its media training for captains "Media

Survival" underscores the hostile and competitive nature between the police and the media.

Bratton believed that great things were about to happen in the NYPD, and that the media would play a critical role in documenting the changes and their impact as they were occurring. John Miller had a more practical explanation for the press strategy. "Listen," he would say, "the bastards are going to get the bad news stories, and they're going to report them, and there is nothing you guys can do about it. They are not your friends, but neither are they your enemies. We've got a lot of good news stories, and we've got to get them out there to help tell our story." He then added, "By the way, they are a bunch of lazy bastards, so let's give them a hand in doing their work."

From the beginning of the Bratton administration, the press was accepted as a fact of life. Members of the press were given a great deal of access, and they reported their stories. The good news stories got out and drew national attention, so it wasn't long before the national media was reporting from One Police Plaza on the important changes and results at the NYPD. Bratton was sometimes criticized as being a media hound, but that criticism was unfair and unjustified. If Bratton really had been a media hound, then only he would have appeared in the press. Instead, it wasn't uncommon to see Joe Borelli, the chief of detectives, conducting a press conference on huge stories of national interest and international implications. And on more than one occasion, I appeared live at a Sunday morning television panel or for a full half-hour interview on some critical issue confronting the department. More important was the number of police officers and detectives who were not only allowed to appear on television but were actually encouraged to appear there or in the papers, explaining this positive investigation or that tragic incident that had just occurred. And how many times did John Miller have the lead detective in an important case go to the media and give out critical information and request citizens' help in solving the case? So many cases were solved with tips as a result of a detective going to the press that Miller began referring to the disposition of these cases as closed by the press (CBP), a play on the official disposition of closed by arrest (CBA). The bottom line was that we had a very aggressive and strategic media policy.

While every police department should have an aggressive media strategy, the chief, above all, must recognize that a media strategy can be a double-edged sword. While we were basking in the positive media coverage at One Police Plaza, the guys and gals at City Hall were not necessarily enamored with our strategy. Some would argue that they were actually angry about the strategy and its focus on the NYPD. On more than one occasion during the first year, they let their feelings be known—and theirs were not warm and fuzzy feelings.

On one of those occasions, Bratton and Miller were reminded by Peter Powers, the first deputy mayor and Giuliani's best friend, that no one gets out in front of the mayor. Cristyne Lategano, the mayor's press secretary, would let the press know that the mayor was a serious man and indicate that those over at police headquarters were less than serious and more interested in getting their faces on television. Cristyne had figured out that if we were having such a good time, we must not be serious or not working very hard. She just couldn't comprehend that you can have a good time while working your ass off.

9

The Beginning of the End

If you want to be number one, you must first become number two.
—SHUCK SEID

At the end of 1994, Dave Scott, the first deputy commissioner, announced his retirement. The day after Scott's announcement, I received a note on red paper from my Chinese godfather, Shuck Seid: "If you want to be number one, you must first become number two." While I certainly wanted the job as first deputy commissioner, there was a huge financial and familial cost. The first deputy commissioner is a civilian position, similar to the police commissioner. There are only two people in the fifty-thousand-person organization who must reside in the city: the police commissioner and the first deputy commissioner. I resided in Rockland County, a suburb northwest of the city with my wife, Noreen, and two teenage children, Christine and Sean. Christine was in her freshman year of high school, and Sean was just about to enter high school. Like most cops, I was living from paycheck to paycheck. If I were promoted, it would mean that I would have to take up residence in the city. Clearly, I could not move the family, and so I would have to get an apartment in the city, which was a huge added expense. There is no pay difference between the chief of department and the first deputy commissioner; this promotion was going to cost me a minimum of $15,000, but as Shuck Seid said, "If you want be number one, you must first be number two."

Shortly after Dave Scott made his announcement, I had a conversation with Bill Bratton. Bill wanted me to be the first deputy commissioner, but he was very aware of the economic cost of the decision, and he understood that I might feel that I had to turn down his offer. It didn't take me long to think about it. I accepted.

Pat Harnett, who had been my executive officer, was promoted to two-star assistant chief, taking over the Narcotics Division, while Marty O'Boyle received his third star and was now a super chief in charge of the Organized Crime Control Bureau. Charlie Reuther moved over to become chief of detectives.

I knew I needed someone smart to handle the job of executive officer to the first deputy commissioner. I reached out to James McShane, the commanding officer of the 47th Precinct. Jimmy was a lawyer, held a master's degree from Harvard, and had been a close confidential aide to Commissioner Kelly. Jimmy's prior experience with Kelly proved to be invaluable, and he took to the job like a fish to water. Bratton didn't know McShane well, but after meeting him and seeing him in action, he liked him and soon asked me to include McShane in many of our meetings, especially those involving discipline.

Jimmy had a great sense of justice, and his legal training was quite helpful in dispensing punishment to officers who violated the rules. Jimmy always talked of the punishment needing to be "proportionate" to the infraction. He despised the tradition within the NYPD of cutting people's heads off, often for violations that did not warrant such harsh punishment. It is interesting that many members of the press believed we did not punish harshly enough. McShane argued that our job was neither to please the press nor to stop its criticism but rather to administer justice. Both Bratton and I appreciated Jimmy's sense of fairness. Administering harsh punishment, dealing with the press, and trying to maintain a sense of fairness would all color the first few months of my tenure as first deputy commissioner.

The First Leg of the Table Is Removed

The last Sunday of 1994 was just like the fifty-one that had preceded it. I got up early and drove my running route to hide the three bottles of water that would come in handy later during my eighteen-mile run. After finishing the run, I showered and then went to the bagel shop for my Sunday morning bagels, coffee, *New York Times*, and *New York Daily News*. Looking down at the newspaper rack, the big bold headlines on the Sunday edition of the *Daily News* screamed out, "Bratton's Juggernaut." "We are fucked now," I said to myself. Operation Juggernaut was the fancy title that Jack Maple and Marty O'Boyle had given to their new antidrug and antiviolence initiative for 1995.

We had had a great first year with double-digit decline in overall crime, but especially in homicides. At the end of the first year, there were 380 fewer homicides, 14,000 fewer robberies, 10,000 fewer burglaries, and a whopping 17,000 fewer stolen cars. While some of the crime strategies accounted for the reduction in robberies and stolen cars, Maple knew that the reduction in homicides was tied largely to our narcotics effort, which had been led by Marty O'Boyle. Jack and Marty felt that more needed to be done on the narcotics front if we were to drive homicides down even further in 1995.

Toward the end of 1994, Jack would smile, rub his hands together, and exclaim, "This bad boy [meaning the organization] is starting to hum. We haven't even broken a sweat yet, and look at the reduction in homicides. When we unleash this baby [Operation Juggernaut], the bottom is going to fall out of the homicide business." And he was right.

About a month earlier, Mayor Rudy Giuliani and his top deputies had been briefed extensively about Operation Juggernaut with an impressive PowerPoint presentation that had the requisite video of police officers ramming doors while executing narcotics search warrants. And of course, it was set to loud disco music that underscored confidence, stamina, and *just a little bit* of testosterone. Giuliani and his deputies seemed quite pleased with the proposal. You might even say they were excited. Giuliani could picture himself in the City Hall blue room unveiling the new 1995 drug initiative meant to end drug dealing and drug trafficking once and for all. The crusading prosecutor had morphed into a crusading cop. Unfortunately, someone had beaten Rudy to the punch and leaked the story to the *Daily News*. And that was the end of Operation Juggernaut. But it wasn't the last we heard of it.

Rudy Giuliani did not like to be upstaged. To quote Mrs. Loman, "Attention must be paid." Speculation ran amok as to who had leaked the story. But my sense was that City Hall laid the blame at the doorstep of John Miller. Over the next month, we kept hearing allegations from City Hall, often through its cronies in the media, about how overstaffed Miller's Public Information Office was. Comparisons were made between the size of the mayor's press office and that of Bratton's press office. Unfortunately for Bratton, the staffing at the press office also included individuals assigned to the police academy, a group whose only purpose was to produce the monthly police magazine. When you looked at the actual number of individuals involved in day-to-day press activities, the disparity was not so great. However, never let the facts get in the way of a good story.

I had become the first deputy commissioner on January 13, 1995. Among the many duties of the first deputy commissioner, as the number two person in the NYPD, was overseeing staffing and budget. For my first two or three weeks in that position, I dealt with veiled threats from City Hall regarding the budget and especially the staffing at Miller's office.

One night I was summoned to City Hall to meet with Randy Mastro, the mayor's chief of staff and also a former federal prosecutor. I took Joe Wuensch, our deputy commissioner for budget. The meeting with Mastro didn't last long. He indicated that they wanted Miller's staff reduced by twenty-one bodies and that it should be done immediately. We knew that there was no sense in attempting to argue or discuss the matter. Minds had been made up and "attention must be paid." I told Mastro that we would go back to headquarters and begin working on the reductions. He insisted that the list of names of those who would be leaving the Information Office be ready the following morning. I just responded, "We'll work on it." As I left City Hall, I knew they were not happy.

The next morning at around 9:00, I received a phone call from Mastro asking, incredibly, "Where's the list?" I said, "We're working on it." He replied, "I need the list now. The mayor is standing next to me." I replied, "When I have the list, we'll get it over to you," and I hung up the phone. About a half hour later, I received a frantic phone call from Mastro wanting to know where the list was. I knew this was getting uglier by the minute. Commissioner Bratton was still at an early meeting, but I finally reached him by telephone. "You had better get back here in a hurry," I said. "Things are starting to turn to shit."

When Bratton returned to headquarters, we had a short meeting at his office, along with Miller and Maple. At this point I was no longer accepting phone calls from Mastro, but my confidential aide, Sergeant Jimmy Cambria, sent a note to me: "Mastro called and he wants the list." The delay in assembling the list was that we were trying to find suitable assignments for those being transferred from Miller's office. Some of these individuals were veteran officers with stellar records and certainly did not deserve to be treated in a shabby fashion by merely assigning them to a random patrol precinct. Nonetheless, City Hall wanted the list with the names and where they were going to be assigned to ensure that we were not playing shell games.

At one point in the discussion, I suggested to Bratton that maybe we should just all walk over to City Hall together and resign. I was quite serious, and Bratton seemed surprised that I would be willing to end my career over a fight between him and City Hall. About five minutes after that statement, Sergeant Cambria arrived with another note from City Hall: "If you guys are looking to resign, we'll accept your resignations." Holy Christ, I thought to myself, they've got police headquarters bugged! A few moments later one of Bratton's assistants came into the office and said, "Miller's on television. He's just resigned."

I had thought Miller was still in the anteroom with Maple preparing the list. We turned on the television, and there was Miller, in the second-floor pressroom, holding a press conference that was being carried live by NY1, the all-news television station. Miller had announced his resignation and in a highly emotional speech talked about the

Public Information Office and the notion that the information coming out of that office belonged to the public. It was neither owned by nor controlled by City Hall. John's statements genuinely moved me, and I naively said to Bratton, "They'll be playing that tape in journalism schools for the next hundred years." I could not have been more wrong.

After Miller's resignation, City Hall began its media spin operation. The results in the following days in the newspapers and on television were shocking, at least to me. Miller was portrayed as a poor manager who had considered Bratton's image-making as his number-one priority, rather than the dissemination of information to the public. The biggest disappointment for me was how Don Imus, the New York City radio shock jock, handled the Miller affair. Imus was not only the most popular radio host in the city—he also had the most sophisticated audience of all of New York's morning radio shows. Unfortunately, Imus bought City Hall's spin hook, line, and sinker. I was a huge fan of Imus and Miller had been a semi-regular on his show. So I was extremely disappointed at how Imus treated Miller.

The Miller episode was a big lesson for me. First and most immediate was the idea that Giuliani and his minions were very serious people on a mission. They played hardball, and they played for keeps. I had worked pretty closely with both the Dinkins and Koch administrations, and while we had had occasional disagreements and institutional clashes, they paled in comparison to the Giuliani administration's "win at all costs" attitude.

The second lesson I learned was both a disappointment and a revelation. Even though I was a twenty-five-year veteran of the NYPD and had conducted countless press interviews and even knew some of the reporters personally, I really was naive as to how fickle the press was and how it, too, could be manipulated. John Miller had been one of the stars of the New York press corps for the prior decade and a half. He was their pride and joy. Some would say he was even their poster boy. There wasn't a reporter around whom John had not helped along the way. Miller is one of the most obliging individuals I have ever met. He doesn't say no, he always has time for the high and mighty, but he has even more time for those who are neither high nor mighty. The silence of the New York press corps was deafening. No reporter or editorial-page writer whom I am aware of came out to support John, even though his fight with City Hall was really about them and their access to information.

The final lesson: while the police department must have an aggressive press strategy, it had also better have buy-in and agreement from City Hall. This would include getting the mayor and the city manager to attend press conferences regularly or, at a minimum, extending the invitation for them to attend. The bottom line is that most mayors enjoy watching their chief and his officers on television because they recognize that the police department's success is a positive reflection of their administration. What mayors don't like are surprises, and so if there's going to be a profile in a magazine or a big Sunday newspaper story, it's important that the mayor hear about it from the chief, rather than read the article for the first time as he's having his Sunday morning coffee.

"Look Who's Sitting on My Right Side Tonight"

When Miller left at the end of January 1995, a very noticeable change in the atmosphere at police headquarters became evident. Our first year was marked by hard work and lots of fun. We lost a little of the swagger and attitude when Mike Julian retired toward the end of 1994 to take a corporate job at Rockefeller Center. Losing Miller a short time later took us down another notch in the swagger department. While we continued to make great strides during the second year of Bratton's administration, it was no longer the fun it had been in the first year. To make matters worse, City Hall took a much more active role in the police department's activities, especially in the area of major press conferences and announcements. During the course of the year, I spent a lot more time at City Hall on a variety of issues that were often contentious.

When I was chief of department during the first year of the Bratton administration, I was often at City Hall, but mostly for ceremonial purposes, when I would perform what I sarcastically referred to as my favorite role of "blue potted plant." I would stand behind the mayor, looking real handsome in my uniform with my four stars and medals. The mayor's press secretary confided to me one day that the "mayor loves having you stand behind him at press conferences." After some of these pressers, Jack Maple would rib me regarding my role: "What would the 44th Timoney think of all this?" He was referring to my days as a street cop in the 44th Precinct. I would reply sheepishly, "The 44th Timoney would throw up if he saw how Timoney had turned out." We would both laugh at the truth of it.

We spent a great deal of time in the second year dealing with the fallout from various corruption scandals, arrests, and near arrests stemming from the Mollen Commission. It was possible that some of the arrests might not hold up in court since they did not meet the criminal standard of "beyond a reasonable doubt" for a guilty verdict. Others might not even meet the criminal standards of "probable cause" for the arrest. Nonetheless, the department was left to deal with these "tainted" officers administratively, where the standard for discipline, usually meaning dismissal, was "preponderance of evidence."

Back in the late 1980s, when Commissioner Ben Ward was faced with similar issues, he chose a very good friend of mine, Inspector John Walsh, a great lawyer and the commanding officer of the 32nd Precinct, to be the department's "special prosecutor," who would deal administratively with the corruption cases. Walsh was assisted by a young, aggressive attorney, Sergeant George Grasso. Walsh and Grasso were very successful in getting some officers to resign and in getting others convicted in administrative trials and dismissed.

Years later, John Walsh and I had long discussions about the over-zealous corruption prosecutors who did not have enough criminal evidence against their targets but expected that the department would rid the force of a "suspected" corrupt cop. If the department resisted these strong-arm efforts by the prosecutor, we were reminded that any future arrests by this "tainted" officer would not be prosecuted because there would be a significant amount of "discoverable" records available to challenge the truthfulness of the officer's story. The prosecutors' arguments were sound but seemed unfair to me.

Nonetheless, I began the process of establishing a Special Prosecutor's Office within the Department Advocate's Office to deal administratively with the "Dirty Thirty" cases and other serious misconduct or criminal cases. There was no sense starting from scratch, and so I reached out to George Grasso (recently promoted to captain), who had been Inspector Walsh's assistant. George formed a new Special Prosecutor's Office and reported to me on a daily basis about the progress of the cases as they moved through the system. George staffed the office with attorneys from the Advocate's Office and reached out to an officer, John Gallagher, who was on leave from the department and working in the Bronx District Attorney's Office to prosecute criminal cases. Gallagher had been a young cop in Harlem's 28th Precinct and had gone to law school while at the same time making dozens of arrests as an anticrime officer. He was smart and tough, but he looked like an altar boy—in both appearance and age. He looked like he was fifteen, sixteen at the most. Gallagher added real weight to the Special Prosecutor's Office with his background as a criminal prosecutor in the Bronx.

The lesson for me with the "Dirty Thirty" scandal was that in the future the department, or any police department, and its chief must be intimate with any large corruption investigation, not to interfere, but rather to ensure that there is no mass roundup of police officers with little regard for how solid the evidence is. Each arrest must be able to stand on its own merits. If there is strong evidence for two officers but insufficient evidence against a third, then the third officer should not be arrested. This is clearly a problematic area for police chiefs, but they must be willing to enter the fray even if they wind up accused of being soft on corruption or brutality. Police chiefs owe this, at least, to the men and women who work for them.

Almost a decade later, I would face the same situation in Miami, where a large group of officers was arrested, before I became chief, and tried in federal court. Some were convicted, and others were not. In one particular case, two officers were found not guilty in the court but faced department administrative charges that could have resulted in their dismissal. I reviewed the administrative case prepared by Internal Affairs prior to the administrative trial. I found that neither officer had done anything wrong, certainly nothing that warranted dismissal. To be on the safe side, I had my assistant chief, John Gallagher, who had by that time left the NYPD and worked as an assistant U.S. attorney, review the administrative cases against the officers. Gallagher concurred with my reading. You could argue that the officers had used poor tactics, but if we were going to arrest and fire every officer who uses poor tactics, we wouldn't have many officers patrolling the streets, including Officer Timoney from Bronx Narcotics. I instructed Internal Affairs to file the case, believing the officers and their families had already suffered enough from the arrest and criminal trial.

At the beginning of the third year of Bratton's administration, rumors circulated that he would soon be leaving. A number of people, like former Mayor Ed Koch, opined that Bratton was fed up with Mayor Giuliani and the daily antics at City Hall. When Bill did announce his resignation, there was, of course, intense speculation about who would succeed him. One paper, in particular, named the five likely candidates, with the odds of each one getting the job underneath his picture. The odds-on favorite, at two to one, was yours truly. Jack Maple's odds were eight to one, and Louie Anemone registered ten to one. In a conversation with me, Bratton indicated that he would recommend me to the mayor, but he wasn't sure if that was a solid gold recommendation or the kiss of death. Only time would tell.

About a week before St. Patrick's Day, I attended the pre–St. Patrick's Day dinner at the Plaza Hotel hosted by the parade committee. There were many dignitaries on the dais, including Cardinal O'Connor. I was sitting next to Peter Powers, the first deputy mayor and Giuliani's friend since childhood. I had gotten along very well with Powers, even though we may have had an occasional argument over an issue. When it was Peter's time to speak to the hundreds in the audience, he made reference to the fact that five years before, the individual who had been seated on Peter's right on the dais, whose name I can't remember, went on to great things. Peter went on, "Then four years ago, Rudy Giuliani sat next to me, and he went on to become mayor." He paused, looked down the dais in my direction, and said, "Look who's sitting on my right side tonight." The crowd burst out in applause with the thought of the Irish immigrant, Timoney, becoming the next police commissioner.

Going home that night, I replayed Peter Powers's words in my head. Was it a signal? Would Powers ever utter those words publicly if he had not already had conversations with the mayor? Going to bed that night, I thought those odds in the paper really might be reflective of my chances at the number one job.

About two weeks later, Mayor Giuliani announced his choice for police commissioner, and it wasn't the first deputy commissioner. I had been naive to think that I actually stood a chance for the job. As I look back, it was not meant to be. On more than one occasion in the past year, I had been engaged in some heated discussions and arguments with some of the mayor's senior staff at City Hall regarding proposed policy changes. I was clearly viewed as Bratton's guy; thus, my loyalty to the mayor was in doubt. However, if there ever was a slight chance of my becoming police commissioner, it was doomed in mid-February by an article in the *New York Times*.

Bratton had taken a week's vacation, and I was the acting police commissioner. The day before Bratton's return, I had a meeting at City Hall with Denny Young, counsel to the mayor, regarding a series of promotions that included the promotion of Jules Martin to a two-star chief. Martin, an African American with a law degree, had been the inspector in charge of Mayor Dinkins's security detail during his four years in office. While Denny had doubts about Martin's loyalty, I assured him that Martin was a good guy and would be as loyal to Mayor Giuliani as he had been to Dinkins. We had some further discussion on other promotions, all to no avail. Bratton was due back the next day, and I was going on a week's vacation to St. Lucia to celebrate my twenty-fifth wedding anniversary. In frustration, I said to Denny, "You can work this out with Bill Bratton when he comes back from vacation. After all, it's his department." Denny snapped back, "No, it isn't. It's Rudy Giuliani's police department." I knew this was one argument I was not about to win, so I left.

When Bratton returned, I briefed him on my conversation with Denny Young. I didn't pay much heed to one of Bratton's senior aides who had been sitting in the corner reading during my conversation with Bratton. The next day I left for the sun and warmth of the Caribbean. The resort where I was staying provided reprints of *New York Times* articles. On about the third day I was reading an article about the NYPD. There in black and white was every word I had said to Bratton and every word he had said to me. I knew the Giuliani team would be furious with me and would conclude, understandably, that I had spoken to this reporter. Of course I hadn't. Bratton had a leak in his office.

Nonetheless, when Giuliani made his announcement that Fire Commissioner Howard Safir would be the next police commissioner, I was hugely disappointed and angry. Later that day, in a telephone conversation with my good friend Mike McAlary, a columnist for the *New York Daily News*, I said things about Safir that I had no right to say. (I called Howard the next day and apologized to him.) I also said things about Mayor Giuliani that I shouldn't have said.

I had told a *New York Post* reporter two weeks earlier that if I did not get the job of commissioner, I would probably retire. So when I didn't get the job, I immediately filed for retirement. However, word got back to me through various sources that Mayor Giuliani was upset about my statements to McAlary (statements that the *New York Daily News* had printed) and was exploring the possibility of reducing me in rank back to my civil-service title of police captain. I don't know if that was true or not, but the police union president, Lou Matarazzo, let it be known that if the mayor attempted such a dirty trick, the police union would have twenty thousand cops on the front steps of City Hall the next day in protest.

I have learned more in my life from my mistakes than I ever have from my successes. This was a huge lesson for me. Clearly, I needed to control my temper and emotions better. People who are very passionate need to bite their tongues or take a time-out. It doesn't mean you have to dial back the passion (that's impossible), but you do have to control it. Over the last decade or so, I have seen other chiefs handle situations similar to mine with class and dignity. I am envious of them, and I've learned from them.

A few days after I left the NYPD, Jack Maple announced that he, too, was leaving. The headline in the *New York Daily News,* in a byline by Michael Daly, Jack's best friend, next to a full-page picture of Jack in his seersucker suit, homburg, and spats, read, "Jack Takes a Walk."

10

Interregnum

Jesus, I wasn't even born when those things happened.
—BIRMINGHAM, ALABAMA, POLICE OFFICER

After retiring from the NYPD on April 27, 1996, I had a few job offers in the private sector, but none was very appealing. I knew in my heart of hearts that policing was still in my blood. So I did the next best thing—I became a police consultant, sometimes with Bill Bratton and at other times with Jack Maple. The NYPD had received a great deal of press attention both nationally and internationally during Bratton's administration, and it continued even after we left. Bill was in high demand as a speaker to talk about the "New York miracle." The press attention was quite helpful in getting us consulting work.

The first gig was with Bill Bratton, who had been asked to do a complete review of the Birmingham Police Department (BPD). The BPD had an interesting history going back to the days of the civil rights movement. Chief "Bull" Connor—whose use of water hoses on demonstrators and whose flagrant use of police dogs to intimidate civil rights protestors in the 1960s—had become a legend, but not in a good way. By 1996, Birmingham had an African American mayor and police chief, and the police department was a fully integrated agency that reflected the population it served. While we expected to see some problems within the department, the issue of race, we believed, was a thing of the past.

We examined the organizational structure of the BPD and its crime-fighting efforts, and there were numerous areas that needed improvement. However, what struck me as most interesting was the attitude of the younger officers, especially those who were African American. In focus group after focus group, these officers did not hold back their frustration with the political administration of the city. They understood quite clearly the history of the city and their department. They knew of "Bull" Connor and the water hosing and how his officers had charged crowds with German shepherds. They knew the history, but it was just that: history. The "new" Birmingham Police Department did not resemble the old Birmingham Police Department of "Bull" Connor. However, the attitude displayed by the city administration and even by some citizens was that the department had not changed. As one African American officer said to me one day, "Jesus, I wasn't even born when those things happened. How can I be held responsible for what happened way back?"

This notion of continuing to pay for past sins is something I would see time and again as I worked with other departments, including those in Philadelphia and Miami. But it was not just an American phenomenon. In 1997, I worked with the Turkish National Police in Ankara, Turkey, along with Jack Maple and Gordon Wasserman, who had been a technical consultant for the NYPD. The negative history of the Turkish police being used as a brutal apparatus of the state dominated any conversation regarding reform. Similar charges would be leveled against the Buenos Aires Police when I worked with that department in late 1997.

In Belfast, Northern Ireland, where Bratton and I traveled to act as observers for the contentious Drumcree March, the animosity toward the Northern Ireland Police (Royal Ulster Constabulary) by the area's minority Irish Catholics was unsettling. In a meeting with us, Gerry Adams, the Irish Republican leader, laid out the demands of Sinn Fein, the political party associated with the outlawed IRA, rather succinctly: the Royal Ulster Constabulary was an illegitimate police force and had to be completely disbanded before any meaningful reforms could take place. When I pointed out that in the worst days of "Bull" Connor and the Birmingham Police, the notion of completely disbanding the BPD was never discussed, that instead the issue was reform of that agency, Adams just looked at me and said, "You don't understand the history here."

Whether Gerry Adams was serious in his demands or if it was just his public posture, it nonetheless underscores the damage a police department can do to the psyche of the people it serves if the people feel estranged from it or, in fact, have no confidence in it. Variations of this theme have affected many departments in the United States, whether it is the episodic bursts of corruption scandals in the NYPD, the brutality of the Chicago Police Department, or the shootings of civilians by Miami police officers, resulting in serious civil unrest. The bottom line is that police chiefs need to be cognizant of the long-term damage that can result when their departments are not performing properly or not making any obvious efforts to deal seriously with issues, especially corruption and brutality, that negatively affect public confidence.

In 1997, I had the opportunity to do a good deal of work in Fortaleza, Brazil, with Bill Bratton. Tasso Jereissati, the governor of the state of Ceará, which encompassed Fortaleza, the state capital, had hired us. He was a businessman who had been educated in the United States and had been impressed with our crime-fighting record in New York. He realized that if Fortaleza was to reach its potential as a business center and a competitor against São Paulo and Rio de Janeiro, he needed to deal effectively with security. At the time, both São Paulo and Rio were suffering significant increases in violent crime from gangs, unnerving much of the business and tourist industry.

I arrived in Fortaleza a day earlier than Bill and met with a retired general from the army who was now in charge of the police. The general, a big and gracious man, asked if I would talk to the command staff from the police department on what it takes to establish a high-performance department. The speech seemed to go well, and after I finished, the general made a few closing remarks. "Did you hear the chief?" he exclaimed. "He spoke about leadership, about authority, about working hard and working smart. Notice he did not speak of salary. It is not salary that gets the police to perform in an effective manner but nonmonetary things like leadership and dedication." Bill arrived the next day, and we spent the week traveling around the city, getting to know the department and its people. We scrupulously avoided offering any advice early on. It is important to take time to assess any police department fully before offering advice. To give advice too early would leave you open to being perceived as, at best, a know-it-all, and, at worst, patronizingly paternalistic. A real review requires asking lots of questions and, maybe just as important, observing the nonverbal communication of those with whom you interact. Often officials will tell you the party line and pretend they agree while their body language screams, "This is the biggest bullshit in the world!"

About two weeks later, Bill and I were having breakfast at our hotel in Birmingham. I was reading *USA Today* and happened to notice a photo with captions that indicated that off-duty police officers in Fortaleza had engaged in a protest for better pay and conditions. The protest went sour, and there was a skirmish between on-duty officers, mostly supervisors, and the off-duty protesting officers. Shots were fired from the ranks of the off-duty protesting officers, and the chief of patrol, a kind man we had met on our first trip, was struck and seriously wounded.

Two weeks later I was back in Fortaleza for the second of many trips. I was to brief the governor on our initial findings and lay out a road map for the future. As I arrived at the governor's office, I was greeted by a general who pleaded with me to explain to the governor that the police officers needed a decent pay increase. The shooting of the chief of patrol had gotten the attention of this general, and now he was on the side of the officers in their efforts to secure a livable wage. It shouldn't take the shooting of a high-ranking officer to convince a chief that police officers need a decent salary, nor should it take a corruption scandal, like that investigated by the Knapp Commission, to argue for livable wages so that the cops "don't have to steal" to supplement their salary, as it was so inelegantly put by the division inspector to our outgoing roll call in the 44th Precinct one day in 1972.

I have made it a point to be quite vocal regarding police officers' salaries, even when it doesn't sit well with City Hall. I believe police chiefs have the moral obligation to speak up when their officers are not properly compensated. Obviously, police chiefs have a fiduciary responsibility to the city that employs them, but they also have a responsibility to those they command. Remember, you get what you pay for. Or, as my daughter Christine says, cheaper is more expensive in the long run.

PART II

Philadelphia

11

Philadelphia, Here I Come

Once you cross the George Washington Bridge, you're out camping.
—LIEUTENANT FRANK MCGEE, COMMANDING OFFICER,
NYPD SHOOTING RANGE

In the late fall off 1997, Mayor Ed Rendell of Philadelphia hired Bill Bratton to do a quick study of the Philadelphia Police Department and to make some recommendations to improve its crime-fighting efforts. As part of his review Bill asked me to read some documents, including a management study of that department that had been conducted prior to Rendell taking over as mayor in 1991. The management study had been conducted by a group of consultants, which included at least one member of the Harvard faculty. Before we went to see Mayor Rendell, Bratton asked me if I would be interested in the police commissioner's job in Philadelphia. I told Bill that it would depend on Mayor Rendell's response to our review. While I did not know Rendell, I knew enough about him to know that I would like working for him.

On a Saturday morning in December, Bill and I gave a presentation to Rendell and his inner circle regarding our findings. We had some recommendations for change that we mentioned to the mayor. "But what about the management study I asked you to review?" Rendell inquired. "Well, Mr. Mayor," I said, "I read the entire report and it's a very nice report, but nowhere in the hundred and fifty-seven pages does it mention crime and what to do about it."

At the end of our presentation Bratton hinted to the mayor that I might be interested in the police commissioner's job in Philadelphia if it ever opened. After some discussions with the mayor, I was hired as the police commissioner to serve under Rendell during the last two years of his second, and final, term.

Mayor Rendell had won national acclaim for his stewardship of Philadelphia. He had taken over a moribund city whose best days looked to be behind it. Rendell single-handedly revitalized the city, putting it once again in the top tier of American cities where it rightfully belonged. He had boundless energy and a temper to fit. But he was a genuinely funny guy and the world's biggest practical joker. Vice President Al Gore dubbed him "America's mayor" long before that moniker was bestowed on Rudy Giuliani after 9/11. The *New York Times Magazine* chronicled Rendell's success in a long piece that featured a picture of Rendell kneeling down in a bathroom stall at City Hall personally cleaning the toilet bowl. The picture said it all: there was no job too hard or too low for Ed Rendell to tackle. And tackle problems he did, and he generally succeeded, with one exception: crime, especially homicides. Unlike some politicians, Rendell recognized he had a crime problem, admitted it, and went about the task of fixing it. He had tried numerous initiatives with little or no success. I was his final initiative during his last two years in office.

While some cities, especially New York, had success in their fight against crime in the mid-1990s, other cities, most notably Philadelphia, Baltimore, and Chicago, did not fare so well. This was a fact often overlooked by the naysayers who decried the crime decline in New York City, arguing that crime was declining nationwide, so why the fuss about New York? In fact, the notion that the police had anything to do with the crime decline was ludicrous, they argued, since the police could do little to affect the root causes of crime: poverty, homelessness, education, racism, and on and on and on.

When I took over the Philadelphia Police Department in March 1998, it was going to be like a great lab experiment to see if the policies and strategies developed in the NYPD were transferable to another city. Philadelphia had a stubbornly high homicide count due to the easy availability of guns. The city was helpless to control the availability of guns. Any effort to pass reasonable gun control legislation by the city, including who could be issued a pistol permit to carry, was regularly overruled by the state legislature in Harrisburg.

For the fifteen years prior to 1998, the Philadelphia homicide count had never fallen below 400 annually. In 1990, when New York City had its record 2,245 homicides, Philadelphia had slightly more than 500 for the same year, which, on a prorated basis, would have been the equivalent of 2,500 had it been the size of New York.

Taking over the Philadelphia Police Department and reducing crime was going to be a large task. Adding to that task would be the Philadelphia Police Department's pure civil-service system: advancement through the ranks merely requires that someone pass a civil-service exam, with absolutely no regard as to how the person performed his or her duties, especially in the midlevel management ranks of captain and above. In fact, in a department with more than seven thousand members, the police commissioner only gets to make two appointments to deputy commissioner.

There are a total of four deputy commissioners in the Philadelphia Police Department. One commissioner, the deputy commissioner of administration, is a civil-service position, which means that it is filled by an applicant who has taken an open, competitive exam. A second deputy commissioner is really an assistant city manager (appointed by the city manager). The final two deputy commissioner positions are appointed by the police commissioner. In other cities the police chief usually promotes all senior officers above the rank of captain and, in some cases, above the rank of lieutenant. In the NYPD, for example, the police commissioner appoints all senior officers above the rank of captain, which means that the commissioner controls the careers of hundreds of senior officers. It is a real meritocracy. Some, however, especially the unions, will argue that it opens itself to abuse and patronage. That could be true. But if a commissioner is interested in doing a good job and keeping his own job, he will promote those who have worked the hardest, have had the best ideas and initiative, have had the most positive attitude, and are driven to succeed.

By the way, did I fail to mention that everyone in every rank up to deputy commissioner in the Philadelphia Police Department is a member of a union—the same union? In the NYPD five unions represented the various ranks, up to deputy chief, which meant that assistant chief and above did not belong to any association. The police officers obviously had the largest union, followed by the detectives union, the sergeants union, the lieutenants union, and finally a union that represented those senior officers from captain to deputy chief. Five separate unions removed the inherent conflict of same-union membership and sometimes created competition, dare I say contention, among and between the various unions, which, in the end, is a healthy sign.

From the beginning in Philadelphia, I realized that the idea of all members of the department belonging to the same union would prove problematic, especially in the area of discipline. Discipline is an integral element in the foundation of any organization, but in semimilitary organizations like the police it is the key element.

It is unrealistic to expect most ranking officers to willingly and actively institute and pursue discipline against their subordinates who belong to the same union. The matter is further complicated when the supervising officer initiates administrative charges against a subordinate officer because the supervising officer must give testimony to and be cross-examined by a union lawyer representing the officer. That same lawyer may be called upon to represent the supervisory officer, should he himself get in trouble and need representation.

Implicit in this arrangement is the message that the lawyer is transmitting to the supervisor giving testimony against a subordinate: "Listen, pal, don't be so difficult, 'cause maybe next time I won't be very aggressive if I have to represent *you*." The whole discipline process was further complicated by the pure civil-service system, which made it difficult for a police commissioner to develop his own team since promotion and advancement through the ranks was dependent on how well one performed on a test, not how well a supervisor performed his or her duties, including instilling discipline in subordinates.

Creating the Timoney Team

On March 8, 1998, I was sworn in as the Philadelphia police commissioner; the large assembly room at City Hall was filled to overflow capacity. The entire top brass of the Philadelphia Police Department was present, as were my family, many childhood friends, and a large contingent from the NYPD. The person present who received the most attention was the author Tom Wolfe, wearing his trademark white suit, accompanied by my good friend, the lawyer Eddie Hayes.

I had asked three former New York City police commissioners to speak: Ben Ward, Ray Kelly, and Bill Bratton. Ward emphasized the importance of education for police officers and informed the audience that this would be part of my agenda; Kelly talked about the importance of leadership; and Bratton spoke about change and what fun the entire department would have making change.

When it was my time to speak, I talked about my plans for the department, what the men and women could expect of me, and what I expected of them. I let the members of the department know that I knew they expected change and that I would not disappoint them: there would be change, lots of change. I then gave another, shorter speech, this time in Spanish, directly to the Hispanic community. The Hispanic community in Philadelphia had a very contentious relationship with the police department for a variety of reasons, including the recent death of a man in police custody in the backseat of a marked police car. The next day the headline in the *Philadelphia Inquirer* read, "In Two Languages Timoney Speaks to the City." We were off to a good start.

At a press conference after my swearing-in, I made a promise to visit every police district and conduct roll call within my first thirty days. Be careful what you say to the press—it sometimes listens. There are twenty-six police districts in Philadelphia. What I hadn't realized when I made that promise was that there are two roll calls for every shift: an early roll call and a late roll call, separated by a half hour. This meant that I would spend at least one hour in each district, which does not sound unreasonable. However, I completely underestimated my time demands for the first month. Also, I had not factored in traveling and traffic to different parts of the city.

It turned out a young reporter for the *Philadelphia Daily News* was tracking my efforts to do all the roll calls as promised. I guess that is what young reporters do. Two weeks into my administration, the reporter, Nicole Weisensee, asked how I was doing with the roll calls. Fine, I said, not letting on that up to that point I had done only ten districts, and even those ten had been a challenge. "By the way," she asked, "are you also doing the roll calls at the specialized units, such as Highway and SWAT?" What is this woman doing in my universe? I thought to myself, but responded, "Of course."

I told my driver, Tony Pino, we had our work cut out for us, but Tony assured me it would be no problem. "Besides," he added, "it gives us more time in the car to listen to Sinatra." Tony and I were big fans of Francis Albert, so it made the drive through traffic much more tolerable, even pleasant. Tony also made the task easier because he knew the city backward and forward. He had been a cop assigned to the Traffic Division and had been one of Mayor Rendell's drivers for years until I arrived on the scene and the mayor graciously gave him to me. Tony was a tremendous asset. He was very loyal, and he said little. He was the epitome of discretion, just what you need in the officer who is around the chief more than any other individual.

The roll calls were quite valuable for me in getting my message out directly to the troops. The repetition allowed me to make corrections and sharpen the message, much the way a writer revises his drafts. Also, the time in between roll calls allowed me to speak informally to some of the civilian clerical and administrative staff to get a better understanding of how the districts functioned, how the paperwork flowed, or how a crime report prepared in the street made its way to the "catching" detective. So the roll calls were not a waste of time and, in fact, were quite valuable, if draining. By day twenty-nine I had completed them all, one day ahead of schedule. It reminded me of reading

Around the World in Eighty Days in high school, except I did not pick up the extra day because of a quirk in Greenwich Savings Time.

During my first week as commissioner, I received dozens, if not hundreds, of cards and letters welcoming me to Philadelphia and congratulating me. I didn't really have enough time to read all the correspondence right away, so I would read a little of it when I had a break between meetings. Many of the letters were from priests and nuns. Divine Providence intervened, the first week, when I opened one letter that had been written by John Gallagher, the young lawyer who had worked indirectly for me in the Special Prosecutor's Office of the NYPD.

John relayed to me that he had left the NYPD shortly after I had retired and had taken a job as an assistant district attorney in a prosecutor's office in one of the suburban counties not far from Philadelphia. John indicated he was bored and would love to come to work for me if the opportunity presented itself. I immediately called George Grasso back at the NYPD to find out what kind of a guy Gallagher was. Grasso didn't hesitate. "He's smart and aggressive. As a matter of fact, he reminds me of a young George Grasso," Grasso exclaimed with great pride. That was enough for me. I reached out to Gallagher, set up an interview, and hired him immediately after the interview.

The next week I hired two additional civilians: Kim Clinton became my personal assistant, and Gordon Wasserman became my chief of staff. Kim had come from a family of New York City cops, and I knew she would not be with me long because she was waiting to be called by the FBI. She was with me for about six months, enough time to straighten out much of the personnel data and staffing, which was a mess when I walked through the commissioner's door.

Gordon Wasserman was an interesting hire, to say the least. Bill Bratton had met Gordon back in 1995 on a trip to London. Gordon had come to England from Montreal as a Rhodes scholar and had studied at Cambridge. After college he entered the British Civil Service System and spent twenty-seven years in the Home Office in charge of science and technology. By the end of 1995, he was ready to retire and inquired of Bill if there was any possibility of a job at the NYPD. Gordon was hired as a per diem consultant with the NYPD, and he and I became fast friends.

Gordon's hire at the Philadelphia Police Department did not go unnoticed. I received a telephone call one day from a reporter from a small Irish American newspaper. The reporter informed me that the paper objected to Wasserman's hiring and was going to do a story about his role in torturing IRA prisoners for British prime minister Maggie Thatcher's goons in the spy services, or some such nonsense. "He's not even English," I objected. "He's a Jewish guy from Montreal who happened to work for the Home Office. Write whatever story you want. Wasserman stays." I added a few other choice words not fit for print and hung up the phone.

To the three civilian outsiders I had hired, I added another: Jack Maple. Jack was hired for a small consultant contract to review the Detective Bureau and make recommendations. These hires were the easy part. What remained was much more difficult and more political. Who would be the uniformed members of the new team?

Complicating matters was the understanding by everyone in the city, including me, that I was filling out the final two years of Rendell's administration. (There are generally three types of police commissioners/chiefs. The first and most common are those who serve "at the pleasure of the mayor," which means that when the mayor's term expires, so does the police chief's term. The second are those commissioners who have a written contract, such as those in Los Angeles and Washington, D.C. The least common type is the third, in which the police commissioner/chief is appointed by the mayor/city manager and can only be terminated "for cause," as is the case in Miami.) In Philadelphia, there was no expectation on my part that I would be continuing as the police commissioner under the next mayor. It was understood that every mayor has a right to choose his or her own police chief. But Rendell had hired me to make changes, and I was going to make changes. The people affected by the changes understandably argued, "Why is this guy making changes? He's only here for two years! Why is he disrupting our lives when he's going to be gone soon?" Bringing about change with an incoming new mayor is difficult enough. Making changes during the last two years of a term-limited mayor is unpalat-able to most.

Before I could determine the makeup and personalities of the new top uniform team, I needed to deal with a few things. I had to get a better understanding of how the organization was structured. Next, I had to keep in mind that I was basically limited to two appointments at the deputy commissioner level because of the pure civil-service nature of the Philadelphia Police Department. I made a commitment to myself that I would take a full month to study the organization before making substantive personnel changes, including transfers.

The immediate problem was the overall structure of the Philadelphia Police Department. At the top was the four-star police commissioner. Under the commissioner were four two-star deputy commissioners. There was no three-star position, and there were no one-star positions. When I asked the question, "Who is my number two?" I was informed that it was the deputy commissioner of operations. When I asked why, I was told, "Because he supervises the most people." That's not exactly a good rationale for being number two. More important, he really wasn't the deputy commissioner of operations; he was the deputy commis-sioner of some operations—two other deputy commissioners also had operational responsibilities. The deputy commissioner of special op-erations, which included the Narcotics and Vice units, and the deputy commissioner of support services, which consisted of the Traffic Divi-sion, SWAT, Canine, Mounted and Aviation units, among others. Are you still with me?

I was determined to create a number two who would be a real dep-uty commissioner of operations, except going forward he would be re-ferred to as the first deputy commissioner and would be given a third star, which would be a first in the history of the Philadelphia Police Department. Now, it would be clear to everyone, both in and outside of the department, who was number two: the guy who was wearing the three stars.

When I looked at Internal Affairs, it was even worse. In any police department the head of Internal Affairs must report directly to the po-lice chief. In Philadelphia, there were three separate Internal Affairs units and none of them reported directly to the police commissioner. To make matters even worse, or "worser" as they say in Brooklyn, the main Internal Affairs unit was headed by a deputy commissioner, who was also responsible for community affairs. The head of Internal Affairs is such an important position in any large department that he or she should have one and only one mission: the integrity of the department. As Ben Ward correctly noted at the outbreak of the 77th Precinct scandal in 1986, police commissioners have never lost their jobs because of an increase in crime. A corruption scandal, however, can send him packing.

On a more practical level, there is an inherent conflict when the head of Internal Affairs also has other units, whether operational or administrative, report to him. How would it be possible to expect a fair and impartial investigation into an operational unit member who also reports to the head of Internal Affairs?

While reorganizing the department, I was looking to make a statement about the future. In the mid- and late 1990s, tremendous strides were being made in science and technology within the police profession. Looking to underscore the importance of these innovations, I created at Gordon Wasserman's suggestion a new position called the deputy commissioner of science and technology. What this meant was that any aspect of the police department that dealt with science or technology would come under the purview of this new deputy commissioner. So the communications section (or 911 center) and the Information Systems Division, along with the Management Information System Division and the Forensic Science Division, would all be under one umbrella.

The beauty of this reorganization was that the Forensic Science Division, commonly referred to as "the lab," was removed from the jurisdiction of the Detective Bureau. This was a little-noticed and underappreciated change that removed the possibility of collusion or even the appearance of collusion between detectives and lab personnel. Over the years there had been periodic scandals across the country when lab technicians were found to have altered their findings to please a detective or to enhance a weak criminal case. We wanted our lab technicians to understand that they were scientists first and foremost and that their primary obligation was to the truth, not to pleasing a detective or enhancing a weak case.

There are two things about American policing that need to be understood. First, how a department is organized, including reporting and jurisdictional authority, will depend on the size of the department. Obviously, in the larger police departments, such as New York, Philadelphia, and Miami, it is feasible to have strict lines of responsibility and accountability—for example, having one individual head up the Internal Affairs Unit or the Detective Division with that being his or her sole responsibility. Second, in smaller departments, senior officers may be required to cover more than one area of responsibility, even when there may sometimes be an inherent conflict of interest. In these smaller departments it is incumbent upon the police chiefs to take a much more active role in the day-to-day operations of those units. In large departments it is obviously unrealistic to expect the chiefs to be involved intimately with the day-to-day operations with every unit in the department. Therefore, they must choose capable people who report directly to them, because while they can delegate authority, they can't delegate accountability.

As I spent my first month learning about the department and the city, I was also learning about the top brass, sometimes in unsolicited ways. Often the unsolicited advice turns out to be the most informative, if counterintuitive. So when every member of the Chamber of Commerce whispers a certain name in your ear, you can rest assured that the person mentioned might have a greater commitment to the Chamber of Commerce than he does to the police department. All good news isn't good: If everybody is advocating for a certain individual, that individual may or may not be the best one to make part of your team.

As I was thinking through the personnel changes, two things were quite clear. First, I needed to create change and make that change noticeable. Second, and most important, I was going to be held fully accountable for any changes I made. In New York I had recommended changes. Bill Bratton as commissioner was free to accept, reject, or alter my recommendations. At the end of the day, whatever decision was made was Bratton's decision, and he would get the blame or the credit. In Philadelphia, I would make the changes, and I would take the blame or the credit. It's not easy being number one, but that's why they pay you the big bucks. Or so they say.

Throughout the first month, I conducted dozens of interviews within the department and outside the department. While I was looking for the correct number two person, I was also looking for talent within the organization, including hidden talent. The Philadelphia Police Department is a unique organization in that it has a unit in which high-ranking officials, captains and above, who run afoul of the administration or somehow get themselves in trouble are assigned to a unit called the Command Inspections Bureau (CIB).

The CIB staff would pull duty in off-business hours and respond to emergencies or major newsworthy events on behalf of the police commissioner. I say it is unique in that other police departments, including the NYPD, have what are known as "dumping" grounds, but they are usually reserved for misbegotten, misguided, and misplaced police officers and, every once in a while, a sergeant for good measure. But Philadelphia had an actual "dumping ground" for ranking officers. I interviewed members of the CIB and found more than a few talented individuals whose only crime was that they had run afoul of the prior administration.

My first find was Inspector Michael Cooney, a man with a master's degree in education, who had worked in many units of the department in his twenty-five-plus years, including a stint as a deep undercover infiltrating the terrorist group from the 1960s known as the Weather Underground. Cooney expressed a desire to be involved with training and education in the new administration. The interesting thing about Mike was that of the dozens of people I interviewed, he was the only person who expressed any interest in that area. I immediately assigned him to my office to head up formal education and training. I knew that if I assigned him to the police academy, he would be outranked and nullified by the chief inspector who was assigned there.

Elizabeth McLoughlin was an Italian American captain who looked like a Native American and had married an Irish American. She also had a degree in English literature from one of those fine universities in New England into which guys like Timoney would never be accepted. Captain McLoughlin was immediately assigned to head up my press office. Inspector Joe Fox, a gravelly voiced street cop, was immediately transferred to command a division in the Greater Northeast part of Philadelphia. These are only three of the talented individuals we resurrected who became part of the Timoney team. It gave new meaning to Napoleon's "careers open to talent."

As I was conducting interviews, one name continued to surface time and time again—Sylvester Johnson, the deputy commissioner of special operations. Sylvester was a soft-spoken African American and a thirty-year veteran of the PPD. He had come up through the organization serving in some of the most prestigious assignments, including the Highway Patrol and the Homicide Unit. Sylvester had many medals, including one for bravery that he had received as a result of a shoot-out with a robber that had taken place while he was shopping with his seven-year-old son. Right away I knew that Sylvester would be an important member of the new team, although I hadn't decided on what his new position would be.

While in a conversation with Mayor Rendell in my first or second week on the job, Rendell mentioned an individual, Inspector John Norris, who had been assigned to one of the Internal Affairs units and was preparing to retire. Rendell believed that John could give me some insight into the department, its players, and its problems. I interviewed Norris a short time later, and we had a long discussion. His keen insights into the department and its problems, especially those surrounding Internal Affairs and how it was constructed, impressed me greatly. Toward the end of the interview, I inquired of Norris if he would consider postponing his retirement. He didn't say no, and so I knew that I had gotten his interest. I let him know that I would be getting back to him.

Within the first two weeks I attended my first CompStat meeting in the Philadelphia Police Department. The department, like many others across the nation, had instituted a CompStat process based on the

NYPD model, after having sent representatives to New York to observe. When CompStat began, Jack Maple was sitting next to me. The deputy commissioner of operations led the questioning, and there was a lot of yelling and finger-pointing. I began to see for myself what many people took, or should I say mistook, from their observations of the NYPD CompStat meetings.

If you were to ask chiefs across the country to explain briefly what they had observed in a CompStat meeting in New York, their reply would usually run something like this: "Yeah, the captains stood up there, they were asked a lot of questions, and then they were yelled at." In Philadelphia I saw this perception become a reality. At one point during the Philadelphia CompStat meeting, I leaned over to Jack Maple and whispered in his ear, "Are you happy now? Look at one of the many monsters you and Louie [Anemone] have created." Jack muttered something to the effect of, "Fuck you, Commissioner Timoney." Nonetheless, I was keenly sensitive to the criticisms of how the NYPD conducted CompStat. I was going to make sure that the CompStat meetings in Philadelphia evolved into a more collegial process with an occasional dose of humor. Regarding who would be my co-chair in leading the questions, I would leave that to whatever boss stepped up to the plate.

As I was conducting my interviews, Gordon Wasserman was looking at the science and technology aspects of the department. Gordon was impressed with the department's computer systems and its lab operation. While there were some issues with the lab, especially regarding space allocation, it appeared to have the requisite, appropriately enthusiastic staff. As Gordon looked at the technology and communications part of the organization, he was dealing quite a bit with Chief Inspector Charles Brennen. Brennen was a very sharp individual with a good formal educational background. He was also thought of highly by other members of the city government outside the police department.

A new team was starting to emerge in my head. But before I made my final decision, I wanted to make sure that the new organizational structure was in place. As the process began, it radically changed the organization. The first step was to take the four major operational units and put them under one person, who would be responsible for all day-to-day operations. There would be a new deputy commissioner for internal affairs, whose sole function would be internal investigations. This meant that the three former Internal Affairs units were collapsed into one. The deputy commissioner for administration and training would remain a two-star chief since it was a civil-service position. However, some of the technology units would be removed from administration and assigned to the new deputy commissioner for science and technology, the first position of its kind in the history of the department.

Before I could announce the new personnel changes to fit into the new organizational structure, two deputy commissioners had to be let go—the deputy commissioner of operations and the deputy commissioner of community relations and internal affairs. I brought them into my office individually and informed them that they would not be part of the new team. Both of the individuals opted for retirement rather than to fall back to their last civil-service rank. Interviews and career discussions of this type are never easy. The individuals involved understandably feel disappointed, having given up a significant part of their life to the organization. Unfortunately, bloodletting is part of radical change and cannot be avoided. I was now ready to name the new team and did so at a press conference at City Hall. Sylvester Johnson, the highly decorated cop's cop, would become the new three-star deputy commissioner of operations, also known as the first deputy commissioner. His executive officer would be the two-star deputy commissioner, Robert Mitchell. John Norris, whom I had talked out of retirement, became the deputy commissioner of internal affairs. Thomas Nestell remained as the two-star deputy commissioner of administration and training. And finally, Charles Brennen was the new deputy commissioner for science and technology.

The four major operational units were going to be headed up by chief inspectors. While there were a total of seven or eight chief inspectors, the four operational chief inspectors would wear the insignia of a one-star chief. Sylvester Johnson and I sat down to choose the four new operational chiefs to head up the operational bureaus. We decided these men would be Chief of Patrol Frank Pryor, Chief of Special Operations Dexter Green, Chief of Detectives Jack Maxwell, and Chief of the

Narcotics Bureau Ray Rooney. Ray Rooney was an interesting choice. He was recovering from a very serious heart attack that he had suffered a month or two earlier. Sylvester Johnson brought him to my office and with a smile said, "He wants to be part of the new team." I looked at Ray and said, "This is going to be a tough ride. Are you up for it?" He replied without hesitation, "Absolutely."

CompStat in Philadelphia

With the new team in place, I ran my first CompStat meeting. One of the unexpected things that I had learned from the CompStat meetings in New York concerned the questioners. While Jack Maple was clearly front and center, other questioners also emerged, namely Louie Anemone, chief of patrol, and Joe Borelli, chief of detectives. Anemone, with his aggressive personality and no-nonsense attitude, was a natural. Although Joe was a seasoned veteran, he was laid back, in a Dean Martin–like way. But as the CompStat process evolved in New York, Borelli took a much more active role, surprising some people, including me.

In Philadelphia I knew I was going to be the main questioner, and I fully anticipated that one of the other deputy commissioners would emerge as the "second seat." Ironically, it wasn't one of the deputy commissioners but rather the chief of patrol, Frank Pryor. Frank's outgoing personality was well suited for the CompStat process. He could ask questions in rapid fashion, and he had a quick wit to match. By and large, the uniformed captains and the detective commanders genuinely seemed to enjoy him. I was thrilled with his enthusiasm and his performance. But I can't say that all of the deputy commissioners were as smitten with Frank as I was.

At the second CompStat meeting, a young captain who had been questioned at the prior meeting was once again reporting significant decreases in robberies and other serious crimes. He was the youngest captain on the force, he was smart, and he had the good looks to match. He seemed to have unlimited career potential. His crime numbers, however, struck me as being too good.

As I was reorganizing the department, I created a unit called the

Quality Assurance Bureau. I chose a chief inspector, Vincent DeBlasis, as the commanding officer. Vince had been the chief of detectives when I walked through the door. To run a Quality Assurance Unit demanded a certain amount of guts because it required, among other things, correcting the mistakes of higher-ranking individuals. Vince had already proven that he had a set and then some—he was a rabid Dallas Cowboys fan. In a city like Philadelphia, that takes moxie, and lots of it.

Unlike most police bosses, Vince understood fully the FBI's Uniform Crime Reporting (UCR) system. The UCR contains the crime statistics submitted on a biannual basis to the FBI by local police departments across the nation. While there is no uniformity in state criminal statutes, the FBI creates eight categories of major crimes with corresponding definitions. The submitting department "converts" its data before submitting it to UCR. For example, while some crimes are uniform from state to state, such as murder and stolen cars, others are not.

The UCR has a category called aggravated assault. New York State has no such crime designation, but Pennsylvania does. New York has three crimes that would fit into the category of aggravated assault: felonious assault, reckless endangerment, and menacing. At the end of each reporting period, the NYPD "converts" all felonious assaults, certain acts of reckless endangerment, and acts of menacing into the UCR format. In Miami, there is a state statute called burglary to a motor vehicle. However, for UCR purposes, it is classified as a theft. These are just some of the many conversions that take place from municipality to municipality across the nation.

When I got back to my office after the second CompStat meeting, I asked Vince DeBlasis to take a look at the crime numbers for the young captain whose numbers were going down. It turned out the captain was underreporting his crimes for the purposes of the CompStat meeting. He was immediately removed from his command and reassigned. Unfortunately for him, some of his enemies in the department leaked his misbehavior to the press, and his case became national news overnight. His career suffered a serious setback.

It was all very sad that the young captain had to go through this humiliation. CompStat was never set up to pressure people into "cooking the books." The process meant to examine crime problems and come up with solutions. Sometimes, the solution to the problem is completely outside the ability of a precinct or district captain. The intractable problem of open-air drug dealing is one example. Here the precinct captain may need the assistance of the centralized Narcotics Division. Another example is when a sophisticated robbery crew is working different neighborhoods of the city; to deal with it, the precinct captain may call on the robbery detectives. But if the local captain attempts to mask these problems at CompStat meetings, then he or she will never be able to deal effectively with them. What made this young captain's case even sadder was how unnecessary his cover-up was. As I mentioned earlier, promotion and advancement in Philadelphia are based on an open, competitive civil-service exam. Crime statistics, going up or down, play no part—nor should they. Over the years, one of the complaints about the CompStat process has been that it puts undue pressure on police commanders to drive crime down and that it implicitly encourages "cooking the books." In the vast majority of these cases, the allegations come from disgruntled union officials or commanders who are just not up to the task of commanding.

I suspected two other districts were not reporting correctly. Both of those captains were also removed. In their cases, it was hard to prove whether their actions were intentional or just stupid. As we moved forward through that year, captains were continually replaced at the districts by other captains who were chosen by me or who had actually sought me out through Frank Pryor looking for their own command and greater responsibility. So much for captains being unwilling to step up to the plate and face the music at CompStat! We had more than enough stars lining up to accept the responsibility, and with it greater accountability.

In late August, as we were preparing to submit the first six months of our crime statistics to the FBI, we noticed that some of the numbers did not make sense. Not only did we notice, but two hard-charging reporters from the *Philadelphia Inquirer* also noticed. These two reporters had been writing about the poor crime-reporting system within the Philadelphia Police Department for at least a year prior to my arrival.

During an interview with these reporters, I acknowledged that I, too, had found deficiencies in the crime-reporting system and that I had ordered a hand count of all crimes for the first six months. Further, I informed them that I would not be submitting Philadelphia's crime statistics for my first six months to the FBI because "I had no confidence in the numbers." Needless to say, that was the headline for the next day.

But here is where the reporters and I disagreed. The reporters concluded that the low count was due to "intentional downgrading" of the crimes by various district commanders. While there had been some commanders who had tinkered with the numbers, those situations had been addressed. As we began to look at the reporting system, I felt that the undercount was much more of a systems failure than the result of deliberate misdirection. As I said to one reporter, "If it was only deliberate intention, that would be easy to fix! I would just get rid of the captain. Unfortunately, most of this problem is a systemic failure. That's much more difficult to fix; it's going to require a hand count as opposed to computer tabulation." The reporter then asked if I was going to go back to the prior year, 1997, to do a recount of those numbers. I let it be known that I was there only for Rendell's last two years and that I was not going to spend my valuable time fixing past mistakes.

By the end of the year, when the final crime numbers were submitted to the FBI, Philadelphia showed a 10 percent increase in overall crime. Somebody could have argued that, with a 10 percent increase in crime, Timoney should have been fired. However, everyone agreed that we were finally getting the numbers correct and that the increase reflected better reporting. My sense was that, in actuality, overall crime had dropped. To prove this, I pointed to two crimes that are most accurately reported in every jurisdiction: murder and stolen cars—murder because you have a dead body and, as the late Jack Maple would say, "We don't have a big police cemetery where we hide the bodies," and stolen cars because stolen cars are accurately reported for insurance purposes and the transmission of nationwide alarms through the

National Crime Information Center (NCIC). When you looked at those two crimes at the end of 1998, murder was down 18 percent and stolen cars were down 16 percent. In fact, for the first time in fifteen years, the murder count in Philadelphia was under 400—well under: 338.

Operation Sunrise

Philadelphia's very high homicide rate was intricately woven with the drug trade. I knew that the Philadelphia drug homicides were no different from the New York City drug homicides and that the strategies to deal with them would be similar. To reduce gun violence and homicides, you had to deal with the drugs in a very serious fashion. As part of our new homicide reduction initiative we assigned hundreds of new police officers to the Narcotics Division and created a multiagency drug operation called Operation Sunrise. The results of this operation were immediate, dramatic, and lasting.

When we made the decision to put the additional police officers in the Narcotics Division, I insisted that each officer go to the police academy for a full week of training to address the many concerns I had, including corruption hazards, because these officers would be exposed to certain temptations in their new assignments. I was also very concerned about confrontational situations between police officers in plainclothes and uniformed officers or between police officers in plainclothes and other officers in plainclothes. In the early 1970s in New York City, there had been a few deadly confrontation situations in which police officers had been killed by other officers who thought the guy in plainclothes was a "perpetrator." I knew that, in addition to the ambiguity of plainclothes, race could be a factor in friendly-fire situations. While these situations appeared to be quite innocent, there was a real need for better training and better policies on how police officers, especially those in plainclothes, both on and off duty, identify themselves when confronted.

I made it a point to address the new narcotics officers during their one week of training. Each classroom was made up a mix of officers that would have never existed when Timoney was a cop. The classes consisted of an even number of black and white police officers, with a significant percentage of female officers. They did not look like your father's cops. During my talks, everything would be fine until I got to the pink elephant in the room, the issue of race. I would begin the topic by saying, "You know, not every white guy with a gun in plainclothes is an off-duty cop. And not every black guy with a gun in plainclothes is a perp." The officers would squirm in their seats, look around, and generally feel uneasy. When I talked to them about how perception can kill, they became even more uncomfortable.

After one class, an instructor from the police academy approached me and said, "You know, Commissioner, you may have had those confrontation situations up there in New York, but we've never had them down here in Philly." I replied, "I'm glad to hear that, but we're going to continue the training. Just humor me."

In late August, I received the phone call I dreaded most from Deputy Commissioner John Norris, the head of Internal Affairs. "Commissioner, we've got a problem," he said. "Two police officers in plainclothes just confronted each other in a back alley in West Philly. Both officers are African American. One officer saw the other officer with a gun and yelled something to the effect of 'Yo, five-oh!' and the other officer unloaded his weapon. Fortunately, he missed the other police officer." These men were plainclothes officers from separate districts and were not part of the new Narcotics Division; as such they had not received the confrontation training. A week later I saw the instructor from the academy after one of my CompStat meetings; "Hey, lad, so much for no confrontations in Philly," I said with a wink.

DNA Testing and the Rittenhouse Square Rapist

In May 1998, the homicide commander came into my office to inform me of the rape and killing of a university student living in the Rittenhouse Square area. The crime was horrific, and the circumstances surrounding the discovery of the body were troubling. The student's body was discovered in the early afternoon by a family member, but the crime had occurred in the early morning hours, and there had been a call made to 911. The detective commander informed me that uniformed officers had responded to the apartment, interviewed neighbors, and, finding everything apparently secure, left the scene. The neighbor who had called 911 told the family member that police had responded but had taken no action. I had been in policing long enough to have seen situations where police responded to similar incidents and had not made any real effort to determine the validity of the 911 phone call or had simply not made a good enough effort in their field investigation. I knew this case was going to be a huge issue for the Philadelphia Police Department.

I ordered Deputy Commissioner Johnson to conduct a full review of how the 911 call had been handled and the actions of the officers at the scene. What he found was that the officers did, in fact, respond and did, in fact, speak to the neighbor who had made the 911 call. The neighbor said he had heard a scream, a thud, and then silence. He went downstairs and knocked on the door of the apartment where he thought the scream had come from and received no response.

When the officers got to the scene, one officer knocked on the door and created enough of a ruckus that another neighbor came out to see what was going on. The neighbor who had made the 911 call and was being questioned by the officers began to equivocate, saying that he was not sure where the noises had come from. The officers checked the doors and windows and saw no obvious signs of entry and so left the scene. Commissioner Johnson added that one of the responding officers had a reputation of being a very aggressive, pro-arrest officer, and it was not likely that he would have given short shrift to a field investigation.

When the family member who found the body met the neighbor who had made the 911 call, the neighbor left the family member with the clear impression that the police had done nothing. However, the second neighbor who had come out to investigate the ruckus in the hallway told the detectives that the responding officers had made a good faith effort but were, in fact, dissuaded by going further by the equivocation of the neighbor who had made the 911 call. This was clearly a horrible situation, but the police officers had taken reasonable action when they responded to the scene.

The problem going forward was that we had a violent rapist/killer on the loose in Center City. I held a meeting in my office with the top bosses, including the commander of the Homicide Unit and the commander of the Special Victims Unit, who was responsible for investigating rapes. "If you think this is the first time this guy has hit, you're crazy," I said. "We need to go back and check all of the cases with a similar MO."

The review established that the same individual had struck on at least four occasions during the summer of 1997, nine months prior to my arrival in Philadelphia. In two cases, DNA evidence had been secured but had not been sent to the lab for testing. The other two cases had been handled improperly by the police department: in one instance by the responding officer and in the other by the Special Victims Unit detective. In the first case, the responding officer did not believe the victim had been raped because the victim had washed herself before reporting the incident. The officer stated that rape victims do not act that way—that is, they do not wash themselves. In fact, that indeed is often the very action rape victims take. I wasn't happy with how these cases had been handled, and I let my feelings be known in no uncertain terms.

The two cases in which the DNA evidence had not been submitted did not violate existing protocol at the time. In the vast majority of sexual assault cases in the late 1990s across the nation, the DNA was not tested on a regular basis. In fact, there are tens of thousands of untested rape tests and other DNA samples sitting in labs all across the United States. Often DNA tests were not conducted until a person was in custody and getting ready to go to trial.

I conducted my own investigation into the workings of the Special Victims Unit. The result was that the commander of that unit was transferred and one of the top captains in the police department, Joe Mooney, was put in charge. Captain Mooney began a top-to-bottom review of the unit and recommended to me that we should transfer almost every police officer out of the unit. They were replaced with real detectives, the best and the brightest. The fact that the Philadelphia

Police Department had assigned police officers rather than detectives to the Special Victims Unit was an indication of that unit's position in the pecking order.

When we looked at the existing DNA protocols, we found them to be unsatisfactory. Basically, there was no protocol. There were so many rape kits and other DNA samples to be tested that the numbers were just overwhelming. It was an impossible task to test all of the DNA evidence, given the meager resources of the department. DNA would generally be tested when a defendant was in custody in order to help the case against him going to trial. But this left the vast majority of the samples untested. Obviously, we were expending the resources to collect the evidence, but unfortunately the lab was overwhelmed with the volume, and so there was no regular management or system of prioritization of what should be tested and what could wait.

To me, this was a clear case of a failure to manage workload. If you thought about it logically, the answer was in the analysis of the data. Seventy-five percent of all rapes are committed by "known doers," that is, the identity of the rapist is known to the victim; it's the next-door neighbor, it's the former boyfriend, it's the incestuous uncle. The issue here isn't identity but rather consent. A judge or a jury will determine whether a rape occurred. The other 25 percent of all rapes are "stranger rapes." These are of grave concern because it is within this category that you will find serial rapists. If you test the DNA evidence of all stranger rape cases, then the first time you have a "hit" you have a serial rapist—a stranger who commits more than one rape. The solution was in finding a way to manage the volume of DNA evidence. Testing 25 percent, the stranger rapes, was a less daunting task than testing 100 percent.

I immediately instituted a policy that all stranger rape cases must have the DNA samples tested. To accomplish this, I doubled the capacity of the DNA testing lab and hired more analysts. In addition, I ordered that all stranger rapes for the prior five years (there is a five-year statute of limitations on rape cases) be tested and that the results be submitted to CODIS, the federal DNA database. This review uncovered an additional serial rapist who was on the loose during 1997.

Meanwhile, we established a Rittenhouse Square Rapist Task Force, and leads came in from all over the country, including Alaska. Because of the lengthy intervals between the rapes, the possibility that the rapist was an employee of a cruise ship was checked out, along with other far-reaching theories, all to no avail. About a year later he struck again south of Rittenhouse Square and made good his escape. He then apparently disappeared from the Philadelphia scene.

In 2002, Fort Collins, Colorado detectives reached out to Philadelphia detectives and indicated that a serial rapist had been involved in half a dozen rapes of students in their area. The DNA tests confirmed that it was the Rittenhouse Square rapist. Good detective work by the Fort Collins Police Department led to the arrest of a man named Troy Graves.

In his confession, Troy Graves admitted to killing the young student in Philadelphia. He stated that he had killed her when the neighbor knocked on the door after hearing noises. Shortly after the knock, before the police arrived, Graves escaped from the apartment. He indicated that he had left a lifeless body on the bed, well before the police officers responded.

An interesting footnote to this saga: when the Rittenhouse Square student was raped and killed, the case detectives and I held numerous press conferences and released a police sketch to the public. I made a personal plea for anybody with any information to come forward or, at the very least, to make an anonymous phone call. After Graves was arrested, two women who had been romantically involved with Graves during his time in Philadelphia came forward and told reporters that they had had suspicions. One admitted that she had suspected Graves was the rapist but refused to admit it. She said she had even discussed it with friends and lamented to a reporter, "I knew in my heart it was him." In cases such as these, often somebody knows or suspects he or she knows who is committing the acts. The great challenge for police leaders is to get the message out in such a convincing fashion that someone with the knowledge will at least make an anonymous phone call. Had that phone call been made by either of the two women, the trauma and damage that the students in Fort Collins, Colorado suffered two years later may have been avoided.

No More "Deliberate Indifference"

I walked through the commissioner's door in Philadelphia on the heels of a police corruption scandal in the 39th District that had resulted in the arrest of eight police officers. This corruption scandal seemed to confirm allegations that were made against the Philadelphia Police Department by the National Association for the Advancement of Colored People (NAACP), the American Civil Liberties Union (ACLU), and other civil rights organizations. The ACLU joined the NAACP in a "patterns and practices" lawsuit against the Philadelphia Police Department. The result was a court-ordered settlement that was signed in 1996. Two years had elapsed, and no discernable progress had been made when I was sworn in as the new commissioner.

The 39th District scandal had damaged the image of the Philadelphia Police Department and had taken its toll on the morale of the men and women of that district. When I began my roll call visits, I made it a point to do my very first one at the 39th District. This area covered parts of North Philadelphia, which had a high crime rate, as well as the working- and upper-class neighborhood called East Falls. This was a symbolic measure to reassure the men and women of that district that a new leaf had been turned and that I was there to support them. I hoped in return that they, too, would support me. As I left the district, the commander, a kindly Italian American gentleman, handed me a crucifix and a scapular medal, wishing me luck and letting me know that he would pray for my success. I was genuinely moved and appreciative of his gesture.

Unfortunately, symbolism and prayer will get you only so far. I was faced with the reality of a consent decree that enumerated eighteen major areas of concern that were to be given my full attention. No excuses accepted. I was fortunate to have John Gallagher, a trained lawyer, to lead our efforts to comply with the decree. John's status as a lawyer caused some contention within the city's Law Department. I was informed that I could not have my own lawyer on staff and that the city's Law Department was my lawyer. Finally, I said, "Gallagher is my special assistant, not my lawyer." Gallagher immersed himself in the consent decree, and he briefed me extensively on its meanings and implications. In our discussion, we both agreed that we should try to take care of the easy items on the list first so that we could get them off the table and then devote our attention to the more challenging ones.

By the end of the first year, we had managed, through Gallagher's tireless efforts, to be in compliance with the majority of the eighteen areas. We also created some new policies; while they were not required in the consent decree, they did, in fact, enhance the goals of the decree. As we had done in New York after the Rodney King incident, we created a policy dealing with physical force, especially deadly physical force. The significant change was the affirmative obligation of a police officer at the scene of an incident to intercede whenever it appeared that another officer was using unnecessary force.

The second change I instituted forbade a police officer from discharging his or her weapon at a moving vehicle unless the occupants of the vehicle were using deadly physical force against the officer or another person present by means other than the vehicle. When an officer has discharged his weapon at a moving vehicle, he will most likely argue that the vehicle tried to run him over. Historically, what we find is that in the vast majority of cases, the bullets have penetrated the side and rear windows, which would indicate that the threat to the police officer had actually passed, literally. To make matters worse, the suspects in the getaway cars who were eventually arrested were usually found to be unarmed. Shooting at fleeing cars was not unique to Philadelphia; it was a nationwide issue that needed to be addressed.

When I introduced the new policy on force and shootings, I went to numerous roll calls to explain the policy and accept any questions the officers had. By and large, the vast majority of police officers accepted the changes in good spirit. They knew the intent was to keep police officers out of trouble and out of the news. However, there was always one guy who would make an extraordinary case of why he should be allowed to shoot at a vehicle that was coming at him to run him over. I would just smile and say, "These are only guidelines. Each case will be judged by its own merits. And if there is a case where you shoot at a vehicle and you can show me the tire tracks on your chest, I will rule your shooting justified." Of course, that answer drew howls of laughter from all present at roll call, including the questioner.

Two months after I arrived in Philadelphia, I had lunch with Jim Fyffe, an old friend from the NYPD. Jim was a professor of criminology at Temple University, but more important, he was the foremost academic expert in the nation on police use of deadly physical force. Jim had written his doctoral dissertation on deadly physical force within the NYPD, focusing on the changes in the number of shootings by New York City police officers after the new deadly physical force policy was instituted on August 22, 1972.

During the course of our conversation, Jim told me that he had been the subject-matter expert in forty-one lawsuits against the Philadelphia Police Department. He leaned his six-foot-seven-inch frame across the table, smiled, and said, "We won forty of them." He went on to say that as long as I was in Philadelphia, he would never side in a lawsuit against the PPD. He said, "I have just one other issue. Did you know that Philadelphia is the last big-city police department that allows their officers to carry blackjacks?" "No," I replied, "but I'm going to address that."

I was fully committed to doing away with blackjacks. They are ten-inch-long pieces of round metal wrapped in leather. An officer usually carries one in the back pocket of his or her uniform pants. However, I needed to come up with a better alternative to offer police officers. And I did: pepper spray. It took the remainder of the first year to purchase seven thousand canisters of pepper spray and to conduct the appropriate training. When the policy announcing the replacement of black-jacks with pepper spray was published, I made it a point once more to go to roll calls to explain the rationale. At one particular roll call, when I opened it up for questions, only one officer seemed to have a problem with the change. The officer stood six feet five, had broad shoulders, and looked like he could have been a linebacker or a defensive end. As he was making his case, the other officers were rolling their eyes. I just looked at him and said, "Why is it always the big, tough guys like you who need blackjacks? Look at these little guys next to you. They're not complaining!" There were laughs and snickers, and the questioning officer shrugged his shoulders and said compliantly, "Yeah, I guess you're right."

About six months after the implementation of the no-blackjack policy, Deputy Commissioner John Norris was in my office giving me a briefing on one of his investigations. At the end of our meeting, he turned to me and said, "By the way, since we instituted pepper spray, we no longer have prisoners showing up at the jails with turbans on." This was a reference to the bandaged head of a prisoner who had been struck with the blackjack while resisting arrest.

One of the eighteen items in the consent decree struck me as particularly odd. The decree directed the Philadelphia Police Department to create a system and form to record each and every pedestrian stop. (In New York these are called Stop and Frisk Reports. In Miami they are called Field Investigation Reports.) According to the decree, an analysis of these reports would be able to pinpoint corrupt or potentially corrupt police officers. The notion that a corrupt cop who rips off a drug dealer after stopping him in the street would take time to fill out this form, and fill it out correctly, is ludicrous. This seemed to me to miss the point or the rationale for creating these reports. The report is meant to lay out the legal justification (reasonable suspicion) for stopping an individual in a public place. A secondary purpose is to make sure that race or another factor is not the sole basis for the stop, as is the case with racial profiling.

In 1998, the issue of racial profiling had begun to heat up largely as a result of New Jersey State Troopers discharging their weapons at a van occupied by four African American and Hispanic students who had been pulled over for an alleged traffic violation on the New Jersey Turnpike. Police shot and wounded three of the occupants of the van. The troopers alleged that the driver had attempted to run them down as he and his partner approached the vehicle. The driver denied this allegation. The incident and the media frenzy surrounding it continued over the next couple of years. The case became a cause célèbre and was soon followed by other ugly incidents in different jurisdictions across the nation that all had the tinge of racial profiling.

As we were working on the new pedestrian- and vehicular-stop policy, it became an increasingly more complex project. Racial profiling had become the buzzword or new rallying cry for many civil libertarians and civil rights groups, much as police brutality had been the buzzword of the 1960s. The racial profile issue dominated every conversation we had over the next year regarding the implementation of the pedestrian-stop policy. The central question for us was, How were we going to capture the data? Who would be responsible for warehousing the data? Who would be responsible for the analysis of the data? And what would be done with the findings? One thing was clear to me: this project was going to require a serious commitment of personnel as it was envisioned.

As if to complicate matters further, the plaintiffs' counsel, whose original lawsuit had resulted in the consent decree, came out with their own study on police pedestrian and traffic stops. They concluded that there was wholesale racial profiling by the Philadelphia Police Department. The problem was that the authors of the report had used racial data from the 1990 Census. Cited in the report were at least two neighborhoods with majority white populations in 1990 that had become, by 1999, majority minority neighborhoods. This made it even more incumbent that we get the data for our project right.

With the invaluable assistance of Sergeant Fran Healy, Gallagher and his team redesigned the form to capture the necessary data. Sergeant Healy was a very capable lawyer, in addition to being an accountant. We informed Stuart Dalsell, the federal judge monitoring the agreement, of our proposed changes and our rationale, and he concurred. Additionally, we connected the pedestrian and vehicle stops to the PPD's 911 system. Whenever an officer stopped a pedestrian under reasonable suspicion, or a motorist for an alleged traffic infraction, the officer was required to transmit a message, via police radio, indicating the location where the stop occurred and the race of the individual stopped.

Before we unveiled the new program, we began a department-wide training regimen on racial profiling as it related to pedestrian and car stops. We then secured a grant of $10,000 from Comcast Corporation to produce a video on racial profiling. Karen Simons, the city attorney assigned to the police department, produced the video and did an out-standing job using the staff at the police academy as role players. The video showed a series of scenarios depicting a variety of pedestrian and vehicle stops that an average officer would encounter during a given day. A copy of the video was given to every police officer on the force.

I then assigned an additional ten lieutenants to Internal Affairs. Their job was to collate the racial data from the reports submitted by the police officers and to check with the 911 call center data as a qual-ity control measure. The goal of the analysis and findings was not to punish police officers but rather to educate them and bring to their at-tention an issue that they may not have been considering.

Toward the end of 2000, after a great deal of hard work, revision, training, and production, Internal Affairs had months of data that they had analyzed. Officers from that division began to conduct informal interviews and provide counseling to those officers who appeared to issue a disparate number of traffic citations to African Americans. As luck would have it, the first two officers brought in for counseling were African American. While it wasn't exactly back to the drawing board, it did create food for thought.

The issue of racial profiling continued to garner national headlines well into 2001. After 9/11, it no longer registered as the foremost issue facing the department or the rest of the nation. The new topic du jour was terrorism. However, by 2009, with no further terrorist attacks on American soil, racial profiling made a comeback in certain areas of the country. In fact, in July 2009, an incident in Cambridge, Massa-chusetts, between a white police sergeant, James Crowley, and a black Harvard professor, Henry Louis Gates, led to charges of racial profiling that went from the streets of Cambridge all the way to 1600 Pennsyl-vania Avenue.

Early in the third year of my time in Philadelphia, Gallagher re-ported to me that the Philadelphia City Law Department was begin-ning to see some very positive results due to the policy changes we had implemented. Lawsuits were down, and the sums of money re-quested in those that were filed were lower. Civil rights lawsuits against police departments are usually based on "patterns and practices" and "deliberate indifference." That is, the plaintiffs' lawyers prove the police department has a history of doing something wrong and that the top command couldn't care less. As a result of our policy initiatives, as well as our full-pledged commitment to the consent decree, no lawyer could make a credible argument of "deliberate indifference." As one federal judge was reported to have said to a lawyer filing a lawsuit against the police department, "There may be a basis for patterns and practices, but there's no deliberate indifference over there"—meaning police headquarters, which was just a block away from the federal courthouse. To put icing on this particular cake, the attorney general of the United States, Janet Reno, recommended five or six of our new policies as national models for other departments across the country to follow.

12

Pugnacious Philly

If I am elected mayor, I will keep John Timoney as my police commissioner.
—*SAM KATZ, REPUBLICAN CANDIDATE FOR MAYOR*

When I accepted the job of commissioner from Mayor Ed Rendell, I did so believing that I would hold that position for his last two years in office and then be off on my merry way because every new mayor wants to have his own police commissioner. After the Democratic primary in May 1999, John Street, the former president of the City Council, won the nomination for mayor. Running against him was Republican Sam Katz. As the campaign began to heat up toward the end of the summer, Katz ran on a platform that included keeping Timoney as the police commissioner. Street was noncommittal, indicating that he would name his own team once he won the election and that no amount of pressure would force him to do otherwise. As the election grew closer, Katz maintained his slight lead over Street in the polls. This was quite unusual in a city where Democrats outnumber Republicans four to one. Ten days before the election, at the final televised debate, Katz reiterated his intention of keeping Timoney if elected. Street responded, "So will I, what's the big deal?" And ten days later, Street was elected mayor and kept his televised promise.

There was intense speculation as to whether the new mayor and I would get along. I never quite understood the basis for this speculation because I had had a very good relationship with John Street when he was the City Council president. I found him to be smart and extremely funny, contrary to the perception: smart guy, not so funny. During my first formal meeting with him as mayor-elect, he informed me that he would run a cabinet form of government with weekly meetings, that I would be a member of his cabinet, and that I would get a pay raise.

Mayor Street's first six months were very effective, if uneventful. As we headed into the summer we began to heighten our preparations for the upcoming Republican convention that was to be held in Philadelphia that August. My relations with the mayor could not have been better, and he showed up at the hospital any time a police officer was injured in the line of duty, day or night.

A year earlier, I had selected Deputy Commissioner Robert Mitchell to work full time on the Republican convention, much as I had done in 1992 in New York. Mitchell was a seasoned veteran who had been the security coordinator for most of the big events held in Philadelphia over the prior decade. I had total confidence in Robert. He was a tough, hard taskmaster, and that's what the job required.

Caught on Tape

About ten days before the Republican convention, I asked my top commanders to give me presentations on how they would handle their particular assignment—traffic, dignitary protection, protestors, convention hotels. The presentations were excellent, and I felt confident about our ability to police the convention with little difficulty. I then spoke to all the commanders and let them know how much I appreciated their individual efforts, and I mentioned that I thought we were in great shape and that police-community relations were also excellent. "But," I added, "as you all know, ours is a volatile business. Things go wrong all the time. So let's keep our fingers crossed so that we get through the next ten days." Fingers never stay crossed for long.

Later that afternoon, I was leaving City Hall when a call came over the police radio regarding a police officer shot and a stolen police car. I then heard that the injured officer was being taken to a local hospital, which was just three blocks from City Hall. My driver, Tony Pino, and I headed to the hospital. We actually arrived before the officer and were there to greet him. He was not seriously injured, with only a gunshot wound to his hand. The police radio continued to crackle, and we were then informed that the subject of the chase was in police custody, so things seemed to be working out fine.

Soon the press began to arrive at the hospital, which was not unusual when a police officer was shot. I had always made it a point to be considerate of the press, especially the TV reporters and camera staff who depend on a live head shot for their stations. Usually, the print media can be a little more patient unless they are running up against deadline. So I had intended to get as much basic information as I could, then do a quick "presser," and get back to them later with more details.

As I was heading to the parking lot, where the TV crews and reporters were assembled, a lieutenant whispered in my ear that one of the TV stations had live video footage of the chase and its aftermath, including the capture of the suspect and some heavy-handed police tactics. "It doesn't look good," advised the lieutenant. Unfortunately, I was already visible to the reporters and couldn't turn back toward the emergency room.

I conducted a short presser and told the reporters I would get back to them with further details as they became available. As I was about to leave, a local reporter from the TV station that had the live video of the chase asked me if I wouldn't mind accompanying him into his video truck to look at some footage. He didn't realize that I was aware that they had ugly video, which I would be forced to comment upon as I viewed it. This is the oldest TV trick in the book, and I was having none of it. I told the reporter that unfortunately I had an injured cop and that I needed to get back inside the hospital to see him. "But it will only take a few minutes," the reporter pressed. I declined and headed back into the emergency room. Clearly the reporter wanted to tape my facial expressions as I was viewing the video. "No thanks!," I thought.

Pretty soon the video was playing on national TV, but I had bought myself some valuable time. I could not be accused of dodging the press since I had held a press conference within one hour of the incident.

However, there was a lot of work to be done, and the mayor was in Baltimore attending, of all things, the annual convention of the NAACP. The suspect we had arrested was an African American named Thomas Jones. However, as the video was shown over and over again, the name mentioned most frequently on television was Rodney King.

I immediately spoke to Mayor Street and told him what we knew so far. And so far, what we knew wasn't much and wasn't good. It was going to require that the mayor return to Philadelphia immediately.

As the mayor was on his way back to Philadelphia, we uncovered several pieces of information regarding Thomas Jones: he was a crackhead with a bad drug problem. Ten days prior to the incident with the Philly police, he had stolen a car from an elderly couple in Northeast Philadelphia. Over the subsequent ten days, he had committed at least one robbery each day to support his drug habit. All the robbery victims were women: black, white, and Asian. On the day in question, he was driving the wrong way down a one-way street in North Philadelphia when he was spotted by a police officer in a marked police car.

The officer followed Jones and ran the license plate through the National Crime Information Center (NCIC). The plate came back as a "felony car," which meant that it had been used in the commission of a felony. The officer radioed to request backup, and the chase began through the streets of North Philadelphia. At some point during the chase, Jones got out of his vehicle, ran on foot, and jumped over a large fence with officers in full foot pursuit. Jones doubled back around the street only to find a bunch of abandoned police cars and no officers (they were behind him in foot pursuit). One of the police cars was still running with the keys in the ignition (a similar mistake I had made during my days in the 44th Precinct), so Jones got in. As he was driving away he was confronted by police officers. Shots were fired, hitting Jones as well as one of the officers who was positioned on the other side of the stolen police car.

Jones sped away in the marked police car through the streets of North Philadelphia with a slew of police vehicles in pursuit and a TV helicopter, from the local ABC television station, capturing great video of the chase for all for the world to see on the six o'clock news!

The pursuit lasted a few minutes, until Jones was surrounded at an intersection by about two dozen police officers. After a short standoff Jones was pulled from the police vehicle, and a rugby scrum developed, with police officers on top of Jones, hands and feet flying. Not a pretty sight.

Howls and cries of police brutality aired on every TV channel and radio station that evening. I continued to be briefed on the case and viewed the chase video in slow motion. The mayor returned to Philly around 8:00 P.M. and was also fully briefed. Clearly we had a problem, and there was no denying it. However, I had also been around long enough to know that any rush to judgment is bad, even if the act in question is caught on camera.

We had a political convention coming up in ten days, and that's definitely not when you want to go on national television saying your cops are out of control. That was one sure way of losing the confidence of the officers before the convention. Besides, I had been in those rugby scrums myself in my career, and I can tell you, when fists and feet are flying, the ones who usually get hit are other officers. The bad guy is usually protected by a blanket of cops. However, there was the videotape, and there was no sense denying that it did not look good.

One of the first things I did was to direct Internal Affairs to go to the hospital to take pictures of Jones once he came out of the operating room. I wanted to document the types of injuries he had sustained in the rugby scrum. Although the photos could show a man with significant facial and body bruises, there was also the possibility that they would show no bruises, if my theory about the protective blanket of cops was correct. Indeed, the photos showed no visible bruising on Jones's body, only the bullet wounds where he had been shot.

Around 10:00 P.M., the mayor and I held a press conference stating the obvious: the video did not look good, but no one should jump to conclusions. There would be a full investigation that would leave no stones unturned. Bottom line: there would be no cover-up.

The next morning I went to my office at 6:30 A.M. The headquarters parking lot looked like a Hollywood back lot clogged with dozens of TV cameras and satellite news trucks. In fact, one of the satellite trucks was parked in the police commissioner's spot, showing no deference whatsoever to the reigning police commissioner: me.

Prior to my arriving at headquarters, I had watched the six o'clock news. Two words had dominated the coverage: *Rodney King*. I agreed to do live interviews with the four major news organizations (ABC, CBS, NBC, and CNN). In each interview I had one simple message: "This was not Rodney King." And the video proved it.

On the video, two sergeants take affirmative action to bring the scene under control, as our policy and training dictated. This allowed me to acknowledge that while it did look ugly, two sergeants had taken action to stop the behavior. This was *not* Rodney King all over again. In fact, it was nothing like the Rodney King case, which had involved a suspect who offered no resistance being struck fifty-six times with batons while a group of officers looked on approvingly. In the Jones case, you had an individual who stole a police car, resisted arrest, and caused a police officer to be accidentally shot during the resulting chase. Finally, in the Rodney King case, a sergeant had actively participated in the beating. In the Jones case, two sergeants had stopped the aggressive behavior.

Over the next few days, there were still calls for the arrest and suspension of the officers who had been involved in the chase. At one point, I asked a community activist a rhetorical question: "Who would you have me arrest based on the video?" He specifically pointed to a big police officer who jumped over the car to join in the "beating" of Jones. However, when you watched the video in slow motion, it showed something entirely different regarding this officer. When you first isolate him, you see that he leaps across the hood of the police car to join in on the beating of Jones. But when you slow the tape down, you see that once he clears the hood of the car, he lands on both feet, stops, and takes no further action. It appears he is saying to himself, "I can't believe I just cleared that car!" So when you look at the video in regular motion, his leap over the car adds to the impression of a free-for-all, but, in fact, he took no action against Jones at all.

The Jones case went to a grand jury in Philadelphia. Many police officers testified without immunity and told the truth about what they witnessed and what actions they took. The grand jury did not indict a single officer and, in fact, ruled that the officers used appropriate, necessary physical force. The grand jury went a step further stating that the police officers would have been justified had they used deadly physical force against Mr. Jones. With the grand jury verdict, I felt the department was exonerated and our training and physical force policy was effective and wise. The two sergeants who intervened to stop the aggressive behavior saved the day and probably saved the jobs of the police officers involved.

Real Cops Don't Ride Bikes? The 2000 Republican National Convention

The policing scheme for the 2000 Republican National Convention was similar to other policing plans used in other cities for similar conventions. The new dimension added for this convention was the use of officers on bicycles to handle demonstrations, particularly those that involved marches. Like most political conventions, provisions were made for protest groups who wanted to exercise their rights to free speech. The convention itself was held at the First Union Center, home of the 76ers basketball team and the Flyers hockey team, three miles south of Center City.

A free speech zone was set up on the west side of Broad Street, one of the main thoroughfares in the city, with the convention center on the east side. Protest groups submitted their permits to demonstrate, but because of the number of competing requests, a lottery system was developed that seemed fair and equitable. There was one group in particular, an advocacy group for the homeless, which requested a special permit to protest in front of City Hall. After the City Hall protest, the group, which was expected to number ten thousand, wanted to march the three miles down Broad Street to the convention center. Once the demonstrators reached the center, the group indicated that it would refuse to enter the free speech zone in Columbus Park across from the center. Instead, the group promised to march on the convention center itself and to disrupt the convention center activities.

The request for a permit to march was denied, and the group leaders indicated that they intended to march regardless. There was a great deal of speculation over the weekend as to what would happen on Monday, the opening day of the convention. The betting was that there would be a showdown and clash with police.

While the convention did not officially start until Monday, there were a fair number of protests in the Center City area on both Saturday and Sunday. Various groups, including so-called anarchists, took to the streets in what appeared to be dry runs of what was to be expected the following week. There was some property damage, including graffiti and vandalism to the District Attorney's Office and other buildings, and there were a handful of arrests. When Monday arrived, I was inundated with phone calls about how I was going to handle the unsanctioned homeless march down Broad Street to the convention center. I played it close to the vest, saying that I had not made a final decision, although I had shared my thoughts and sentiments with Deputy Commissioner Sylvester Johnson and Deputy Commissioner Robert Mitchell.

I arrived at City Hall on my bike around 11:30 A.M., accompanied by my two bike partners, Officers Clyde Frasier and Ray Felder. We joined up with the other members of the bike squad that would form the Mobile Protest Unit. The temperature was in the high eighties and was expected to reach the nineties by 1:00 P.M. There wasn't a cloud in the sky. Philadelphia in August is a cross between a hot sauna and a cup of warm milk. And there were, in fact, around ten thousand protestors gathered, just as had been predicted.

The leader of the protest group, a local homeless advocate, held a press conference on the steps of City Hall, indicating that she would lead the group on a march down Broad Street to the convention center, without a permit, and would disrupt the activities at the convention center. There were dozens of members of the press in attendance, print as well as television. As I approached the leaders of the march on my bike, I was surrounded and then engulfed by the members of the media and their cameras. It dawned on me that the novelty of the situation, having the chief of police out on a bike, handling protestors, was too good a picture for any reporter to miss. It's tough enough to answer a question when three reporters are asking you the same thing in

English, but when twenty or thirty reporters are asking the same question in ten or fifteen different languages, it's hysterical. Officer Frasier rode up next to me and whispered in my ear, "Commish, we can't get this thing started with you standing here with all of these reporters. We gotta move." With that, Officer Frasier, Officer Felder, and I rode south on Broad Street to allow the unsanctioned march to begin.

About three blocks into the march, I met up with Deputy Commissioner Robert Mitchell, who informed me that we had approximately three hundred police officers north of the convention center, at Broad and Washington, to stop the march if I gave the order. I told Robert to hold off on any decisions and, since the protesters were moving along with few problems, I would let them continue for now, leaving all of my options open.

The crowd continued to make its way down Broad Street and arrived near the convention center around 3:00 P.M. The sun beat down heavily on protestors and police alike and took its toll on both groups. As the protestors reached the last intersection before the convention center, they were funneled into the free speech zone by a phalanx of a couple hundred cops. As the protestors entered the park, most did not go near the free speech zone, but rather sought shelter from the sun under the first available tree. More than a dozen protestors and police officers were treated for heat exhaustion. The protest basically ended without much fanfare.

The press seemed particularly upset that there was no clash between the protestors and the police. I held a short news conference, at which I was peppered with a series of questions. One local reporter challenged me, asking, "Commissioner, you said you were not going to allow the unsanctioned march, and yet you did. Why?" I responded, "The protest leaders said they were going to march down to the convention center and disrupt the convention activities. They marched to the convention center, but they did not disrupt the activities." This seemed to answer the reporter's question and also amuse others.

On Tuesday, there were more protests, but the day was largely uneventful. During Wednesday morning's briefing, we were informed by our intelligence officers that groups of anarchists were planning protests and disruptions beginning at 4:00 P.M. At around 2:00 P.M. Frasier, Felder, and I left police headquarters to patrol Center City on our bikes. My intention was to go down to the convention center later that night.

At 4:00 P.M. sharp, the police radio crackled with a report of more than a hundred demonstrators shackled together at the corner of Broad and Walnut in the heart of Center City, bringing traffic to a complete halt. Within seconds another protest group blocked the entrance to the highway leading to the Benjamin Franklin Bridge, which spans the Delaware River between Philadelphia and New Jersey. We responded to the Broad and Walnut location and began to unshackle the protestors and place them under arrest. We had to use special tools to cut through their "sleeping dragons," the handcufflike chains they had used. As those arrests were in progress another group of about a hundred protestors ran along Locust Street in Center City, assaulting pedestrians. We made some arrests there. Felder, Frasier, and I then proceeded on our bikes to the entrance of I-676 at around Sixteenth Street, off the Benjamin Franklin Parkway. Additional arrests were made, and one lieutenant was seriously assaulted by a protestor while other protestors tried to get his gun. It was a chaotic scene, but it was under control by 6:00 P.M.

The remaining hundreds of protestors reconvened at Fifteenth Street and Market, on the west side of City Hall. A stalemate ensued for the next two hours. There were minor skirmishes with no major issues. Around 8:00 P.M., the protestors prepared for another assault on police lines, and a decision was made to disperse the protesting groups with a phalanx of a few hundred police officers with Mounted Unit officers leading the formation. Protestors strung a long wire across Fifteenth Street, meant to knock the mounted officers off of their horses. Police officers moved to disperse the crowd and a group of about a hundred protestors broke away, running at full speed toward the vicinity of Rittenhouse Square.

The protestors' efforts to get to Rittenhouse at Eighteenth Street and Walnut were stopped by a group of officers using their bikes as barricades. The group then went south on Seventeenth Street, where

they damaged civilian cars and set a Dumpster on fire. The bike officers, myself included, paralleled the protestors on Eighteenth Street. A
few blocks south, we encountered a civilian driver, an older gentleman
in a black sedan, who had been physically assaulted by the marauding group. We then confronted the group on Seventeenth Street, where
there was another skirmish, and Officer Felder was knocked uncon-
scious. A few arrests were made, while the rest of the group continued
south on Seventeenth, then west on Spruce, then left the area.

While all of this was occurring, protesters in a separate breakaway
group made their way, unnoticed, to the Ben Franklin Parkway. They
vandalized at least a dozen marked police cars that had been parked
and left unattended.

At the skirmish on Seventeenth Street, where Ray Felder was injured, I also got banged around. I did not look too pretty on the eleven
o'clock news that night. After the press conference at City Hall, the
mayor and I visited Ray Felder in the hospital. As we were leaving, the
mayor said to me, "I don't want you going out there tomorrow. You've
become the target, and we are not in the risk-taking business." At first I
was taken aback, but after a minute I realized the man was right.

The next day I stayed in my office doing routine paperwork while the
men and women of the Philadelphia Police Department, especially the
bike cops, patrolled Center City. That night I went down to the convention with Mike Julian, who had come to visit me from New York. When
the convention was over, Mike and I went to a restaurant in Rittenhouse
Square with John Miller, then a correspondent for ABC's news program
20/20. While we were sitting at the outdoor restaurant, about a hundred police officers in columns of two, on their bikes, led by Lieutenant
Billy Schmidt, rode through Center City to the applause and standing
ovations of the patrons of the nearby restaurants. It was a very proud
moment for me, because just ten days earlier, the Thomas Jones case
had gotten us international notoriety for all the wrong reasons. Leading
up to the convention there were some—dare I say many—doubters who
thought we could not handle policing the convention without giving
the city another black eye. Comparisons were being made to Chicago in
1968. We proved them wrong. The men and women of the Philadelphia

Police Department had stepped up to the plate and hit a home run. My cold beer and cheeseburger had never tasted better.

The use of bike officers to handle protests and marches was new in the police profession. The convention was the first time that they were used, not only operationally but also tactically. Over the next few weeks, we received numerous phone calls from police departments across the nation, inquiring how to establish bike squads and the concomitant training. Of all the phone calls, the most pleasing was the one I received from the chief of police of Atlantic City, New Jersey. The chief explained to me that he had been trying for years to have his police officers ride bikes to patrol the busy boardwalk there. The officers had always resisted this move, complaining that real cops don't ride bicycles. The chief went on to say that when his officers saw the Philadelphia Police Department officers on television handling protests while on bicycles, he had been inundated with requests from his officers that they be allowed to patrol the boardwalk on bicycles. Imitation is the sincerest form of flattery.

"Top of the World, Ma!"

As 2000 came to a close, I looked back on John Street's first year as mayor and considered it to have been a pretty good one. Crime was under control, and the biggest event of the year, the Republican National Convention, had been a major success, bringing credit and acclaim to the city. The Thomas Jones case had obviously been a black eye, but it had been handled well and could have been much worse than it had been. As the new year came and went, I was feeling pretty good about the department and how my team and I were running it.

Don't get too comfortable on your pedestal, Mr. Timoney. Things are about to change.

In February, I received a phone call from a *Philadelphia Inquirer* reporter who wanted to interview me about a disciplinary case involving a captain assigned to the Homicide Unit. The reporter had a complete copy of the Internal Affairs file, which had been leaked to him by someone in the department.

The case involved an off-duty accident in which the captain, who was driving his take-home, unmarked police car, had a collision with a pillar that supported elevated train tracks. The accident happened in February 1998, a month before I became the police commissioner. The captain was returning home from a police promotion or retirement party a few blocks from headquarters. Two police officers and a patrol lieutenant responded to the accident scene and suspected that the captain may have been drinking prior to getting behind the wheel of his car.

There were no injuries to the captain, just damage to the police car. The lieutenant, it was alleged later on, instructed the two responding police officers to handle the matter as an ordinary accident with property damage.

Sometime later, one of the police officers, feeling guilty about having engaged in a cover-up, went to Internal Affairs, which began an investigation into the accident.

After I was sworn in as police commissioner, there were dozens of issues on my plate. This case was not one of them. It was only a few months later, while being briefed on a host of Internal Affairs investigations and their status, that I became aware of this investigation for the first time. There was nothing especially startling about it; it was being investigated properly, and once the investigation was completed, the District Attorney's Office would review it to confirm whether to proceed criminally or administratively.

It was more than a year later when the case finally came to me for the final disposition. The District Attorney's Office had passed on it, which indicated that there was no criminal violation, or if there was one, it would be too difficult to prove. The charges against the captain basically indicated that he had had a car accident off-duty and may have been drinking. The responding lieutenant had also been charged with covering up the accident.

During my first few months as police commissioner, I had not met the captain, to the best of my knowledge. On homicide matters I mainly dealt with his supervisor, who was an inspector. However, as the months went on, I began to notice the captain, especially at CompStat. I was also briefed by him on a number of homicides. He was a very impressive individual who was smart and had a street cop's toughness. If central casting were looking for an ideal homicide captain, he was your man.

By then I had become aware that Internal Affairs was investigating him. I wondered why he had not been transferred from homicide by my predecessor when the allegations regarding his accident first surfaced. But I never gave it much thought after that. As the months went on, the captain became more impressive with his work habits, his diligence to duty, the steadfastness with which he completed tough investigations, and most of all with his results. In addition, he was one of the few bosses whom I had met in my career, especially a detective boss, who took his responsibility to control overtime seriously. While he made sure that detectives had all of the overtime they needed to work their cases and solve the crimes, he also made sure that the overtime "gravy train" was not abused or misused.

The captain's steadfastness in curtailing overtime abuse, however, did not sit well with some of his homicide detectives or their cohorts over at the union hall. That made me like him even more. When his disciplinary case finally came before me, his stellar performance and the amount of time that had elapsed blurred the seriousness of the incident, at least in my mind. I don't believe termination from the Philadelphia Police Department ever entered my thinking. I had actually terminated Philadelphia police officers, only to have all but one of them returned to full employment. And that one had soured my relationship with the union forever. So I imposed a four-week penalty on both the captain and the lieutenant. And that was that.

A year later, when I received the phone call from the *Philadelphia Inquirer* reporter, I was not overly concerned. It was only when the reporter began to delve into the issue of the disparity of discipline given to cops versus their bosses that I knew this was not going to be a good story. When I picked up my copy of the *Inquirer* that Sunday morning, it was clear that this case was a hell of a lot more serious than I had ever really considered. The quotes selected from the Internal Affairs investigative report created a pretty ugly picture.

By Monday, every television station in Philly and every other press outlet were hot on the trail, and my judgment was called into account.

The feeding frenzy became so intense that the mayor put together an outside panel to investigate the case more broadly and to examine the entire disciplinary process. I actually welcomed this panel, because up to this point, I had viewed the disciplinary process in Philadelphia as a complete joke. I guess some could say my decision had added to the laughter.

The first great lesson in situations like these is that you quickly learn who your friends are. On the third night of the frenzy, I received a text message from Mayor Street to the effect that "We all make mistakes. However, what you've done for this city, no one can argue with. You are in my prayers." That was the second time in my life that I knew everything would be okay as a result of a phone call or text message. The first was when I retired from the NYPD, in what one might describe as a bit of a huff, and I received a telephone call from the archbishop of New York, Cardinal O'Connor, letting me know that everything would be okay and that he would be praying for me.

Of the many phone calls of support I received that week, none was more revealing of the reality of the disciplinary system in Philadelphia than that from former mayor Ed Rendell. "Johnny," he said, "you screwed up. You should have just fired the guys. Then the arbitrators bring them back, and everyone's satisfied. That's how it works in Philadelphia."

The District Attorney's Office maintained that they had never passed up on the possible arrest of the two officers and that they had not approved the case to be handled administratively. The records indicated that not only had they sent the case back, but they had signed off on it as well. When confronted with this information, they maintained that they had sent it back only for further investigation. At any rate, the District Attorney's Office arrested the captain and the lieutenant and took them to trial; they were then found not guilty and put back to full duty, just as Ed Rendell had predicted.

Another of the great lessons I learned from this incident was that, even when an infraction happens before you take office, if the final matter comes before you for disciplinary action, you are fully accountable for the discipline you impose. And my lesson was much more difficult: you can't allow time and performance to cloud a decision. There is no doubt in my mind that in the time between the date of the infraction and the time when the case came before me for disciplinary action, the seriousness of the charge had somehow dissipated. The captain's stellar performance during this period further clouded my decision. It was one of the low points in my long career. Fortunately, you can survive the low points. It just takes time. And performance.

9/11

My normal daily routine saw me getting up at 5:00 A.M., having a couple of cups of tea, and then driving over to Boathouse Row to be on the Schuylkill River by twenty minutes to six with my rowing partner, Mark O'Connor. The row would last an hour, and then I would go back home, prepare for work, and would usually arrive in my office around 8:15 A.M. The deviation from this routine occurred on Tuesdays, when Mayor Street held his weekly 9:00 A.M. cabinet meetings at City Hall.

City Hall was located equidistant from my apartment on Rittenhouse Square and police headquarters, the "Roundhouse." So on Tuesdays I would leave my apartment later and go straight to City Hall for the cabinet meeting.

September 11, 2001, started just like any other Tuesday, except it was more glorious. It was a crisp but warm morning, and the sky was clear blue. As I was leaving my apartment around 8:50 A.M., my wife, Noreen, pointed to the television and indicated that a plane had just struck one of the towers of the World Trade Center. I paid it little heed, assuming it was a small, single-engine plane that had veered off-course from Teterboro Airport, which was a short distance across the Hudson River in New Jersey.

Ten minutes later, I was in the mayor's conference room with other cabinet members waiting for the mayor to enter. He was running a little late, as he was finishing up a phone call in his office. I received a phone call from my wife telling me that a second plane had struck the World Trade Center. I immediately knew this was no accident. We were under attack. There was no doubt in my mind that this was a terrorist act; by whom I did not know. The one question that came immediately to mind was, How could this happen? As I headed toward the television in the corner of the conference room, the mayor entered, and I motioned for him to join me. We watched together, stunned as the North and South Towers were engulfed in flames. We immediately went into emergency mode, activating the city's Office of Emergency Management. I called my office and ordered that all off-duty personnel be directed to report to work immediately.

Amid all of the excitement in the mayor's conference room, I kept one eye on the television, listening to my old buddy, John Miller, who was reporting from the ABC television news desk on who was likely to be responsible for this awful act. As the television camera focused on the South Tower, it, incredibly, collapsed. I had a difficult time believing what I was seeing.

I had been a deputy chief in the NYPD at the time of the first bombing of the World Trade Center in 1993. A few days after the bombing, I had the opportunity to visit the site, and what I saw amazed me. From the garage, where the U-Haul truck carrying the bomb had been parked, a gigantic hole had been blown through the ceiling and up through two or three additional floors. This created an inverted craterlike image. I was stunned that the building was still standing after such an explosion.

Months later, at a meeting with other city and state agencies, a structural engineer who worked for the Port Authority of New York and New Jersey (which owned the World Trade Center complex) pointed out, almost boastfully, that the World Trade Center towers were constructed to withstand hurricanes, tornados, explosions, and anything else you could think of.

When I saw the South Tower collapse, I was incredulous and thought back to my conversation with that Port Authority engineer in 1993. We continued working the phones, attempting to get hard intelligence regarding the attack. There was none. After one phone call, the mayor motioned for me to look at the television. "The second tower just collapsed," he exclaimed. When I saw a replay of the collapse, I told him that was just a replay of the South Tower collapsing. "No," he said, and explained that the North Tower had also collapsed. When I realized that the second tower had, in fact, gone down, too, I just kept asking myself, How could this happen?

Then an announcement came over the television that a plane had crashed in a field in western Pennsylvania. That was followed by an announcement of a plane striking the Pentagon. There was no doubt that we were under attack; we were left pondering how many more planes were involved and how long the attack would last.

On the television John Miller kept referring to the exclusive interview he had conducted with Osama bin Laden back in 1998. Bin Laden had promised a spectacular attack on the United States. I had seen John's interview and had also read his *Esquire* piece about the interview and his trials and tribulations leading up to it. I don't believe that I ever felt that bin Laden's threats would become a reality. Certainly not in the form I was seeing unfold before my eyes as I watched television in the mayor's conference room. As the morning wore on, Miller was more than convinced that this was the fulfillment of bin Laden's promise to strike at the heart of the United States. Bizarrely, no government or law enforcement official was offering a counter-opinion.

At about 11:30 A.M., I left City Hall and headed to police headquarters. The streets surrounding City Hall were jam-packed and traffic was at a virtual standstill as people attempted to leave Center City. The scene reminded me of the old Japanese *Godzilla* movies, in which all of the terrorized motorists are headed away from the monster. When I arrived at headquarters, many of the off-duty officers had already arrived and were being deployed with hundreds of on-duty officers to intersections throughout the city.

At around noon, in a telephone conversation with members of the FBI, I was given an update. Basically, they were attempting to ascertain the location of all planes within the continental United States and all of the planes that were expected to land within the United States that had originated from overseas locations. The federal authorities had been unable to make radio contact with a plane that had left Madrid and was scheduled to land in Philadelphia sometime after 1:00 P.M. They told me that if they got any further information, they would get back to me. By

1:30 P.M., I had not gotten any updates about the plane, so I assumed it had been located and that everything was fine.

I took a walking tour of Center City with Tony Pino, my driver. The entire area was like a ghost town. There were cops at every intersection, but there were no civilians to see them or to engage them in conversation. I knew this was going to be a long day, so we looked for a place to get something to eat. Every commercial establishment was closed. We gave one final try and went to Matt Pagano's Pizzeria and Sandwich Shop in the basement of Strawbridge's Department Store. I was a regular at Matt's, along with the federal judges and prosecutors who worked across the street. On a normal day there would be at least a hundred people eating lunch there. As we walked in, just one patron was eating a sandwich in the corner, and Matt and his staff were cleaning up, getting ready to close for the day. Matt whipped up my regular chicken cutlet hero, and we sat together for ten minutes discussing what was happening ninety miles to the north of Philadelphia in my old hometown.

Later that afternoon, I made numerous attempts to contact my brother, Ciaran, a lieutenant with the NYPD, with no success. I was also informed that my nephew, police officer James Carroll, was missing after responding to the attack at the World Trade Center. He appeared a few hours later, having been trapped in one of the buildings across the street from the complex. I got home late that night and watched the continuous replay of the towers collapsing.

I went in to work early the next morning and repeated the process we had begun at midday Tuesday—that is, putting uniformed officers at key intersections and iconic buildings and institutions to show the flag. I knew in my heart that a uniformed officer standing post in front of a signature building could do little to thwart a terrorist attack, but there were no other feasible options because the intelligence coming across the transom was nil.

Within a few days, the magnitude and sadness of what had happened on that beautiful, clear Tuesday morning began to set in. An awful, sinking feeling remained in the pit of my stomach. The routine of the police commissioner's job—paperwork, telephone calls, and meetings—all seemed irrelevant. As the names of the dead became public, I realized how many of the victims I knew—some intimately. Amazingly, of the dozen and a half NYPD officers killed, I knew only two. However, I knew most of the top fire department hierarchy who had perished. They had been my colleagues and planning partners over the previous decade for many of the major events that New York City had hosted. Each story and each life lost was sadder than the previous one, but none was sadder than when I found out that the only son of Shuck Seid, my "Chinese godfather," had died.

In Irish culture, irony is a prized commodity. In death, it is priceless. John P. O'Neill, an assistant special agent in charge with the FBI, who was a friend of mine but an even better friend of John Miller's, had spent the past half dozen years hunting down Osama bin Laden. Unfortunately, he was unsuccessful. But not from lack of effort. John had recently retired from the FBI and was working as the head of security at the World Trade Center. On September 11, John was on his second day on the job and found himself rescuing people from the burning inferno when he was struck and killed by a falling piece of one of the towers. A lot has been written about John's death, but one thing is for certain: when the planes struck those buildings, there was no doubt in John's mind who was the mastermind behind the dastardly act.

A few weeks after 9/11, I took the Amtrak train from Philadelphia to New York's Penn Station to attend the Irish wake of John O'Neill at Elaine's. Elaine's had been our hangout during the Bratton years, and its denizens included writers, actors, cops, and lots of gawkers. On a normal Friday night, getting to Elaine's from Penn Station would take a half hour at minimum. But this time, the trip took under fifteen minutes. There was very little traffic. When I got into a cab on Thirty-third Street, the driver was of obvious Middle Eastern decent and was probably of the Muslim faith. The entire windshield of the cab was covered with an American flag. There was barely enough space for the cab driver to see the road. Here was this cabbie using the symbol of the American flag to protect himself against reprisal for the acts of others who had meant to destroy everything that flag stands for.

While Irish wakes are meant to celebrate the life of the deceased, there was little joy that night at Elaine's. Every conversation, every statement, every verbal utterance always led back to the inevitable discussion of what had happened on that awful Tuesday morning. Riding back to Philadelphia that night on the train, I felt for the first time that I could finally breathe, that I was free of the conversation surrounding the attacks. Philadelphia is only ninety miles south of New York City, but in terms of the effect of the attacks on the psyche of the average Philadelphian, it could have just as easily been a separate planet. The next morning, I was back on the river with my rowing partner, Mark O'Connor, breathing the fresh air along the Schuylkill River, away from the torment and depression that had become New York City.

A week or two later, I, along with some other big-city chiefs, was asked to testify before Congress regarding the preparedness of cities to deal with terrorist attacks and also the gathering and sharing of information between the FBI and local police. I had conducted a few television interviews in the weeks following 9/11, during which I had expressed my frustration with the lack of intelligence and intelligence sharing by the FBI and other federal law enforcement agencies. As I concluded my testimony before the congressional committee, I made a final observation: that the next piece of information I received from the FBI would be the first. A few hours later, I was in the office of the new FBI director, Robert Mueller, for a prearranged meet and greet. Mueller had taken over the FBI one week prior to 9/11, so obviously my criticism was not directed at him. Nonetheless, as I entered his office he confronted me, saying, "Timoney, I am fed up of looking at your mug on television, criticizing the FBI." He half smiled and shook my hand and promised that things were going to change. And they did.

By the end of October normalcy had returned to policing in Philadelphia. That meant the old fights with the police union resumed, now more fiercely than ever. Additionally, I was being severely criticized on talk radio stations for my interference with police officers in their fight against terrorism. You see, two years prior to 9/11, as a result of a rash of robberies and killings of Chinese deliverymen, I had changed the police department's protocol in dealing with illegal aliens. My new policy reflected one put into effect almost twenty years earlier by Mayor Ed Koch in New York City.

A simple premise in fighting crime is the idea that in order to fight the crime, you have to know about it. Many of the Chinese immigrants in Philadelphia who had been the victims of robberies and other crimes often did not report those crimes, sometimes because of their resident-alien status. Because they refused to come forward and cooperate with police, they only encouraged more similar crimes. The new policy basically said that if you were a victim of crime, you should report it to the police and that under no circumstances would the police inquire about your resident-alien status. The protocol went on to say, however, that if you were an illegal alien who was engaged in illegal activity, the appropriate federal immigration authorities would be notified.

The policy was fair as far as I was concerned. But many people in the land of talk radio, with the support of cops who had fed them bad information, had a field day at my expense. The notion that I would inhibit police officers in their fight against terrorism is ridiculous. Nonetheless, the charges flew. I reached out to the number one talk-radio personality in Philadelphia, Michael Smerconish. He agreed to have me on his program for a full hour so that I could explain the policy and its intention. At the end of the interview, Smerconish characterized the policy as "reasonable," and that seemed to deflate the hot-air balloon that had surrounded the issue.

There were other fights, including the perennial favorite, "reasonable" gun control, which is a perennial loser. When I first came to Philadelphia, I assumed that the state of Pennsylvania would be filled with quiet, peaceful Quakers. I knew from my experience in New York that some of the crime guns recovered by the NYPD came from Pennsylvania. However, I assumed that was just the result of proximity. Typically, the states that were the big sources for guns were southern states such as Florida, Georgia, and Virginia. What a surprise when I found out that Pennsylvania was the second leading gun ownership state, with Texas being number one. While the police commissioner had the responsibility of issuing permits for concealed guns, the commissioner was powerless to refuse a permit to applicants unless they had certain criminal convictions or had some certifiable mental condition. The city administration had tried to get the lawmakers in Harrisburg, the state capital, to give the police commissioner more power and discretion, but to no avail. I also argued issues surrounding gun shows, where it appeared there was little or no regulation regarding who could buy guns. Finally, there had been efforts, especially by Mayor Rendell, to pass some legislation limiting gun purchases to one a month. Or, as he would say, "Twelve guns a year! Why would you need more?"

At one point, sometime in November 2001, as I was making a mental list of all of the fights and battles I was involved in, I wondered to myself if all my opponents were wrong, or if I just liked fighting. And if so, had I become fed up with the fighting? I wasn't sure of the answer to that question, but I knew I was ready for a change. Suddenly, an opportunity in the private sector, working for Beau Dietl, an old friend of mine in New York, presented itself. (Beau and I had worked together in the 25th Precinct in East Harlem, and he had been quite a cop.) While 9/11 had had a tremendously negative impact on New York's business community, the security industry was an exception to that. I thought I would enjoy returning to work in New York, and in the process I would make a decent salary.

When I informed Mayor Street of my intention to leave by the beginning of the new year, he seemed genuinely shocked and upset. We had had an excellent working relationship, contrary to what had been written in the press. Even though the mayor tried to convince me to stay, my mind was made up: I was returning to New York.

PART III

Miami

13

Paradise Found: Miami

I have a vision for this city, and I am putting together a team to make that
vision a reality. You can be part of that team, and we can do this together.
—MANNY DIAZ, MAYOR OF THE CITY OF MIAMI

In late November 2002, on a typically cold day in New York, with the
temperature hovering in the high forties, I received a telephone call
from Patrick Kelly, chief of police of a town called Medley, a small
hamlet just west of the city of Miami. I didn't know Chief Kelly, but
he indicated that he had been following my career over the years. He
went on to say that the city of Miami was conducting a search for a new
chief of police and that in the course of a conversation he had had with
Miami's mayor, Manny Diaz, my name had come up. The purpose of
the phone call was to relay a message from Mayor Diaz to me, to see if
I would be willing to come to Miami to speak with the mayor and the
city manager. I'm not the brightest guy in the world, but the opportunity to leave chilly New York to visit tropical Miami for a few days on
someone else's dime was a no-brainer.

In early December, I found myself in Miami for the first time in
my life. I met with Mayor Manny Diaz and the city manager, Carlos
Jimenez. The mayor explained that he was just finishing his first year
in office and was looking to hire a new chief of police since the current chief, Raul Martinez, had announced his retirement a few weeks

earlier. Carlos Jimenez indicated that the new chief of police would be his last hire, as he intended to retire in early January 2003. The meeting with both men went very well, and they indicated that they would get back to me, which they did the following week.

I returned to Miami once more and again met with the city manager and the mayor. I was offered the job of police chief, with the caveat that they could not match the salary I was earning in the private sector. Of course I understood that. What impressed me most was my conversation with the mayor. He had a great vision for the city and a clear path from which to achieve his goal of making Miami one of the top-tier cities in America. He said it would be great if I would be a partner with him in achieving his goals and fulfilling the dream.

I accepted the offer, and we agreed that I would assume the new position in early January 2003. As soon as the formal announcement was made in early December, I received a number of phone calls congratulating me. I also received a few phone calls from people in law enforcement inquiring if I had lost my sanity. The consensus of these callers indicated that Miami had a troubled police department and that reform would be a heavy lift, even for a strong-willed guy like me. I knew nothing about the city of Miami except what I had read in the press and seen on television—and that had not been good. The image was that of a city with a huge drug problem and a concomitant high homicide rate. Miami had a history of bad police shootings that sometimes resulted in major civil unrest and riots. In fact, in the prior twenty-five years, Miami had had more riots as a result of police shootings than any other city in the United States.

In 1980 and 1981, Miami led every major U.S. city with the highest homicide rate, driven by the drug trade with the advent of the "Cocaine Cowboys" in the late 1970s. In 1980, fuel was added to the fire with the forced expatriation from Castro's Cuba of 125,000 people in the Mariel Boatlift. The vast majority of the 125,000 were normal, everyday Cuban citizens who had relatives in the United States. However, Castro took the opportunity to reduce the populations of his prisons and mental institutions by forcing Cuban American boaters to take the criminals and mentally ill people in their boats to America with them. As one

Miami Police Department (MPD) captain explained to me, in 1980 he was a young police officer and he and his cousin drove their boat to the Port of Mariel to pick up his young nephew and bring him to the United States. As his nephew boarded the boat, Cuban soldiers, with rifles pointed, directed the young MPD officer to take two complete and total strangers with them in addition to his nephew. This scenario was repeated hundreds of times. The opening scene of the movie *Scarface*, where thousands of immigrants are crammed into large tents that were erected under the highways of Miami, graphically captures the tidal wave of people who had landed on Florida's shores.

The dramatic increase in violent crime led the Miami Police Department to go on a police officer hiring binge, with little regard to qualifications and background checks. The police chief at the time, Kenneth Harms, lamely proclaimed that he had been forced to disregard qualifications due to the politics at City Hall. The mayor, Xavier Suarez, responded that the chief of police had established the standards and qualifications used in hiring the new officers. The massive hiring binge would haunt the Miami Police Department over the next decade with scandal after scandal, the most notorious being the "Miami River cops." In this case, uniformed Miami police officers in 1985 boarded drug-laden vessels on the Miami River, stealing hundreds of pounds of drugs and transporting them from the scene in the trunks of their marked police cars. When the police officers boarded the ship, six crewmembers, fearful for their lives, jumped overboard. Three drowned.

Around 1990, Miami again made international headlines as a result of hundreds of tourist robberies, including one in which a German tourist was killed. Toward the end of the decade, the final nail was driven into the coffin when the city declared bankruptcy. The once tropical paradise, which had been a vacation venue for many Americans, became a place to avoid at all costs.

Over the previous decade, many of the white residents of Miami had fled north to Broward and Palm Beach counties. A popular, racist bumper sticker read, "When the last American leaves Miami, please turn off the lights." Miami began to be referred to derisively and under the breath as a "banana republic." In fact, in one cruel joke, someone drove a truck up to the front entrance of City Hall and dumped a load of bananas to underscore the pernicious epithet.

It was against this backdrop that Manny Diaz ran for mayor in 2001. Like some other new mayors of the twenty-first century, Diaz's background was not in politics but in business. Against all odds the businessman, Diaz, beat four other politicians to become mayor of the city. He was committed to reforming the politics of the city, improving the business climate, and creating a rational model for future development. Diaz, who is also a lawyer and a civil rights activist, was gravely concerned with the workings of the Miami Police Department. Shortly after becoming mayor in January 2002, Diaz wrote a letter to the U.S. Department of Justice, Civil Rights Division, requesting that they come to Miami to conduct a "patterns and practices" review of the MPD's day-to-day operations and the department's policies and protocols.

By the end of 2002, while I was interviewing with the mayor and the city manager, the city of Miami was preparing for a federal criminal trial of a dozen police officers who had been arrested on a variety of charges surrounding police shootings. These arrests seemed to be part of a recurrent theme that had created an indelible image of the Miami Police Department as a corrupt and brutal organization. And it was this image that had prompted so many phone calls to me from my former colleagues.

As the interview and hiring process were taking place, I was in daily contact with John Gallagher. John had left the Philadelphia Police Department in the fall of 2000 to become a White House fellow in the Clinton administration, where he worked under Attorney General Janet Reno. He finished his fellowship in August 2001 under the new attorney general, John Ashcroft, and got a job as an assistant U.S. attorney in Albuquerque, New Mexico.

Once I had accepted the chief's job in Miami, I called John to offer him the position of assistant chief of police for administration. He accepted immediately, which suggested to me that he was bored with the life of a federal prosecutor in New Mexico and was looking for the opportunity to get back into big-city policing. Around the same time

I received a telephone call from Louie Vega, my trusted confidential aide when I was chief of department in New York. He was now a deputy chief at the Hartford Police Department in Connecticut. Louie and Sergeant Jack Casey handled many of the super-sensitive operational issues for me when I was chief of department. I trusted both of them with my life and my career. Louie indicated that he would like to become part of the new team in Miami, and I accepted his offer without hesitation. I knew I was going to need someone tough like Louie to run Internal Affairs.

"If They Expect Change, Don't Disappoint Them"

The Miami Police Department is more similar to the NYPD than it is to the Philadelphia Police Department, even though the Miami Police Department, with twelve hundred officers, is much smaller than the seven-thousand-strong police department in Philly. Like the police commissioner of New York, the Miami police chief has the discretion to promote all senior officers above the civil-service rank of captain. Philadelphia, as you may recall, because of its rigorous civil-service system, has only a few discretionary promotions under the control of the commissioner. So team building in Miami, in many respects, was going to resemble that of New York in 1994.

There are two things that need to be understood regarding the New York and Miami system versus the Philadelphia system. In New York and Miami, because the police chief has the power to promote, he really can create his own team. In the process of creating that team, there is a high degree of buy-in and congruity with the chief's vision and his goals to achieve that vision. Because of this, it is likely that the changes made will stick and become part of the department's culture and traditions. However, in the Philadelphia system the commissioner builds his team with players who already have their rank and position due to the civil-service system and not at the discretion of the commissioner. You can build some loyalty in a system such as this, but there will be more than a few high-ranking officers who will just "wait you out." Therefore, although creating radical change by sheer dint of personality is possible, that change often does not become part of the culture or tradition of the department once that personality moves on.

In Miami, unlike New York, I knew none of the players. Therefore, I was going to spend at least the first month conducting interviews of most of the officers above the rank of lieutenant. I was also going to make sure that I abided by the number one commandment for any police chief taking over a new organization, especially a troubled organization: when people expect change, don't disappoint them. While I was conducting interviews for the new team, I also assessed the old team that was still in place and concluded that, indeed, some personnel changes needed to take place. And that meant people would be forced to leave.

Serendipity did play a role as I began my tenure in Miami, and that was in the person of Angel Calzadilla, senior executive assistant to the chief of police. Angel was one of those people who knew everybody and everything. He had a stellar career as a patrol officer in the Little Havana neighborhood of Miami, winning numerous medals and awards. He had also been a top hostage negotiator for the department. Prior to his elevation to senior executive assistant, he had spent a few years working in the Public Information Office, where he was known, literally, by almost everybody in Miami due to his frequent appearance on television on both English and Spanish channels. I had actually seen Angel on television, on *Larry King Live*, when I was the police commissioner in Philadelphia.

Angel became the face of the Miami Police Department during the 2000 crisis surrounding young Elián González, the seven-year-old Cuban boy who had become a cause célèbre for the Cuban nationalist community in Miami. The González affair marked another contentious chapter in the history of the MPD. In November 1999, young Elián had left Cuba for the United States with his mother and twelve others in a small boat. The attempt ended in disaster, with Elián's mother and ten others drowning, and Elián and two survivors found clinging to a tube floating in the ocean off Florida's coast. Young Elián was united with relatives in Miami. His father in Cuba asked for his return and on April 22, 2000, he was forcibly removed from his relatives' home in Little

Havana by armed immigration officials who were apparently assisted by a Miami police official. Many in the Cuban expatriate community felt betrayed by the Miami Police Department, and numerous days of civil unrest followed the forcible removal of the child. There was real tension and distrust in the Cuban American community regarding the MPD. Up to this point the Cuban American community had always been the staunchest supporter of the MPD. Now the two major communities, the Cuban American community and the African American community, were at odds with the police department. It was against this backdrop that I saw Angel on television attempting to explain to Larry King the no-win situation in which the police found themselves. He even articulated quite eloquently and forcefully the internal conflict that he, as a Cuban American police officer, faced with the Elián situation. He was obviously sympathetic to the young boy's cause, but he was also a police officer sworn to uphold the law. On the Larry King show Angel powerfully articulated the conflicts that police officers often encounter during their career: sometimes it's an African American police officer, handling a civil rights protest, who may be required to make an arrest of civil rights protestors toward whom he feels very sympathetic; sometimes it's a Catholic police officer who has to arrest a priest or a nun at an abortion clinic. Whatever it is, it may make that police officer uncomfortable, but nonetheless the law must be enforced.

Angel was a critical aide, especially during the early months. He helped me navigate the political waters. The respect with which he was held within the Cuban American community, especially among the elders, was instrumental in getting out many of my early messages on Spanish radio and television stations. More important was his loyalty to the Miami Police Department and to the leader of that department, whether it was Raul Martinez or John Timoney. Some people confuse or misunderstand the notion of loyalty. Some think loyalty to an individual is paramount, and that's wrong. What's most important and most crucial is loyalty to the organization, no matter who is in charge.

There is no science to creating a new team to run a police department in a major American city, or any city for that matter. Many variables come into play. Macro variables include the demographics of the city, the history of the police department, policing scandals, the influence of politics on the department, and recent elections, including major campaign promises. The list goes on and on. The micro influences will usually deal with the people and personalities under consideration. What are their pedigrees? Are they known innovators whose loyalties are beyond reproach, or are they creative thinkers who play the game of politics first and foremost? Do they have what the military refers to as "command presence"? This includes not only how they look in uniform, but whether or not they exude a confident manner. Or are they smart but shy? Are they good listeners in addition to being good talkers? Do they show the requisite deference without being a sycophant? Are they looking for a challenge and a chance to rock the boat, or are they merely looking to steer to avoid collision?

A key to assembling the right team also depends on previous successes or failures. If a chief maintains that he or she has always made the correct team selections, that chief is not being fully honest. Every chief makes some mistakes in the personnel selection and promotion process. The key is to have many more successful appointments than failed appointments. You should always learn from your mistakes but never be risk-averse in your decisions for fear of making a mistake.

A week before taking over the Miami Police Department, I sat down for a few hours with the outgoing chief of police, Raul Martinez. He was a twenty-five-plus-year veteran of the MPD, and he was a decent and thoughtful fellow. It was very gracious of him to spend the time with me; most outgoing chiefs would not have done the same. He gave me an in-depth briefing of some of the issues facing the department, and we also went over the profiles of each and every staff member. Chief Martinez played no favorites and was careful to keep his personal opinions to himself. He made no recommendations, but he did tell me one story in particular that struck me as quite insightful. It concerned Commander Frank Fernandez.

Apparently, a boat with more than two hundred Haitian refugees had landed on the beach on Key Biscayne, outside of the MPD's jurisdiction. The Haitian refugee problem had become quite political over the prior few years, with allegations that Haitian refugees did not receive the same favorable treatment that the Cuban refugees received. Some police commanders will steer clear of politically thorny situations, such as this one, even in their own jurisdiction. It appeared that no one was in charge, and to make matters worse, it was being covered live on television via a news helicopter. Commander Fernandez took a group of Miami police officers to the scene and established order while awaiting federal immigration officials. After the officials arrived, Commander Fernandez remained at the scene and continued to give his operational guidance. "Fernandez saved the day," said Chief Martinez. "That situation could have blown up in all of our faces." Fernandez's actions reminded me of the oft-quoted "man in the arena" speech given by Teddy Roosevelt, in which he refers to the whole notion of being a risk taker versus being risk averse.

About a week later, I began conducting more than two dozen interviews of individuals who could be part of the new team. One individual, not surprisingly, stood out heads above the others: Commander Frank Fernandez. Frank was a Neighborhood Enhancement Team (NET) commander, the equivalent of a district commander in Philly or precinct commander in New York. He was smart, confident, and competent; when he entered the room, you took notice. He had "command presence," which had clearly helped him in the Haitian refugee fiasco. In addition, he had a good formal educational background and was presently finishing a master's degree. When I first interviewed Frank, I knew he would be part of the new team; the exact role, however, had yet to be determined.

After Commander Fernandez left my office, I had a conversation with Angel Calzadilla regarding the progress of the interviews. Angel mentioned to me that Commander Fernandez would be leaving in two weeks to spend three months at the FBI's National Academy. I instructed Angel to reach out to Commander Fernandez to let him know that he was going to be part of the new team, the exact position undetermined, so that he might want to consider postponing his gig at the FBI academy. Angel returned to my office within fifteen minutes to tell me that Commander Fernandez had just canceled his trip.

As the interviews progressed I had a good feeling: there was a great deal of talent within the middle-management ranks in the Miami Police Department. It was going to be difficult to select the immediate members of the new team. I suffered from an abundance of talent, not a bad ailment to have. I knew from experience that I would get plenty of other opportunities to make promotions, but the initial selections are very important because often they will set the tenor and send the message you want to get out regarding the new management team.

Selecting the new team is one thing; when to announce it is more problematic. There is no "perfect" time to make the announcement. For example, if you announce your new team within the first week, you will be accused of rushing the process and of not taking time to hold proper interviews and assessments. If you take too long to make the announcement, the old team that is still in place will get comfortable and entertain the notion they may be part of the new team. Additionally, there is the difficult task of informing members of the old team that they will not be continuing in their positions.

In Philadelphia, I knew the time had come to make the personnel changes when I received a call from a reporter: "Hey, Commissioner, I guess you are keeping so-and-so as the number two," he said. "Really," I replied, "and how did you determine that?" "Well," the reporter went on, "I just saw so-and-so with your guy Jack Maple at the Palm restaurant having lunch. That means the deal is sealed because the Palm is the place in Philly where all the political deals are done," he boasted. "That's interesting," I replied. "I have never been to the Palm. I eat in South Philly in cheap Italian restaurants."

I knew immediately after that call I had to do two things. First, bring in my number two and let him know he would not be part of the new team. Second, and very important for going forward in Philadelphia, I needed to explain to the South Philadelphia restaurant owners that I hadn't meant to denigrate the fine South Philly Italian restaurants as "cheap" but should have used the adjective "inexpensive." As someone once remarked, "Timoney only opens his mouth to change feet."

In Miami, the decision day for personnel changes came when Tom

Ridge, the former governor of Pennsylvania and future homeland security secretary, came to Miami on January 30, 2003, to announce the establishment of the Department of Homeland Security. The Port of Miami was used as the backdrop for the announcement. I knew Governor Ridge from my Philadelphia days, and we got along great. I went to the announcement with Mayor Manny Diaz. It was a beautiful sunny day, and all the security logistics went flawlessly. As we were leaving the port, I had a conversation with the chief of field services and the chief of detectives. Both of them were justifiably pleased with how the security operations had been handled. But for me, I knew it was time to make my announcement. I could see that they were getting comfortable.

I immediately called my administrative assistant, Angie Ruiloba, and had her direct the two chiefs to report to my office that afternoon, at separate times, fifteen minutes apart. I also asked Angie to have Commander Fernandez come to my office fifteen minutes after the second chief left, and then the other six members of the new team at fifteen-minute intervals after that.

When Commander Fernandez came to my office, I informed him that he was my new number two—the three-star deputy chief of field operations. Chief Fernandez's elevation mirrored my elevation in the NYPD when I was promoted to the position of four-star chief of department. Like me, Frank had just jumped past all of his colleagues and all of his former bosses in one giant leap.

I then had Major Gerald Darling come into my office and told him he was going to be the new chief of detectives. Gerald had been a major in the Detective Division and also had a great deal of experience in patrol. He would be the third two-star assistant chief. John Gallagher would be the two-star chief of administration; Louie Vega would be the two-star chief of Internal Affairs. Three other commanders, Juanita Walker, Craig McQueen, and George Cadavid, were all promoted to major. This was the starting lineup for the new team, and as I've said, I knew I would be making additional promotions as the year progressed. But I believed I had a solid foundation from which to start.

Confronting Police Shootings

When a new chief takes over a police department, crime is usually the number one issue. This was not the case when I took over as the chief of the Miami Police Department. Miami's worst crime days were in the past. A record number of homicides had occurred back in the early 1980s (1980, 1981, 1982). A high rate of robberies, especially tourist robberies, had occurred in 1989 and 1990. So the number one issue confronting the Miami Police Department when I walked through the door in 2003 was not ordinary street crime, but rather crime within the department, especially police shootings.

The day I was sworn in, thirteen police officers were beginning their federal criminal trial on charges resulting from police shootings of civilians. (Two officers had pleaded guilty and testified against the other eleven officers to get a lighter sentence.) The scandal surrounding these shootings and the resulting press attention had severely damaged morale within the department. I knew that any change in the department's shooting policy could be viewed by some officers as giving aid and comfort to the enemy (in this case, the media). There was also the distinct possibility that change could further alienate and demoralize the already demoralized force. Nonetheless, police shootings had to be dealt with in order to help mend the rift between the police department and the citizens of Miami, especially those in the African American community.

I knew from my prior experiences in New York and Philadelphia that a strong, restrictive shooting policy, along with proper training, could help reduce police shootings. I had witnessed the reduction of police shootings by 80 percent in New York over a period of two decades, and shooting fatalities had gone down from ninety a year to around a dozen a year. Philadelphia saw similarly positive results during my four years there. The average of fourteen people killed each year as a result of police bullets was reduced to an average of two. I knew similar results were possible in Miami. More important, I knew that these reductions in police shootings could be achieved without endangering police officers' safety.

Rather than wait to have my new team in place before implementing the new shooting policy, I literally began the changes, verbally, my first week on the job. At numerous roll calls, I let it be known in no uncertain terms that the MPD's shooting policy would be changed and strengthened. Police officers would be forbidden from shooting at motor vehicles unless the driver of the vehicle were using deadly physical force against the officer by means other than the vehicle. So while the new policy was not yet officially written, it was announced and being discussed at roll call where the officers had the opportunity to ask questions.

In the early weeks, I also met with Al Cotera, the head of the police union—the Fraternal Order of Police—and informed him of the many changes that would be forthcoming in the department's expanded shooting policy. When I explained to him that my job and every supervisor's job was to keep officers out of trouble, out of the headlines, and out of jail, he concurred. He had been particularly moved by the sight of those thirteen police officers, some of whom had been his good friends, on trial in federal court. After the difficult time I had had with the police union in Philadelphia, it was a pleasant surprise to be dealing with an individual who was not looking to confront management at every step toward reform.

In my first month as chief, I happened to be riding my police bike on a Sunday in the neighborhood of Coconut Grove in the southern part of the city. I came upon about a dozen police officers working an off-duty detail at a street fair. Stopping to chat with them, I had a very pleasant but surprising conversation with Officer Walter Byers. Officer Byers was an instructor at the police shooting range. He was a respected, seasoned veteran who told me that he had heard about the proposed new shooting guidelines, and he concurred that they were long overdue. A week or so later, I had the occasion to meet with Officer Byers's supervisor, Sergeant Armando Valdez, and had a similar conversation with him. I felt heartened by these two conversations. It struck me that it was very important to have allies such as the two officers who actually train police officers at the shooting range.

Training police officers in firearms proficiency should not deal solely with the mechanics of getting a good score. Part of the responsibility for the range instructors is to imbue officers with the philosophical underpinnings that all life is sacred and that deadly physical force should be used as a last resort. My conversations with Officer Byers and Sergeant Valdez convinced me early on that my message would get out firmly and correctly. Police officers may not fully embrace a new change in shooting policy from the chief of police. But if these officers get the message from the range instructors, whom they respect, then the chances of that message taking hold is that much greater.

I also wanted to take the shooting policy to the next level. Standard police shooting policies delineate when an officer can and cannot shoot. For example, an officer is forbidden from firing warning shots and is not allowed to shoot at cars. But I also wanted to address those situations when you could shoot. Even if you are within the parameters of the policy and the law, do you absolutely have to shoot? Have you put yourself in a position where you have no other choice but to shoot? Many times police officers are too brave for their own good. They will rush toward a dangerous situation (thank God), but we need to teach them to slow down, think strategically, take cover, and give themselves an extra half second to determine whether to shoot or not. I know it is an extreme tactic, but can you, like Mike Julian did in Brooklyn, run around a car to avoid being stabbed by a mentally disturbed sixteen-year-old rather than shooting him? When I talked about this philosophy, I tried to couch it in human terms. "You don't want it on your conscience that you let a shot go from your weapon at a moving vehicle that strikes and kills a sixteen-year-old unarmed car thief whose only real crime was fleeing from the police. That's not what you signed up for. You don't want to go through the hell, nor do you want to have your families dragged through the hell, of newspaper stories about your killing an unarmed sixteen-year-old car thief."

There is an Irish joke that goes as follows: a Catholic priest is riding his bike along a country road when he comes upon a farmer named Murphy. Murphy has a tree branch in his hand and is continuously hitting his donkey with it because the donkey has decided not to pull Murphy's cart to market. The priest is shocked, and says, "Murphy, what in God's name are you doing?" Murphy replies, "Father, the donkey just sits there refusing to move, and I have to get this produce to market before it closes." "Murphy, that beast is one of God's creatures," the priest replies. "He needs to be loved and treated with care. He needs to be cajoled, and you need to explain to him why he needs to pull the cart to get your produce to the market." "Really?" the farmer says. "Could you show me how to do that, Father?" The priest gets off his bike, picks up the tree branch, and smacks the donkey with a big wallop to the side of the head. Murphy, shocked, says, "Father, I thought you said that he was one of God's creatures and that I had to love and cajole him and explain to him why it was important for him to pull the cart to the market." The priest replies, "All that is true. But first you have to get his attention."

The arrest and trial of the thirteen police officers had gotten the undivided attention of every man and woman in the Miami Police Department. In their heart of hearts, they knew something had to be done. Something had to change.

As our new shooting policy was officially issued, we also ordered hundreds of controlled electronic devices (CEDs), commonly referred to as Taser stun guns, to give police officers an alternative to using their firearms. The Taser weapons were critical to the success we ended up having in reducing police shootings my first year in office. If you look at police shootings from city to city, you find that sometimes there is community reaction. For example, two guys armed with guns go in and stick up a liquor store. In the process of making their escape, they wind up being shot and killed by responding police officers. Most of the time, there is no reaction. The average citizen concludes that is the cost of doing business for the robber. However, when you have an emotionally disturbed adult who is very dangerous, armed maybe with a butcher knife or a tree limb, and he gets shot and killed by police, there is often a huge public outcry. Couldn't the police officer just have disarmed the disturbed person without shooting and killing him? the public asks. Couldn't the police officer have just kept a safe distance until the backup unit arrived? In city after city across the United States there are stories of emotionally disturbed people (EDPs) killed by police bullets. Regardless of the fact that EDPs can be quite dangerous, their deaths always cause a public reaction. While we in policing often feel that this criticism is unfair to police officers, we also know that we have to do a much better job of dealing with these situations without having to resort to deadly physical force.

The city of Miami is located in Miami-Dade County. For a variety of reasons—especially the weather—Miami-Dade County has the highest proportion of mentally ill "street people" of any county in America. Some of these street people are not only emotionally disturbed but are also on occasion quite dangerous. They can be armed with a knife, a baseball bat, a tree limb, a two-by-four. However, they are almost never armed with a gun. In street encounters with this population, the Taser weapon is a godsend. It allows the police officer to maintain a safe distance, up to twenty-five feet, and still disarm the dangerous person with a burst of electrical current. In at least three of these situations during my first year in Miami, had the police officer not possessed a Taser, all three of the street people could have been shot.

Another critical component in how we dealt with the EDPs were the Crisis Intervention Teams (CITs). These are specially selected and trained police officers who respond to scenes to handle EDPs, much like trained hostage negotiators respond to hostage situations. Interestingly, the CIT program in Miami is spearheaded by a local criminal court judge, Steve Leifman, who was moved by the number of mentally disturbed individuals who were brought to his court having committed a serious felony, sometimes involving injury. The judge correctly understood that there needed to be a non–law enforcement vehicle for handling these dangerous situations. As a result of his work and dedication in this area, he has received multiple national awards. But for him, knowing that his program has saved even one life is its own reward.

The final and maybe the most critical key to reducing police shootings was the buy-in by the executive staff and also the leadership of the SWAT Unit. Deputy Chief Frank Fernandez had been a SWAT officer for more than a dozen years and had been involved in dozens of situations where deadly physical force could have been used but was not. When someone like Frank Fernandez endorses a more restrictive shooting policy, it carries a great deal of weight. Similarly, the SWAT supervisors, Lieutenant Armando Guzman and Sergeant George Velez, also embraced the reforms.

There was one episode involving Sergeant Velez, captured on live television, which underscored the notion of assuming good defensive tactics that allow an officer that extra half second to make a decision about whether or not to shoot. The incident involved an armed, barricaded subject who was holding hostages. The building was a four-story project with balconies encompassing every floor. As Sergeant Velez took up his defensive position, the armed subject burst from the apartment pointing what appeared to be a revolver at Sergeant Velez and the other responding SWAT members. The subject then quickly ducked back in to the apartment. A half hour later he surrendered.

Reviewing the television tape the next day in my office was quite revealing. When you slow down the video you see the man come out of the apartment and point an object directly at the SWAT officers, as if he were going to shoot. Upon closer examination, the object in the subject's hand was a cell phone. Why he would point this at police officers as if he were going to shoot is anybody's guess. Clearly, the man was distraught, and this could have been a "suicide by cop" attempt. Only this time the cops did not oblige.

As a side note, how many times have I heard or read of a situation in which a police officer shoots a person who he thinks was pointing a gun, only to find out later that the "gun" was, in fact, a cell phone? When the average citizen hears stories like these, they are incredulous. And it is understandable. However, when I viewed the video of the man pointing the cell phone at the SWAT team, it was confounding as to why they didn't shoot.

Around July 2003, as I looked at the various statistics for the first six months of the year, I noticed that no Miami police officer had discharged his or her weapon at another person. This was extraordinary. By November, I began to realize that there was a chance we could finish the year without firing a single shot at a citizen. This was not the result of "depolicing"—that is, the result of officers making fewer arrests, engaging the public in fewer contacts, and being less proactive. In fact, quite the opposite was happening. Police officers were being much more proactive, and arrests were up significantly for the year.

Going into the final week of 2003, the Miami Police Department still had not discharged a single bullet at a citizen. But was that about to change? Reports came over the police radio of a man barricaded in his home, shooting through the window at responding officers. There was a standoff at the scene with SWAT officers assuming defensive positions around the house. I had a chance to speak by phone to the SWAT commander at the scene, Lieutenant Armando Guzman. "How is it going there, Armando?" I inquired. "Things are tense but okay," he replied. "The guy let a few rounds go at us, but nobody's hit, and we're taking it from there." With a mild attempt at gallows humor, I asked Armando, "Is this guy aware of our record?" Armando replied, "I don't think so, Chief. But I am. And I'm going to try to keep the record going." A few hours later, the gunman surrendered peacefully to Lieutenant Guzman and his officers.

We finished the year 2003 without any police officer discharging a single round at a citizen.

In late January 2004, a promotion ceremony was held in the lobby of police headquarters. It was a large ceremony, and there were dozens of family members, including children, in attendance. In my address to the promotees and their families, I spoke about the tremendous job that the men and women of the MPD had done in 2003. I then mentioned the record of no shots fired at a citizen. Family members burst out in wild applause, and I noticed lots of smiles and expanded proud chests from the police officers present. It was one of those special moments in my police career.

In the first couple of months of 2004, the no-shooting streak continued. Police officers spoke openly about the record and embraced it and were proud of it. For the first eight months of 2004, not a single bullet was discharged at a citizen. We had gone a full twenty months, an extraordinary record. In September, Hurricane Charlie hit the city. An armed robber who was obviously impervious to the additional police officers out on the streets during the storm took it upon himself to stick up a grocery store. Nearby police responded, and the armed robber was shot and killed.

Over the next year, there were a handful of additional police shootings, all of which were justified. The department then went another twelve months without discharging a single bullet at a citizen. During the second no-shooting streak, Michael Putney, the senior and most respected political reporter in Miami, made the following observation to me. "Chief, there has been a real cultural change in the Miami Police Department. I have worked in this city for over twenty-five years and I never thought I would see such a change."

The Shenandoah Rapist

In June 2003, the chief of detectives and the commander of the Special Victims Unit briefed me on a case involving the rape of three young girls that had occurred over the course of a week. The girls were eleven, twelve, and thirteen, and the MO left no doubt that the same individual had committed all three of these awful crimes. We immediately began the process of community notification, including a press release and an artist's rendering of the description of the attacker.

When I asked the detective commander if any similar cases were on file, he replied that there were not. I countered with, "If you think this is the first time this guy has hit, you're mistaken." I directed the commander to go back over all of the old cases, especially those involving stranger rapes.

While the review of past rapes was being conducted, we created a Shenandoah Rape Task Force with all available resources dedicated to capturing the individual before he struck again. As the task force detectives followed up leads and conducted their investigation, Deputy Chief Fernandez, Assistant Chief Gallagher, and myself, along with other ranking officers, spent a great deal of time riding the neighborhoods on our police bikes, interviewing and reassuring residents and handing out sketches of the perpetrator.

Meanwhile, detectives went back through all of the old cases of stranger rapes, and if there was DNA evidence available, it was immediately hand delivered to the lab for testing. As a result, we received two additional hits. One was the rape of a seventy-nine-year-old woman that had occurred three months prior to the assaults on the three young girls.

At that time, the MPD's protocol for when and how to test DNA was similar to most other departments' protocols. That is, DNA evidence was often secured but not tested in any regular fashion. The DNA would be tested if someone was in custody and the request was made by the prosecuting attorney to test the DNA in order to strengthen the evidence for the trial. While this protocol seems okay, it misses the central point of DNA testing, especially in stranger rape cases. The idea is to submit all DNA obtained at the scene of a stranger rape. The purpose is not to strengthen some future criminal case, but rather to try to identify the rapist. When you get a second hit on a stranger rape, you know you're dealing with a serial rapist.

I had a sick feeling in my stomach that this was Philadelphia all over again; the Shenandoah rapist had eerie similarities to the Rittenhouse Square rapist. When I was informed of the two latest hits, I directed the detectives to continue going back over old cases, including those from the prior year. There were two more hits. One in September 2002 and another in December 2002. The reviews uncovered at least two other cases in which no DNA evidence had been secured, but there was no doubt it was the same individual. In one of those cases, a seventy-one-year-old woman had been sexually assaulted.

I had spent more than thirty years in policing, and I had never encountered a serial rapist whose victims spanned such an age difference, from eleven to seventy-nine. The case not only shocked the community but also paralyzed with fear many of the female residents within the Shenandoah and Little Havana neighborhoods where the past victims had lived.

The manhunt continued through the summer of 2003. Leads were followed, all with negative results. It was becoming a race against time before the individual struck again. The only two solid facts we had were his DNA profile and his status as a Honduran national. Some of the victims had been Honduran nationals, and the perpetrator had used certain words that were idiomatic. We finally got our first real break, but it was at the expense of another attack.

Over two months had passed since his last attack. One day, in the early afternoon, a young mother was in her backyard hanging laundry. A man approached her and inquired about renting a room in the house next door. As the woman was explaining to the man about the rental, he suddenly grabbed her in a chokehold and attempted to drag her into her house. The woman screamed, and her husband, who was inside, came to her rescue, grabbing the perpetrator in a chokehold. He was in the process of choking the individual when his young daughter appeared and pleaded, "Daddy, Daddy, please let him go. You're going to kill him!" As the father loosened his grip on the perpetrator's neck, the perpetrator bit the husband's forearm, causing a deep laceration. The assailant fled out onto the street and jumped into a double-parked, black car that had the flashing hazard lights on.

The husband ran after the assailant but was unable to catch him. The man sped away through the residential neighborhood. However, the husband had a good description of the assailant as well as of the black getaway car. This new information renewed the spirit of the detectives, who had become somewhat frustrated with the lack of progress. Over the next two weeks the search intensified. We now had a better idea of whom we were looking for and, more important, what type of car he was driving.

Detectives broke the Little Havana neighborhood into a grid, with each detective responsible for a particular section. On a late Friday afternoon, about two weeks after the failed attack, Detective Sergeant William Golding observed a man, acting suspiciously, who fit the description of the rapist in a car that also fit the description. It was a two-way residential street, and the detective observed the man looking down alleyways. As their cars passed each other, the detective made eye contact with the subject. The subject immediately averted his eyes, which every police officer knows is a sign of guilt but which is extremely difficult to explain to a judge in a court of law. It's called "cop instinct." The detective, in his unmarked car, whipped a U-turn and followed the subject in the black car. The subject accelerated the car at one point and blew a stop sign. Game on!

The detective put on his lights and pulled the black car over. As both cars came to a stop, the subject put on his flashing hazard lights. Sergeant Golding had an even stronger feeling this was the right guy because in Miami no one uses hazard lights when double-parking.

The subject was questioned and taken into custody. His DNA sample was immediately sent to the lab for testing, and it confirmed that he was the Shenandoah rapist. I received a phone call from the detectives early that Saturday morning to tell me we had our man in custody. When his identity was confirmed, I immediately notified the mayor, the city manager, and the city commissioners; we scheduled a press conference for one o'clock that afternoon to announce the arrest.

Earlier that morning, along with nineteen other police officers representing the Miami Police Department, I had raced in the Miami Dragon Boat Races held on Biscayne Bay. After receiving the call, I returned to police headquarters, still dressed in my race outfit, and exited my car. As I crossed the parking lot, a detective approached me, stating, "He wants to speak to you." "Who wants to speak to me," I asked. "The rapist," he replied as he pointed to the stairwell of police headquarters. I entered the stairwell to find two other detectives with the handcuffed prisoner. He was about five feet, five inches tall and was sobbing uncontrollably. He apologized profusely, and at one point he indicated to me that he had seen me on television, patrolling on my bike and handing out the police sketch and that he felt awful that he had caused so many headaches and grief. "Can you forgive me, Chief?" he pleaded. I told him, "Only God can forgive you," and continued on to my office to shower, change into my uniform, and prepare for the press conference.

At 1:00 P.M., a large press conference was held at police headquarters to announce the arrest of Reynaldo E. Rapalo, a Honduran national, for the rapes committed in the Shenandoah and Little Havana neighborhoods. Women and young girls of Miami could finally relax knowing that this monster was now behind bars, probably for the rest of his life. They were safe again. Or were they?

Fifteen months later, I received a phone call informing me that Rapalo had escaped from the Miami-Dade Detention Center just west of downtown Miami. It turned out that an ordinary citizen driving past the jail had observed bedsheets tied from end to end, hanging down the side of the building. The citizen, knowing that the hanging sheets were not part of the jail decor, went into the jail reception area and told the clerk, "I think you've got a problem. There are some bedsheets hanging from the side of your building."

When new police officers get sworn in for the first time, I make it a point to speak to them and their families, letting them know that the life of a police officer is anything but normal. While other family members are celebrating a birthday or a baptism, police officers often get called away from these occasions to respond to the call of duty. Other times, such as Christmas and New Year's, while everyone else is having a wonderful time with their families, police officers are scheduled to work. When the Shenandoah rapist escaped a few days before Christmas, I knew that a lot of police officers and detectives and a police chief would not be enjoying Christmas with their families. The second manhunt for the Shenandoah rapist was under way.

With teams of detectives and dozens of police officers in cars and on bikes, we patrolled the streets of Little Havana through the Christmas holidays. It was bizarre, to say the least, especially riding my bike on Christmas Day. A few days later, acting on a citizen's tip, Rapalo was found hiding in a strip of shrubbery on the side of LeJuene Road outside of the Miami city limits. I headed to Miami-Dade police headquarters with Mayor Diaz and Deputy Chief Fernandez to take part in the "presser" announcing Rapalo's rearrest.

Before the press conference, I took the opportunity to go into the room where Rapalo was being held. He immediately recognized me and smiled. But I didn't recognize him. He was slimmer, and his hair was straight where a year earlier it had been curly. I realized that I would never have recognized him had I encountered him on the street during our manhunt. He looked that different. As he was being led from headquarters to an awaiting police car to be taken back to jail, he smiled radiantly at the news cameras, as if he didn't have a care in the world, fully enjoying the fact that at that moment he was the center of everyone's universe.

A little over a year later, Rapalo went to trial and was convicted of all charges. When the first guilty charge was announced by the jury foreman, the lead detective on the case, Fernando Bosch, who had spent over two years of his life chasing Rapalo, closed his eyes and clasped his hands as if to thank God for justice rendered. As each successive count was announced with a corresponding guilty finding, tears rolled down Detective Bosch's face as his emotions clearly got the best of him.

At the defendant's table, Rapalo sat there in his chair with a smirk on his face. When the first guilty charge was announced, the smirk became a grin. As each successive guilty finding was announced, his grin became a full-toothed smile. Once again, Rapalo was the center of the universe. The juxtaposition of emotions was confounding. Normally, you would expect the case detective to be grinning and happy with the conviction. Similarly, you would expect the defendant to slump in his chair, head down, tears rolling down the sides of his face. But not in this case.

From the time he was recaptured after his escape, up to and including the trial, Rapalo had an almost constant grin on his face. He clearly enjoyed the attention that he was receiving. He had taken Andy Warhol's fifteen minutes and stretched it to fifteen months. The question for me remained, What about the Rapalo I had first met the day after his original arrest? What about the tears streaming down his face and his plea for forgiveness? The textbooks indicate that the sociopath is capable of displaying these wide-ranging emotions convincingly. It is my sense that the original Rapalo I met was a phony. The real Rapalo was the one with the evil grin, laughing at the world and sucking up all of the attention.

When the detectives were going back over the old stranger rape cases, that laborious process underscored the need to have a policy in place that requires the case detective to hand-deliver all DNA evidence in stranger rape cases directly to the lab. Similar to Philadelphia, DNA testing of a stranger rapes became mandatory. Had this been the existing practice prior to my arrival, the MPD would have known that it had a serial rapist on its hands the same month I was being interviewed by Mayor Manny Diaz to become the new Miami police chief.

Even today, there are tens of thousands of untested rape kits and other DNA samples that hold the identity of serial rapists across the nation. Clearly, there is a need for funding, especially federal funding, to fully take advantage of forensic technology. But there is also an obligation to manage the workload. For example, are we collecting too much DNA, especially in property crimes, where there is almost no possibility of that DNA ever being tested? Are we creating our own backlogs by overcollecting? Are our policies and practices too focused on collection and not enough on prioritization? Should testing be idiosyncratic, based on the initiative or lack of initiative of the case detective? Or should policies and procedures clearly delineate what is a priority and what must be tested, even down to the description of what tasks the case detective must perform (hand delivery of DNA evidence to the lab)?

Finally, the CompStat process, where both commanders and detectives are present, is a perfect venue to check and verify that policies are, in fact, being adhered to. At every MPD CompStat, the commander of the Special Victims Unit is questioned regarding any stranger rapes or stranger sexual batteries that have occurred in the prior reporting period. If a DNA sample has been obtained on a stranger rape, you can be sure that the commander will indicate that the DNA sample was hand delivered by the case detective to the lab.

An interesting side note. When I first became the chief of the Miami Police Department, I attended a CompStat meeting. I did not ask any questions for the first two hours but just listened and observed. Toward the end of the session, the lieutenant in charge of the Homicide Unit reported on a homicide that had occurred in the Overtown neighborhood. I decided to ask a few questions because two weeks earlier I had a meeting with federal Alcohol, Tobacco, Firearms, and Explosives (ATF) officials that gave me some concern. I asked the lieutenant, "Did we recover any ballistic evidence at the scene?" He replied in the affirmative. I asked, "Did we submit the bullet casings to the ATF IBIS system?" (The IBIS system checks the "fingerprints" of bullet casings and looks for matches nationwide.) The lieutenant replied that the detective whose job it was to make these submissions was sitting next to him. He introduced the detective, whom I asked, "Did you submit the casings to IBIS for testing?" "Yes," he assured me. "We do that in all cases," he said, with a patronizing air. "Really," I replied. "That's interesting. I had a meeting with ATF officials last week, and they complained that you hadn't submitted anything since last August."

The room became silent. Eyes were cast downward toward the floor. The embarrassed detective said something to the effect that he would "check on that." Angel, my executive assistant, said later that the message had gone quickly through the department after that CompStat meeting not to lie to Timoney because he already knew the answers before he asked the question. Not a bad message.

14

Free Trade, Free Speech, and the Politics of Policing

Chief, I understand that there is talk of a "blue flu" among the officers. That they think you are taking this thing too lightly.

—MIKE KIRSCH, TELEVISION REPORTER

As a police chief you will sometimes hear allegations made about you and motives ascribed to you that will leave you scratching your head. In February 2003, I became aware that the Free Trade Association of the Americas (FTAA) was going to hold a meeting in Miami that coming November. I may have heard of the FTAA before that, although I honestly can't remember. The reason why it is important to put a date to when we began security preparations is because of some of the outlandish allegations that were made after the event was over—to wit, that John Timoney was hired specifically to handle the FTAA meeting. Some even opined that I would be leaving Miami directly after the FTAA meeting had concluded. The fact that the FTAA meeting never came up in any of our conversations during my interview with Mayor Diaz is just that: a fact. As John Miller, the famed reporter and good friend, often said, "Never let a fact get in the way of a good story."

Policing an event like the FTAA meeting is similar in many respects to policing a political convention. It requires a significant number of police officers, both in uniform and plainclothes. This had not been an issue for me in New York and Philadelphia, because both of those departments are big enough that I could peel off a few thousand officers without shutting down the rest of the department. There may be five or six police departments in the United States that can supervise these big events without relying on assistance from outside police departments. All other departments will require the assistance of outside agencies under the concept of "mutual aid."

Sometimes, however, mutual aid can become mutual destruction. The World Trade Organization (WTO) meeting in Seattle in December 1999 underscores this notion. About two thousand hard-core violent protestors, sometimes referred to as anarchists, infiltrated fifty thousand peaceful union protestors. The ensuing melee between police and protestors was captured on national television, and the resulting blowback cost the Seattle police chief his job. When you view some of the ugly video footage of police officers mixing it up with protestors, you assume you are watching Seattle police officers. However, many of those police officers were not city of Seattle officers, but rather officers from surrounding jurisdictions who had come to help under the auspices of mutual aid. Some help. So policing the FTAA meeting in Miami was going to be something new for me: I had never had to rely on outside help for any large event in New York City and Philadelphia.

The policing of the FTAA meeting was made more challenging by three other factors. First, the WTO meeting in Seattle had alerted police departments hosting big events that, in addition to regular protestors and demonstrators, also present would be so-called anarchists, whose sole goal, it appeared, was to disrupt the event and cause as much property damage as possible. Property damage in the anarchists' twisted thinking is not a crime. Second, in a post-9/11 world, all large events provide an opportunity for terrorists to make a statement. While planning the 1992 Democratic convention in New York and the 2000 Republican convention in Philadelphia, terrorism had been a backburner issue. For the FTAA meeting, however, it was front and center. Third, the FTAA was the first event of this nature after the establishment of the Department of Homeland Security in the spring of 2003. Therefore, any national security event, such as the FTAA meeting, would require working closely with Homeland Security and some of the units under that department, including the U.S. Coast Guard.

In late February, I designated Deputy Chief Frank Fernandez the overall security coordinator of the FTAA meeting. Frank had a great deal of experience in handling demonstrations, and he was obviously familiar with the notion of mutual aid, having participated on both sides, sometimes as a member of the agency receiving aid, sometimes as a member providing aid. Frank put together a top-notch team that included Captain Tom Cannon, who would be the overall incident commander for the four-day event. Major Adam Burden commanded all of the special operations units, while Lieutenant Armando Guzman headed up the SWAT detail. Major Juanita Walker and Lieutenant Steve Caceres handled all of the community-relations aspects of the event. Major Tom Roehl and George Wysong, a legal adviser, handled much of the contentious negotiations between the city and groups looking to protest. Other commanders were responsible for logistics, intelligence, and various operational support functions.

By September, the planning and training for this event had begun to take form. Deputy Chief Fernandez and his team briefed me on a regular basis, and a good security plan appeared to be in place. As expected, more than two dozen mutual aid agreements were drawn up and signed with outside agencies. I had only a few concerns going into the event.

When planning to police these large events, it's imperative that the top command understands their dynamic and ever-changing nature. Over the past decade, I had noticed a change in how the media covered the protests surrounding these events. I was also aware that these events increasingly became entangled in the tentacles of the legal community.

The Tompkins Square Park Riot in New York in 1988 was the first time in my experience where handheld video cameras became an accessory of the people engaged in civil disobedience and other forms of unlawful behavior. The graphic footage from these cameras provided great fodder for local television stations' newscasts. It also provided entrepreneurial lawyers with great leverage in their attempts to extract justice, in the form of U.S. currency, for their clients. Over the next decade, these handheld cameras were augmented with the advent of cell phone cameras. Beginning with the Rodney King incident, video footage of egregious police misconduct became a staple on the evening news. With the advent of twenty-four-hour cable news stations, the footage was not only more valuable, but actively and aggressively sought by the various networks: hearing their nightly plea for anyone with any footage of an event to please submit it became commonplace. Recently, with the advent of YouTube, video footage and its outlets seem boundless.

The WTO fiasco in Seattle in 1999 and my experience at the Republican National Convention in Philadelphia in 2000 had led me to think about these large security events. My conclusion is that these events have three parts. If you were to view the event as a game, there would be a pregame plan, a game plan, and a postgame plan. Traditionally, in handling these events, police departments have focused almost all of their attention on their pregame and game plans, with little regard for the postgame plan. The pregame plan involves the planning, training, and logistics preparation for the event. The game plan is the event itself: how demonstrations are handled and how arrests are effected. The postgame plan involves two institutions outside the influence of the police: the media and the legal community. I believe that the postgame plan has become the most important part. The planning for the event may take a month or six months. The event itself may be a day or four days. But the postgame plan goes on and on and on. Six years after an event, a police official will find himself sitting across the table from a lawyer, answering questions about minutiae regarding what may or may not have happened on a certain corner at a certain hour.

The role of the legal community is perhaps understandable even though it continues forever. The media, however, is an entirely different animal. It is entirely possible that the police official and his department will receive positive reviews as the events are occurring. The department will be praised for its bravery and restraint under great provocation and duress. About a week or two after the event, the tone

will start to change. "Maybe those guys weren't so great. You know, I
think I saw a police officer use his nightstick. And why did they have
to arrest that poor old woman who happened to get in the middle of
all of those bad boys?" And so it goes. If you compare a newspaper account from the day after an event with one a month after, you would
think the reporter was writing about two different incidents. If you
ask reporters about the difference in the coverage, they will reply with
something about their "watchdog role." I like to remind them that it
sounds more like their "lapdog role," in that they lap up everything
that they are told.

To deal with an event's postgame plan, police departments need to
keep impeccable records, including their own video footage of what
transpired. You will spend the rest of your days on the postgame plan,
so your records must document every action and every decision made
throughout. This is necessary, first, to prevent embarrassment, and
second, to mitigate the monetary damage that the city may suffer if a
ruling or a finding goes against the department.

The pregame plan, the game plan, and the postgame plan are not
limited to the police. The so-called anarchists have *their* own plan. They
train in how to provoke a police officer on the front lines. They train in
how to engage in "un-arrest tactics" designed to assist in freeing one
of their arrested colleagues from police custody. And, of course, they
train in how to take the best video shots of police officers looking their
worst. Finally, when arrested, they train not to cooperate with authorities, not to give their name, date of birth, or home address. The motive
here is clearly aimed at clogging the criminal justice system. They then
document this for their postgame plan when they sit down with their
lawyers to sue the city for false arrest and spending three days in jail,
disregarding the fact that they could have spent three hours in jail had
they only identified themselves.

Another major concern had to do with the personal appearance of
police officers and the rules of engagement concerning necessary force.
You quickly find out that under a mutual aid agreement there is only so
much the requesting chief can demand or expect. I wanted to ensure
that police officers reporting for duty did not turn out in their personal

protective gear from the outset. I thought it was important from a PR perspective that it not look like we were preparing for battle. I also understood the necessity of having that gear available in the event that a demonstration turned ugly and violent. I was not about to advocate that police officers take unnecessary risks just for PR value.

The rules of engagement regarding necessary force were also a sensitive matter. I had handled many demonstrations in my career and had been involved in serious, violent confrontations. However, I had never been in a situation where tear gas was used. The use of tear gas in the NYPD is a last, last resort. Some view it, myself included, as a sign that things are out of control. I met personally with some of the chiefs who would be participating in the FTAA event, including Carlos Alvarez, the director of the Miami-Dade Police Department, and Sheriff Ken Jenne of the Broward County Sheriff's Office. There was absolutely no disagreement on the rules of engagement and the appropriate posture for this event. I felt quite positive as a result of these meetings as we headed into the final month before the FTAA meeting.

Just because somebody at the top feels good doesn't necessarily guarantee that this good feeling will be transmitted to those at the bottom. About two weeks before the FTAA meeting, a local television reporter, Mike Kirsch, came to my office to interview me regarding the upcoming event. Before the formal interview began, he asked me to view some raw video footage and interviews that he had conducted in New Orleans with a group of anarchists. The anarchists who were interviewed would give some of the most despicable movie characters a run for their money. Their language would make a sailor blush. It even made me blush, and I'm no shrinking violet. The bottom line was that these characters, and one in particular, who pointed into the camera with his warning, were coming to Miami to kick Timoney's ass and the collective ass of all of his cops. The reporter then interviewed me, trying to get my reaction to the provocative taunts. I had no reaction. However, the reporter did get a rise out of me when he suggested that some of my police officers were talking about engaging in the "blue flu"—a work slowdown—because they felt that Chief Timoney was not taking the potential violence seriously enough and was looking to downplay what was, in their opinion, sure to take place. My response was the truth. I would never take action or not take action that would jeopardize the safety of my police officers.

Many businesses and institutions, including the federal courts, announced that they would not be open for business during the week of the FTAA meeting. I found this a little surprising, since I personally had gone to numerous meetings with different members of the business community to share with them our plan for policing the event and the resulting traffic disruptions they might face. However, I reassured all of them that their safety would not be in jeopardy and that there was no need to panic. Not only did I deliver this message, but my downtown commander, Willie Alvarez, also went to additional groups and gave the same reassurances.

Unfortunately, there was an outside force at work that not Timoney, Fernandez, or Alverez could counter: the media. Day after day and night after night, the local television news networks aired videos of violent confrontations between police and protestors at prior economic summits—in Davos, Switzerland, Cancún, Mexico, Seattle, Washington, and other such exotic locations. The not-so-subliminal message was quite clear: Armageddon was right around the corner. As if the weekday newscasts weren't bad enough, the Sunday morning talk programs got into the act. I took part in a television panel with two other civic leaders discussing the upcoming event. For almost the entire half hour of the program, as we spoke, our faces were not shown. Instead, it was Timoney's voice-over, with the ugly scenes of protest from Davos, Cancún, and Seattle. If a picture is worth a thousand words, it is my sense that these ugly videos more than overshadowed Timoney's attempt to get everyone to calm down.

As we drew closer to the event, I went to many roll calls and training sessions, once again reassuring police officers that things would be fine, that we had a good plan in place, and that we had the proper leadership to implement those plans. Not once did I ever get a sense of uneasiness on the part of officers. They appeared ready for the task at hand and also seemed to appreciate the nuance involved in not appearing overly militaristic.

Monday was the first day of the FTAA meetings, and no trouble was expected. At 7:00 A.M., I met Mayor Diaz for coffee at the Hyatt Hotel, which was outside the "frozen zone." The zone had been created around the main location where the FTAA meeting was being held—the Intercontinental Hotel—with ten-foot fencing encompassing the entire hotel and some of the surrounding streets. Only properly credentialed persons could enter the frozen zone. When the mayor and I finished our coffee, we walked outside the Hyatt to get a breath of fresh air. A field force of thirty police officers from a nearby jurisdiction arrived at the Hyatt to assume their duties just as we exited the hotel. The police officers then began to don their personal protective gear. I was a little surprised by their actions since we weren't expecting trouble, and I knew people would use this as an opportunity to portray the police as unnecessarily provocative. I had a short conversation with the captain of the field force, and he understood perfectly the image we were trying to portray.

This incident, although minor in nature, underscores the difficulty of policing major events by use of mutual aid. Mutual aid is just that: aid. The requesting agency doesn't get to demand the top ten police officers from each assisting agency. It doesn't get to dictate the attire that the officers will wear or the equipment they will carry. As the chief of the Miami Police Department, I had the ability to impose discipline on any member of the MPD who didn't follow orders or directions. I had absolutely no authority over a police officer from an outside agency, even if he was policing an event within the jurisdiction of the city of Miami and under the auspices of a mutual aid agreement. Thus, there are limits to the efficacy and effectiveness of mutual aid agreements. Some, especially in the legal community, will argue that when an outside agency enters into a mutual aid agreement, that agency subjects its officers to the rules and regulations, protocols, and policies of the lead agency. While that may be a nice sound bite or argument in a lawsuit, in reality it's specious.

I was fully confident that our police officers would perform with great professionalism and restraint. I was so confident that I had created an embedded media strategy whereby local print and television reporters were to be included with various units to give them a bird's-eye view of the events as they unfolded. Two were even embedded with the bicycle squads, which included Deputy Chief Fernandez, Assistant Chief John Gallagher, and me.

Monday and Tuesday, the first two days of the FTAA meeting, were uneventful. On Wednesday, the head of the American Federation of Labor and the Congress of Industrial Organization (AFL-CIO), John Sweeney, came to Miami and held a meeting and rally at the Guzman Theater downtown. After the meeting, he led a group of about two thousand union members on a march from the theater to the Bayfront Park Amphitheater, where his union would hold a huge rally the next day with an expected crowd numbering in the tens of thousands. Mayor Diaz and I escorted Sweeney and his group to the amphitheater. I had known Sweeney during my New York days, and, in fact, we had both graduated from the same high school, Cardinal Hayes in the South Bronx. Sweeney and his union colleagues indicated to us that they were quite pleased with the planning and preparation for the event. He went out of his way to say nice things about his fellow Hayesman. That sentiment wouldn't last twenty-four hours.

Later that night, a rally was held at the amphitheater. Speaker after speaker railed against the FTAA. The rally was well attended and peaceful. However, at the end, an individual took the stage and informed the crowd that a "direct action" was planned for the next day. He invited everyone to attend. It was understood that the "direct action" in question would be an attempt to tear down the security fence surrounding the Intercontinental Hotel, as had been done at prior meetings of this type.

At 7:00 A.M. Thursday, two separate protest groups numbering about nine hundred people in total assembled in different parts of the city. One group met at the county office building downtown, while the other group emerged from a convergence center or safe house in Overtown. The Overtown group marched north, then east to Biscayne Boulevard, obstructing morning traffic in the process. Eventually, this group met up with the group from the county office building. The larger group then marched east on Flagler Street, its destination being the security fence on Biscayne Boulevard. Numerous skirmishes with police took place along the way, and some arrests were made. When members the group reached the fence, they attempted to pull it over using grappling hooks. They were defeated in their efforts by the Miami police field forces. This was not the end but rather the beginning of a long day of cat and mouse/assault and response.

The union rally to be held at Bayfront Park would begin with dozens of buses discharging their passengers at the park. These logistics had been worked out weeks prior to the event. However, the actions of the violent protestors that morning impeded the ability to get all of the buses to the amphitheater, and unfortunately some elderly union members had to disembark from their buses a few blocks away and walk to the amphitheater.

The AFL-CIO eventually held its rally and then marched through the city streets, although the length of the march was shortened by the AFL-CIO leadership as a result of the violence committed by the anarchists. At around 2:00 P.M., as I stood by the grassy knoll next to Bayfront Park, I noticed a young man and woman, part of the group that had conducted the violent demonstrations earlier, now picking up garbage, including empty bottles and cans, and placing them in large, green plastic bags. It was obvious to me that this garbage was to be used against police officers, but there was little we could do at that point. Any action taken by police against these two could have led to the charge that the Miami police were so bad, they wouldn't even allow environmentally conscious youngsters to help clean the park of debris.

About a half hour later, my cop instincts were proved correct when the same two environmentally conscious twentysomethings used the garbage they had collected to start a huge bonfire in the middle of Biscayne Boulevard. A civilian passing the bonfire attempted to extinguish it and was assaulted and knocked to the ground for his civic effort. At this point, it became clear that this crowd was quickly getting out of hand and needed to be removed from the boulevard. Over the next few hours, police field forces methodically attempted to move the crowd of a couple hundred people off the boulevard to prevent further violence. Every police warning was met with the crowd throwing objects and missiles. There were dozens of arrests, and eventually calm was restored. Within twenty-four hours of the end of the FTAA meeting, charges of police brutality and other acts of misconduct were levied against the Miami Police Department and its law enforcement partners.

Within days, the AFL-CIO filed a series of lawsuits. It was their contention that the Miami Police Department either refused to allow busloads of union members to drive onto Biscayne Boulevard or actually directed them north on I-95 toward Orlando. They also sued the MPD for not allowing the peaceful union protestors who were inside the Bayfront Park Amphitheater to leave after the rally. They neglected to point out that there was a riot outside and that the union folks could have been injured. In fairness, some legitimate lawsuits were filed on behalf of individuals who may have received injuries at the hands of the police while the officers made use of their less-than-lethal weapons to disperse the violent crowd outside the amphitheater. In one instance, a photographer who was just trying to do his job was accidentally struck on the side of one of his eyes, causing a serious injury. A few days later, Deputy Chief Frank Fernandez, Assistant Chief John Gallagher, and I went to his office and apologized to him. I assured him it had been an accident, but I also let him know that I understood he would sue us and that there were no hard feelings.

There is a great deal of irony involved in these demonstrations and protests. There is a bit of a game afoot. You can't prove it, but it's there. A local reporter confirmed this in a conversation with me the week of the FTAA meeting. He said, "Do you think we [the press] would be here just to cover the lawful protest of the union members of the ALF-CIO? They have no drawing power. We're here because of the anarchists. Because we know they'll engage in outrageous and illegal behavior that will provide good footage for the six o'clock news." The bottom line is that the anarchists need the peaceful protestors, and in a perverse way the peaceful protestors need the anarchists. That's how you draw attention to your cause.

A few months later, amid all the allegations and threatened lawsuits, Deputy Chief Fernandez seemed exasperated. He pointed out all of the efforts we had made to ensure that the police officers were properly trained and how we had emphasized restraint and patience and professionalism. Yet, Frank pointed out, the MPD was still criticized. "I understand, Frank," I replied. "But imagine what we would be dealing with now if we had not have taken all of those precautionary steps. Unfortunately, it's the zeitgeist."

A Clean Bill of Health from the Feds

In the early spring of 2003, Alex Acosta, the head of the Justice Department's Civil Rights Division, and a team of investigators met in my office with Deputy Chief Fernandez, Assistant Chief Gallagher, and me. Acosta had assembled the team as a result of a letter from Mayor Diaz in 2002 requesting a federal civil rights investigation of the MPD. The team laid out a series of concerns that they would be looking into over the next few years. The concerns revolved around police misconduct, police corruption, police use of force, and other similar issues that John Gallagher and I had already tackled, as a result of the consent decree, back in Philadelphia. The meeting was very positive, and it was clear that the posture of the Justice Department was one of facilitating change. I never felt for a moment that the Justice Department was coming in to make unreasonable demands or attempting to garner cheap headlines, as some have alleged has occurred in other cities.

At the end of the meeting, I assured Acosta that he and I were in total agreement that reforms needed to take place within the MPD and that affirmative steps had already been taken to address some of his concerns. I pointed out the new police shooting policy, which, as best as I can determine, was the most restrictive shooting policy in the nation.

Over the next two years, under the leadership of Deputy Chief Fernandez and Assistant Chief John Gallagher, new policies and procedures were developed to deal with the concerns of the Justice Department. For example, Internal Affairs would now be leading the investigation into all police shootings. The record-setting reduction in police shootings, including the twenty-month span during which time not a single bullet was discharged at a citizen, received the most media attention. What didn't receive nearly as much attention was the dramatic decrease in police dog bites.

Someone once joked, "Timoney, you may be able to get your cops to shoot less, but can you get your dogs to bite less?" The short answer was yes. In 2002, the year that Mayor Diaz wrote his letter to the Justice Department, sixty-eight people were bitten by Miami police dogs. In 2003, that number was reduced to forty. It was reduced further to twenty-six in 2004, then to twenty-four in 2005, just as the Justice Department was concluding its investigation. In each of the past three, there have been fewer than twenty dog bites.

A more aggressive drug-testing policy was implemented to ensure that police officers remained drug free. Within two years of the new policy, six police officers were terminated for failure of a drug test or refusal to submit to a drug test. In addition, we created the first-ever comprehensive program for identifying poor performers, officers demonstrating disciplinary problems, and officers with "fitness for duty" issues. One of the most effective deterrents was a test Deputy Chief Fernandez created for police officers with misconduct and other bad behavior. He also devised a Supervisor Accountability Program, which required a patrol supervisor to respond to any scene and put himself/herself "in command," then radio in and report the same.

This proved to be a very effective tool in holding supervisors accountable and also letting officers know that a supervisor was on the scene and in charge. I made it a point to let every single sergeant know that, if something went wrong at an incident or scene, my first question would be directed to the supervisor. If the police officer has done something wrong, I will deal with that later. But first I want to know what the supervisor did.

It is heartening to listen to the police radio and hear supervisors getting to a scene in a hurry and immediately getting on the air with their car number and the statement, "In command." In those few incidents when a supervisor doesn't notify police radio that he or she is in command, the police radio dispatcher immediately attempts to raise the supervisor on the air. If that fails, the ranking officer at police communications is notified. This seemingly minor change has had a profound impact on how scenes or incidents are managed. It has significantly reduced the number of incidents that can go awry when there is no supervisor present to give guidance and direction, especially to younger officers.

In February 2006, three years after the Justice Department began its investigation into the MPD, the department closed its investigation, stating that all of the its concerns, which were laid out in early 2003, had been addressed. The department commended the "leaders and the men and women of the Miami Police Department for the many improvements the MPD, specifically under your direction, had made to its use of force policies over the course of our investigation." In a telephone conversation regarding this letter, Shanetta Cutlar, chief of the Special Litigation Section of the Department of Justice, informed me that the Miami Police Department was the first police department in the nation to get a full clean bill of health from the Civil Rights Division of the U.S. Department of Justice.

While we had made great strides in reforming the department in many areas, we also had great success in fighting crime and in improving the quality of life for the citizens of Miami. Crime was reduced every year beginning in 2003, with homicides reaching a low not seen since the mid-1960s. There was an increased appreciation of the work done by the police officers of the MPD, and police-community tensions reduced considerably. The men and women of the department felt rightfully proud of their efforts. They were finally receiving positive press for their actions, as opposed to the daily bashing for missteps that had become seemingly de rigueur.

The Benefits of a Vote of No Confidence

As the reputation of the Miami Police Department improved, it gained national attention, and requests for assistance and guidance came from all quarters, including other police departments in the United States and abroad. It was a very good feeling for all involved that the department was being held in such high esteem and was being viewed as a model to be emulated. The success in Miami resulted in requests for members of my team and me to travel overseas to explain how the MPD had achieved its reforms and accomplishments.

At one point, Jeb Bush, the governor of Florida, requested that I take a team of Miami police officials to Haiti to see if we could assist the interim government in its policing efforts. We produced a report with some of our findings and recommendations that was submitted to Governor Bush and to the commanding officer of Southern Command (SouthCom), General John Craddock. A short time later, I returned to Haiti with General Craddock to meet with the interim president, Gérard Latortue, to see how we could advance our recommendations.

A few months later, General Craddock asked me if I would accompany him and a group of U.S. senators to Guantánamo Bay, Cuba, to look at the prison conditions for the more than four hundred suspected terrorists who were detained there. My executive assistant, Angel Calzadilla, accompanied me on this trip. Republican senators Chuck Hagel of Nebraska and Pat Roberts of Kansas were part of the delegation as well. This mission was an eye-opener. The squalid camp conditions depicted in some press reports were not so squalid. At one point during our tour of the prison, after visiting the medical facilities, Senator Roberts opined wryly, "These prisoners have better medical care than almost everyone in the state of Kansas." A week later, Deputy Chief Fernandez accompanied Democratic senator Ted Kennedy and other senators on a similar mission to "Gitmo."

The following year the U.S. Senate established the Jones Commission, whose task was to travel to Iraq and report on the military progress of Operation Iraqi Freedom and the progress of the Iraqi police forces. The commission was headed by retired four-star general Jim Jones, the former Marine commandant. There were a total of twenty members of the commission, fifteen military and five police. I was a member of the police fact-finding team, which also included Chuck Ramsey, the retired Washington, D.C., police chief who would chair the police group in Iraq; Terry Gainer, the former head of the Capitol Police and now the Senate sergeant at arms; Assistant Chief Constable Duncan McAlister, from the Police Service of Northern Ireland; and

Mike Heidingsfield, retired chief of police of the Scottsdale Police Department and colonel in the Air Force Reserves.

On returning from Iraq after spending more than a week touring that nation, one quite naturally reflects on how fortunate we Americans are to live in this country, free of the violence and carnage that plague that war-torn nation. Looking closer to home, I realized how fortunate we were in Miami to have a high-performance police department, with little or no obvious problems. Or so I thought. While things appeared to be running smoothly within the MPD and the city, there were some who were looking to disrupt the calm.

About two weeks after I returned from Iraq in August 2007, I received an inquiry from a local reporter regarding the Lexus SUV I had been driving. It was clear from the questions that the reporter believed he had a hot story about the chief of police getting free use of a Lexus SUV.

I had been a Lexus owner since 2002, when I worked in the private sector in New York. When the three-year lease on my New York car was up, I leased another Lexus from a dealership outside the city of Miami. The owner of the Lexus dealership was an Irish American guy from New York whom I had become friends with through a mutual friend, a retired NYPD lieutenant. One day the dealership owner called me and said that the Lexus Corporation was providing new hybrid SUVs for promotional trials to some customers, and also to some noncustomers in the Miami area. At least two other high-profile individuals, along with other friends of the dealership owner, would be receiving the cars.

I drove the car on a regular basis, including to work every day. It was no secret within the department that I was driving the Lexus SUV. I never thought I was doing something wrong since I was a Lexus customer and I was paying my monthly lease fees. At one point, I had attempted to make arrangements to return the vehicle to the dealership, but the manager at the Lexus dealership, upon finding the low mileage I had accumulated, laughed and told me I hadn't even given the hybrid a proper breaking in. The mileage was low because police headquarters was less than two miles from my residence. Nonetheless, I should have returned the car at that time. Being careless, I continued to drive the SUV in lieu of my original leased vehicle.

When the reporter submitted his questions about the car to the MPD's Public Information Office, the commanding officer came into my office with the police department's legal adviser, which was standard protocol. I explained to them that I had an existing lease with the Lexus dealership. In fact, I showed the lease to the lieutenant so that he could feel comfortable in telling the reporter that he had actually seen it. While I knew this was not going to be a good news story, I was completely unprepared for the reaction and the spin on the story. The reporter went on television that night and indicated that I initially denied having the car, which was completely untrue. He made no mention of the fact that I had a current lease with the Lexus dealership.

Once the story hit the airwaves, it generated interest from other media outlets, including the *Miami Herald*. The story had "legs," as they say. I immediately requested an opinion from the Miami-Dade Ethics Commission regarding any violation I may have committed. I then purchased the SUV for its full showroom sticker value. Additionally, I calculated "the benefit" I received from driving the SUV instead of my leased Lexus sedan. It came to $3,900. I then wrote three checks to three different charities for a total of $4,500 to cover this "benefit." The next day I wrote a letter to the *Miami Herald*, in which I apologized to the citizens of Miami and to the men and women of the Miami Police Department for my stupid, careless mistake. But the maelstrom was far from over.

A police officer got word to me that the Lexus fiasco had been orchestrated by the police union (the FOP), which had leaked the story. The union's goal was twofold: First, it wanted to get rid of Chief Timoney. Second, it wanted to ensure that Deputy Chief Frank Fernandez did not become the next chief of the MPD. My source further indicated that the police union was going to issue a vote of no confidence at its next meeting, only a few days away. The vote would be against both Deputy Chief Frank Fernandez and me. It appeared their main gripe was that the discipline we had issued over the past few years had been too onerous.

I was quite taken aback by the actions of the FOP. I had certainly had a very good relationship with the former union president, who had been there for my first three years in office. I assumed I had a good relationship with the new president, because Deputy Chief Fernandez had worked very closely with him and his team during the union contract negotiations with the city. Deputy Chief Fernandez was my representative at these meetings, and on numerous occasions the union had begged him for his assistance, which Deputy Chief Fernandez graciously gave, and I concurred. In fact, prior to the contract negotiations, I had had numerous conversations with the mayor and the city manager at which I stressed the importance of the officers' receiving a good contract and benefit enhancements, including additional compensation for formal education achievements. When the contract was finally signed, it made Miami police officers among the top-paid police officers in the state of Florida. A Miami officer's starting salary is around $44,000 per year, and a five-year veteran is paid around $65,000 annually.

As we tried to piece together a timeline for these events, it appeared that the FOP had hatched its plan when I was in Iraq with the Jones Commission. I could recall having only one negative interaction with the FOP. That was when the current union president, Armando Aguilar, came to my office for his first and only visit. He requested that I not fire a police officer who was a friend of his and who had been caught shoplifting at a local department store. Obviously, the FOP president was not happy with my decision.

About a week after the vote of no confidence, the FOP held another press conference. This time the union alleged that the NET commanders were forcing police officers to downgrade crime. For example, they alleged that robberies were reduced to larcenies, and burglaries were reduced to vandalisms. They were not the first police union to make such an accusation. It has happened quite often in different departments across the nation. I had prior information that the FOP was going to make those allegations, so even before their press conference was held, I wrote a letter to the Florida Department of Law Enforcement (FDLE) requesting an audit of our crime statistics by either their experts or the experts at the Uniform Crime Reporting (UCR) section of the FBI.

Not to be outdone by Timoney, the union then demanded that the FDLE conduct a criminal investigation into the downgrading of crime. The union maintained that thousands of crimes were not being recorded as crimes but were being recorded as "noncrimes," listed for the purpose of "information." For example, a wife who called the police to complain that her husband had taken the car and had not come back would be reported by the responding officer as an "information" report. A stolen car report would not be prepared, nor would a nationwide alarm be transmitted.

Six months later, the FBI completed its audit and found that the MPD was over 99 percent compliant with UCR standards. This was well above the national standards for compliance in this area and a complete vindication for my team and me and, for that matter, for every man and woman in the MPD. Sadly, the union had effectively charged that its own members were intentionally downgrading crime, which is a crime in itself.

At one point after the vote of no confidence, a reporter asked me my feeling about the vote. Votes of no confidence had become a ploy by police unions across the United States to undermine sitting chiefs. Many chiefs had received votes of no confidence, and none had ever lost his or her job as a result. Actually, if you thought about it rationally, a vote of no confidence by a union almost guarantees that a chief will remain in office, at least in the short term. No mayor or city manager is going to succumb to the mob mentality involved in a vote of no confidence. In a perverse sense, the vote should really be titled the Guaranteed Employment Act for Chiefs. Many chiefs joke that if you haven't received a vote of no confidence, you haven't been doing your job.

Nonetheless, I wanted to answer the reporter's question, and I replied, "The only vote of confidence I need is that of Mayor Manny Diaz. He is the reason I am here, and he is the reason I stay." Just to be sure, I called Mayor Diaz, and Deputy Chief Fernandez and I met him at a television station as he was finishing an interview. The three of us rode together in Deputy Chief Fernandez's car, and I asked the mayor straightforwardly, "Do you still have confidence in Deputy Chief Fernandez and me?" Without hesitation, the mayor replied, "You both have my full confidence and backing." The city manager at the time was Pete Hernández, who had succeeded the former city manager, Joe Arriola. Pete had been in the position less than a year, but he, too, indicated his strong support for Deputy Chief Fernandez and me.

In July 2009, after almost two years of a criminal investigation involving more than 150 police officers and thousands of hours of testimony, the FDLE submitted its final report responding to the allegations of the downgrading of crime. It found no evidence whatsoever that even one police officer had behaved in such a manner. Upon reading the report, I realized how utterly ridiculous the FOP charges were. For example, they alleged, "Chief Timoney never attends CompStat meetings." However, they also alleged that I put too much pressure on commanders during CompStat meetings. The bottom line is that I have never missed a CompStat meeting; in fact, I actually rearrange the scheduling of CompStat meetings to fit my busy schedule. And finally, I have never put pressure on any person to fudge the crime numbers. I am and always have been opposed to quotas. My philosophy is quite simple: work hard, and the numbers will take care of themselves.

I had mentioned earlier that I have learned more from my mistakes than I ever have from my successes. That doesn't mean mistakes are good. Mistakes are bad, but they do teach. The Miami-Dade Ethics Commission conducted its investigation and ruled that there was nothing illegal about my use of the Lexus. The commission pointed out that there was no quid pro quo and that the dealership had no business with the city of Miami and, in fact, that the dealership was located outside of the jurisdiction of the city of Miami. However, the use of the SUV was viewed as a "gift" and should have been reported on my annual financial disclosure form. For failure to report the gift, I was fined $500.

Assault Weapons and the Death of Detective James Walker

When I entered the New York City Police Department in the late 1960s, the gun that a police officer was most likely to encounter in the hands of a bad guy was known in the vernacular as a Saturday night special. These were small revolvers, often not very well made and sometimes held together by electrical tape. Occasionally, a police officer might come across a zip gun, which may have been crafted in someone's garage. Obviously, there were better guns, including semi-automatic pistols, but these were the exceptions. Throughout the 1970s and 1980s, the guns carried by criminals were increasingly becoming more powerful and more numerous. By the end of the 1980s, the NYPD was confiscating more pistols than revolvers. In fact, 1989 was the crossover year where, for the first time, the NYPD confiscated more pistols than revolvers.

The increase in the number of powerful weapons in the hands of criminals was not limited to New York. It had become a national epidemic. Police departments all across America began to address the issue of police officers' being outgunned by their opponents. More and more departments switched from their six-shooter revolver to 9-mm semiautomatic weapons with a magazine clip that could hold at least twice as many rounds.

The NYPD resisted the pressure to arm its officers with more powerful weapons. The main argument was that in a highly concentrated urban area like New York City, giving police officers more powerful weapons would actually endanger public safety. Mike Julian and I certainly held that opinion. The hit rate of NYPD officers was 20 percent. That is, for every five bullets officers discharged, one hit the intended target, and the other four missed. Assuming that you tripled the number of bullets fired due to the increased magazine capacity, that equaled tripling the number of missed shots that could strike an innocent bystander. However, the pressure to switch from the revolver to the semi-automatic pistol finally became too great, especially after a young New York City police officer, Scott Gadell, was killed by a drug dealer armed with a more powerful weapon. Gadell's body was found in an alleyway. It appeared he had been attempting to reload his revolver. This killing underscored the fact that NYPD officers were outgunned on the streets of New York.

In late 1992, Raymond Kelly became the NYPD police commissioner, succeeding Lee Brown. Kelly used to ride at night on an ad hoc basis with different police officers in different neighborhoods of the city. Between answering calls for service he would chat with them, trying to gauge their concerns and entertain their suggestions. One morning, over coffee, the commissioner confided to me that it made no difference what neighborhood he was in or what conversation he tried to strike up, all roads always led back to the officers' lack of firepower. This also became a major issue in the gubernatorial election of 1993. As a result, the sitting governor, Mario Cuomo, allocated several million dollars to purchase 9-mm weapons for NYPD officers. There were no more reasons to resist the pressure to switch. In 1993, the NYPD, with financing with the governor, made the change. For the moment, both sides were even. But it was an ephemeral leveling of the playing field.

In 1994, the Congress of the United States passed a law banning the importation and sale of assault weapons. President Bill Clinton signed the Assault Weapon Ban (AWB), but it had a sunset provision whereby it would expire ten years hence unless the Congress reintroduced it. In 2004, the AWB expired and the law was not reintroduced in Congress. Coincidentally, in Miami and all over South Florida we began to see an increased use of AK-47s, especially among warring drug gangs. Many city leaders, especially mayors, advocated a restoration of the federal assault weapon ban, but no one in Congress took the initiative to reintroduce the legislation. Clearly, the tactics of some progun lobbyists had scared some members of Congress who had advocated for the 1994 legislation. Some of those members had lost their seats, so the message was quite clear.

The issue of the restoration of the federal ban on assault weapons has become intertwined with the Second Amendment and the right to bear arms. Most reasonable Americans understand and support the Second Amendment. Clearly, people have a right to own a firearm to defend themselves. Obviously, hunters have a right to own rifles and shotguns for hunting. But it is extremely difficult to articulate a rationale for the easy access and easy availability of assault weapons that are meant to do one thing and one thing only: kill people, lots of them. On September 13, 2007, a Miami-Dade police officer, Jose Somohano, was shot and killed by a violent thug carrying an AK-47. This AK-47 had been manufactured in China and was now on the streets of Miami.

Four months later, on January 8, 2008, an off-duty Miami police detective, James Walker, literally drove into a gun battle between rival drug gangs. Detective Walker managed to get off one shot, but he was felled and died instantly from the powerful bullets from the felon's AK-47. This AK-47 had been manufactured in Romania. In conversations with ATF officials over a year prior to Detective Walker's death, I had been informed that an increasing number of AK-47s being recovered on the streets of South Florida were recent imports from the old Soviet bloc countries. Tens of thousands of these weapons had been stock-piled in salt mines, and, with the expiration of the federal ban on the importation of assault weapons, AK-47s began flooding the market. Two things immediately took place: their availability increased, and their price decreased. The AK-47 used to kill Detective Walker had been purchased legally for around $300 by a nineteen-year-old, who then handed the weapon over to an eighteen-year-old, who then passed it on to the twenty-year-old who killed Walker. You need to be twenty-one years of age to purchase a pistol or a revolver. But because AK-47s are classified as rifles, purchasers need only to have reached their eighteenth birthday.

Increasingly, AK-47s have become the gun of choice of many of the drug gangs in South Florida. There is a disturbing casualness to their use. As I witnessed the increase in the use of AK-47s in gang-related shootings and homicides, and as the confiscation of these weapons by my police officers increased, it became clear to me that something had to be done. Police officers had once again become outgunned on the streets; we were again engaged in an arms race, with the bad guys leading the way. I had an obligation to protect my officers and to give them a fighting chance.

Six months before Detective Walker was killed, I had asked my staff to research and make recommendations to me regarding the issuance of high-powered weapons to our police officers. The recommendations were that we make available to our officers AR-15 assault weapons, which would give them a fighting chance. I took no satisfaction in making that decision, but it was a decision I had to make. I found my-self in the same position that New York City police commissioner Ray Kelly had found himself in over a decade earlier when he made the switch from revolvers to pistols. Back then, I opposed the change from the .38-caliber revolver to the 9-mm pistol. I now realize that it is easy to opine when you don't have the ultimate responsibility. When you are the police chief or commissioner, you don't have the luxury of idealism. Even though I know that over 99 percent of the time, police officers will not need or have easy access to their AR-15 (it is kept separately in their squad cars), there have been times and there will continue to be times when the availability of the AR-15 levels the playing field. At other times there is a psychological reassurance for the police officers who know they now have that rifle available. Therefore, there's not only a utility factor but also a psychological factor. And that is not unimportant.

In June 2008, Mayor Manny Diaz became the president of the U.S. Conference of Mayors. Mayor Diaz and other brave mayors like him have led the fight to restore the federal ban on assault weapons. As Mayor Diaz correctly points out, these weapons are not meant for hunting or target shooting. These are weapons of war. "They have no place on the streets of our cities."

My concern is for the present and the future. Today, far too many assault weapons are in the hands of violent criminals. They are too easy to get and too cheap to resist. When I think back over what I confronted on the streets of the South Bronx in the late 1960s and 1970s and compare that to what the police officers of Miami face today, there is no comparison. And what about ten years from now? How about twenty years from now? What will our police officers face? Will Rambo have become reality?

Miami Police College

In 2002, the citizens of Miami approved a Homeland Security bond that provided hundreds of millions of dollars to finance capital projects, including the construction of a new police academy. Miami police recruits had previously trained at the Miami-Dade Community College School of Law Enforcement. While the college prepared young recruits academically for their new profession, there seemed to me to be a disconnect between the classroom and the policies and procedures to which the officers were required to adhere once they hit the streets.

Building a new police academy and staffing it with Miami police officers would go a long way toward reducing the gap between academics and real-world policing. For example, at the MPD Police Academy, police recruits would learn both the state law concerning deadly physical force and the Miami Police Department's policy, which is much more restrictive. There would be other tangible benefits to having our own police academy, including imbuing police officers with the notion of service and instilling in them sorely needed discipline. The ability to expose recruits to real-life practitioners, whether they're veteran police officers working patrol or seasoned detectives working the Burglary Squad, is invaluable. The advantages were numerous. However, there was one major drawback. We didn't hire enough recruits on a yearly basis to sustain a police academy the full twelve months of the year. Something needed to be done to enhance it so that it would be a viable institution and not a part-time school that opened and closed for every new police recruit class.

The Miami Police Department has provided training on an informal basis to many Latin American and Caribbean countries. Over the past decade, the demand for this training has increased. Unfortunately, the MPD was not equipped to meet this increased demand, even though doing so is now more important than ever.

If one studies the development of these countries over the last forty years, certain facts emerge. In the 1960s, 1970s, and 1980s, many of the countries ruled by dictators or military juntas transformed into emerging democracies. A key to a thriving democracy is strong democratic policing that respects human rights, protects minority rights, and combats widespread systemic corruption. The clearest sign of a struggling democracy is a police force that is poorly trained, poorly paid, and often corrupt. Instead of preventing crime, officers are themselves engaged in crime, whether it's kidnapping or drug dealing or facilitating others who are involved in those illicit trades. These corrupt and ineffective police organizations threaten the very survival of the struggling democracies. Interestingly, many of the government officials and businesspeople of those countries look to the United States for guidance and assistance. It seemed to me that building a new police academy would provide an opportunity to formalize and expand in a very structured fashion the prior relationships and training that had taken place between the MPD and these countries.

The idea was to create an Institute for Democratic Policing within the MPD Police Academy that would focus on training middle- and upper-level police managers from overseas. The MPD is quite fortunate in that more than half of its members speak Spanish. We are also fortunate to have the largest number of Haitian-speaking police officers outside of Haiti. For Miami, this seems like such a natural fit.

When the idea of an Institute for Democratic Policing was presented to public officials and private citizens who have a stake in Latin America and the Caribbean, the response was overwhelmingly positive. Similarly, when the idea was presented to some officials in Washington, it was equally well received.

As we began to lay out the plans for the academy, I happened to meet Dr. Rudy Crew, the superintendent of the Miami-Dade School District, at Mayor Diaz's office. Dr. Crew and I had become acquainted in New York back in the mid-1990s. At that time we had spoken about creating a criminal justice high school in New York City that would begin training teenagers for careers in law enforcement, ranging from policing and corrections to lawyering and forensics. As I was explaining the plans for our new police academy to Dr. Crew, we again began to speak about establishing a criminal justice high school. Only this time, the high school would be built in conjunction with and become part of the new police academy.

There was enough land next door to police headquarters to double the footprint and square footage to accommodate both the police academy and the criminal justice high school. Certain parts of the complex—such as the gym, the auditorium, and the cafeteria—would be shared facilities. Other parts—such as the shooting range—would be secured and off-limits to the high school students.

In the summer of 2008, a groundbreaking ceremony was held, and construction of the new facility began. Both the academy and the high school opened their doors to new students beginning in the fall of 2009. It is the only school of its kind in the world. It created an excitement within the city of Miami, with the school superintendent assigning a new school principal and his assistant to their positions a full year in advance, allowing them to be on site for the construction and to develop closer ties with the MPD and the surrounding law enforcement community such as the courts, corrections, and the federal and state District Attorney's Offices.

The construction of the police college was a great achievement in 2008 after five years of research and a lot of hard work by Deputy Chief Frank Fernandez and the chief of administration and training, Adam Burden. Later in the year we had another major achievement in the area of homicides, or should I say lack of homicides. The city of Miami went through the entire month of October without a single homicide, a circumstance the city had last seen in 1966. Actually, we went a full forty days without a homicide, which was quite remarkable. Going a week or even two weeks without a homicide could mean you are just lucky. Going forty days without a homicide is more than just luck. It is design and hard work. All units within the department have to be working in a focused and coordinated fashion. The officers in the police cars and on the beats have to do their job—and they did. The narcotics officers have to do their job, and of course they did. The detectives must be aggressive in their investigations, especially in the area of aggravated assaults surrounding the drug trade. They need to treat an aggravated assault with the same seriousness they would a homicide, recognizing that effecting an arrest for aggravated assault may interrupt a cycle of violence—where one shooting is followed by a retaliatory shooting, which is then followed by another retaliatory shooting, resulting in dead bodies on the pavement. It's a novel concept: prevention through apprehension.

Police and Politics

In June 2007, I was elected president of the Police Executive Research Forum (PERF), a think tank for progressive police administrators in the United States and abroad. The executive director of PERF is

Chuck Wexler, a PhD from the Massachusetts Institute of Technology who has almost thirty years of experience in the police profession.

PERF was one of the police groups that helped garner support for the Community Oriented Policing Services (COPS) legislation in 1994 that put a hundred thousand more police officers on the streets throughout the United States. President Clinton signed the legislation—which was sponsored by Senator Joe Biden of Delaware—into law. For the rest of the decade, the benefits of this legislation became apparent across the States. While the 1980s and early 1990s had a justified reputation for lawlessness and violence, the later part of the 1990s became known for the historic reduction in crime nationwide, especially violent crime. A good deal of the credit for this has to go to the COPS legislation and the establishment of the COPS office within the Department of Justice.

When President George W. Bush was elected in 2000, most pragmatists understood that he would not fully embrace COPS, which had become one of the prior administration's very successful programs. Every administration wants to place its own imprimatur on new legislation and initiatives. The expectation was that President Bush would have his own law enforcement agenda. There is no way of knowing if that would have, in fact, developed. What we do know is that 9/11 happened, and all eyes and attention in Washington turned first to Afghanistan and then to Iraq.

The COPS office remained open, but the funding declined year after year. It was no exaggeration to say that Afghanistan and Iraq sucked all of the oxygen out of the room. There were some indications by 2006 and 2007 that crime was beginning to creep back up around the nation. There was also some evidence of a weakening of the American economy. It seemed clear to most observers that the so-called urban agenda, which included cops and crime, was no longer part of the national agenda. Mayors and police chiefs had had a seat at the table during the Clinton administration. That seemed no longer to be true.

In the fall of 2007, in a conversation with Mayor Manny Diaz, we discussed his upcoming ascendancy to the position of president of the U.S. Conference of Mayors. "You are going to be in a position to have a seat at the table and to influence the urban agenda of the next administration, whether it's Republican or Democrat," I said to the mayor, stating the obvious. The mayor concurred. Over the next few months, the mayor, along with his chief of staff, Suzanna Valdez, and I discussed issues that we should try to get before the candidates of each party. Suzanna had worked in the Clinton White House and was attuned to national politics.

In June 2008, Mayor Diaz took over as the president of the U.S. Conference of Mayors and hit the ground running, not as a jogger but more as a sprinter. The mayor laid out five core areas that he wanted the next administration, whether Democratic or Republican, to focus on and create a strategy to deal with. He set up five task forces, each headed up by a mayor, to deal with the following issues: infrastructure, crime, the environment, the arts, and poverty. Each task force was to have a meeting in a different city and come up with findings and recommendations for the next national administration. Obviously, I was interested in the crime task force.

This task force met in Philadelphia in early August of 2008. Mayor Diaz asked me, as his chief of police and the president of PERF, to assist in this meeting. Hosted by Mayor Michael Nutter of Philadelphia, the task force was chaired by Mayor Jerry Abramson of Louisville, Kentucky, who had been the president of the U.S. Conference of Mayors when the original COPS bill was passed in 1994. Attendance was strong, with about fifty mayors and chiefs present, and the enthusiasm at the meeting was a clear indication of Mayor Diaz's influence and leadership. Senator Joe Biden was the keynote speaker. In his speech, Senator Biden made it clear that he was representing the sentiments of the Democratic presidential candidate, Barack Obama. Biden's words inspired the attendees and gave them a reason to be hopeful.

An invitation to attend the meeting was also extended to the campaign of the Republican presidential candidate, Senator John McCain. The campaign sent a staffer to attend the meeting.

After the lunch, Senator Biden stuck around and had informal chats with the mayors and the chiefs, including Mayor Diaz and me. I had gotten to know Senator Biden from my days as the Philadelphia police commissioner, and we had developed a very good relationship. Chuck

Wexler, the executive director of PERF, kids me about this relationship, stating, "You two guys have this Irish thing, and you're oblivious to the Jewish guy on the sidelines."

The other four task forces held their meetings, and by the end of August, Mayor Diaz had a complete package to present to both campaigns at their political conventions. The staff at the U.S. Conference of Mayors learned what the staff of the city of Miami Mayor's Office already knew: Mayor Diaz is a workaholic who moves at breakneck speed and demands the same from those around him. Either get on board or step aside. That is his operating philosophy, and I concur wholeheartedly.

In November 2008, the American people elected a new president, Barack Obama, and a new vice president, Joe Biden, just as the national economy tanked. Bank and business failures mounted, while unemployment increased. Cities and their coffers took hard hits, and layoffs and furloughs were the order of the day. The two months after the election, normally a time for respite and team building, were instead a time of economic chaos and confusion. As they say in Brooklyn, "Things kept getting worser and worser."

In early January 2009, Chuck Wexler and I had a meeting with Vice President–elect Biden. Mr. Biden spoke about an economic stimulus package, a Great Depression–style program meant to jump-start the dying American economy. The future vice president assured us that a reinvigorated COPS office and other pro–law enforcement initiatives would be an integral part of the new legislation. A month later, after President Obama and Vice President Biden were sworn in, the new stimulus package passed with all of Vice President Biden's promises intact. President Obama and Vice President Biden deserve most of the credit for the passage of the stimulus package, but Mayor Manny Diaz deserves recognition for his work to ensure that the package included funds to address the concerns of the country's major cities.

In March 2009, proving he was a man of his word, Vice President Joe Biden came to Miami to hold a press conference at Miami Police Headquarters. The vice president acknowledged the great work of Mayor Diaz and the U.S. Conference of Mayors in lobbying for the reinvigoration of the COPS office and the national conversation on policing and crime. To back up his words, he presented the mayor with a check for over two million dollars for the hiring of additional police staff and the purchase of equipment and technology. He indicated that more money would be forthcoming. And once again, true to his promise, in July 2009, the city of Miami received 11.2 million dollars for additional police hires.

During my last two years as chief, I had made it quite clear that when Mayor Manny Diaz left office, I too would leave. In November 2009, Mayor Diaz ended his mayoralty due to term limits. On his last day in office, I submitted my letter of resignation. Big-city chiefs usually last three to four years; seven years was more than enough.

I had always felt certain that Deputy Chief Frank Fernandez would succeed me as chief. Frank is in a class by himself and is among the finest police officials in the United States. Unfortunately, as a result of a political deal, the new mayor did not choose Frank as the next chief. However, Frank will be a big-city chief some day soon. Such talent cannot go unrecognized. I think that Frank must feel similar to the way I felt when I was not chosen to be the police commissioner of the NYPD after Bill Bratton's departure. Regardless, I went on to lead two major departments, and I am confident that Frank Fernandez can look forward to a similar fate.

Conclusion

Where We Were, Where We Are

The Cambridge police acted stupidly.
—PRESIDENT BARACK OBAMA

Over the course of my career, I have attended numerous community meetings and have obviously conversed with thousands of police officers. Two refrains—or should I say laments—always appear and reappear without fail. Whether it was when I was a young officer patrolling the streets of the South Bronx, a midlevel manager rising through the hierarchy of the NYPD, the police commissioner of Philadelphia, or the chief of police of Miami, the lament of veteran police officers was always the same: "They don't make cops like they used to." The community member laments that "the only thing I really want is a cop on the beat, like the guy who patrolled the streets when I was growing up."

The first time I heard the lament regarding officers who knew their community was when I was a young police officer walking a foot beat in the South Bronx in the early 1970s. The sentiment seemed to make sense, but as I thought back to when I was a young teenager growing up in Washington Heights, I didn't remember a police officer walking the beat. I do remember police officers in police cars who broke our chops on a daily basis for playing stickball in the street or curveball underneath Mrs. Lemondrop's window. I concluded that the reason I didn't remember a specific police officer in my community on his foot beat was because foot beats must have stopped in the late 1950s and thus were a thing of the past. Fast-forward twenty years: as a captain and later as a deputy chief, I continued to hear the same lament from people who were aged forty or fifty—my age!

In Philadelphia and then again in Miami, the longing for the days of the foot beat officer who knew everyone in the neighborhood and who chastised wayward children and settled disputes between neighbors and family members without ever having to resort to making an arrest continued to be voiced at community meetings. I vowed to myself that I would find this ubiquitous foot beat officer. After much research, what I did find was that this lament was not of recent vintage. The case of Police Commissioner Louis Valentine is illustrative.

Valentine entered the NYPD as a rookie in 1902. His rise through the ranks was periodically stalled as he ran afoul of different police administrations due to his desire to see a corruption-free NYPD. Eventually, Valentine became the police commissioner under New York's reform mayor, Fiorello LaGuardia. In his autobiography, *Nightstick*, Commissioner Valentine lays out what his priorities were when he became police commissioner in 1934. First and foremost among his goals was to return to the days when he first came on "the job," about 1903, when the police officer on the beat knew everyone in the neighborhood, and everybody in the neighborhood knew him. . . . You get my point.

My research took me to Hollywood, where I think I found our missing beat officer. His name was Officer McShane. He walked a foot beat in the 1945 movie *A Tree Grows in Brooklyn*. Officer McShane knew the problems of the people on his beat intimately. He was around day and night, and he looked after the neighbors on his beat, including the family with the alcoholic father and exasperated wife and two adorable little girls. Eventually and predictably, the father dies from his affliction and Officer McShane is there to ease the widow's pain. As the movie ends, the viewer is left with no doubt that Officer McShane will continue looking after the family, and, in fact, he's such a good beat officer that it is clear that he will wed the widow and be the new father to the two little girls.

Yes, I found the beat officer, or should I say, I found the myth. There is nothing wrong with this myth. It is really an ideal that most people have regarding police officers in their communities. Most people like police officers or want to like police officers. It is the job of every police officer and every police chief to help make the myth a reality, or at least make the ideal a goal.

The first lament, "They don't make police officers like they used to," is one that I heard from veteran cops time and time again in all three cities. My instinctive reply was, "Thank God." Unlike the second lament regarding the mythical beat officer, this refrain is not necessarily a desirable goal. Police officers today are better educated, more diverse, more humane, more professional, less brutal, and certainly less corrupt than their predecessors. The history of the NYPD is one of periodic corruption scandals every quarter of a century. In between the commissions established to investigate and put an end to police corruption has been a continuous series of negative issues, especially those involving deadly physical force. Sometimes this force has resulted in serious civil and community unrest. Other times it affected only the family and friends of the person who was subjected to it.

When I was a teenager in my freshman year at Cardinal Hayes High School, I worked as a dishwasher at Saint Elizabeth's Hospital in Washington Heights alongside my mother, who worked in the kitchen. A young guy named George, a high school dropout, worked at the hospital full time as a freight-elevator operator. George was older than I, maybe eighteen. He was a bit of a knucklehead who was into cars, including, sometimes, stealing them. One night, George was stopped in a stolen car and subsequently shot twice in the stomach by an NYPD police officer. George returned to work a few months later, and he didn't appear to hold any animosity toward the police officer who had shot him. But when he showed me the colostomy bag with his guts in it, attached to his stomach, it seemed to me that that was a pretty extreme punishment for driving a stolen car.

The senior police officers whom I met when I first entered the NYPD were not bad officers—a lot were quite good. They were brave beyond belief, and many of them had served their country honorably in World

War II or the Korean War. They were the right men for that time. But almost all of them looked like me: a white guy, probably Catholic.

The social and civil unrest of the 1960s demanded change in almost all of our institutions, whether government or private. Some of these institutions resisted change, and some of that resistance is still evident even today. However, two very conservative institutions that were among the quickest to embrace change and, in some cases, to lead change, were the military and the police. While this change had many facets, the overarching goal was to create more inclusive, more professional, better-educated institutions. By and large, this also meant greater racial and gender integration.

The military has its own story. From a segregated military under President Harry Truman in the early 1950s to a fully integrated military—with General Colin Powell leading the way—thirty years later: it is an extraordinary American story. The police profession has an equally great story to tell.

When I entered the NYPD in 1967, very few African Americans or Hispanics worked in the department. In fact, when I arrived at the 17th Precinct in Midtown Manhattan, there were, if I remember correctly, only a handful of African Americans. Back then the department had few, if any, civilian employees, white or African American.

As a result of the civil rights movement of the 1960s, but especially as the result of the large-scale civil unrest in many American cities, recognition grew for the real need to integrate police forces throughout the United States. In the parlance of the time, the goal was to have police departments reflect as much as possible the populations they served. The practicality of this goal was brought home to me early on in my career in the 44th Precinct in the South Bronx by none other than a seasoned and salty veteran white police officer.

There was a block called Davidson Avenue within the confines of the 44th Precinct whose residents were all African American. To say that there was a great deal of tension between the residents and the police officers from the 44th would be an understatement. It was not unusual for a simple dispute call to turn into a huge donnybrook between police and residents of that block. One day, while discussing a prior incident with the veteran officer, he mentioned how different the neighborhood response was to police when the newly assigned African American sergeant was on the scene. It appeared to the veteran that when the residents observed a fellow African American supervisor on the scene giving orders and directions, the residents were more responsive and respectful. To the veteran it made sense, and it made his job a lot easier. I agreed!

While there was a push to hire more African American police officers in the early 1970s, there was a simultaneous push for greater civilian participation within the organization. This was meant to free up armed police officers from routine clerical duties and reassign them to patrol the streets—the reason they were hired in the first place.

The move toward greater civilianization brought many African Americans, mostly female, into an organization that was almost entirely white and male. The effort to recruit more African American police officers proved more difficult, but some progress was made. The hiring of a significant number of African American civilians had a salutary affect on the workplace, especially in precinct station houses. The largely white police force began working on a daily basis with non-white, largely female coworkers and had to behave accordingly. It was no longer okay to use locker-room language or make racially insensitive remarks. An officer might still harbor a private prejudice; however, he knew to keep his private thoughts to himself.

The early 1970s saw some very big classes of new police hires and some progress in getting more minorities in these classes. Understandably, most of these minority hires were assigned to largely minority precincts. It seemed to make sense to assign an African American police officer to one of the Harlem or North Brooklyn precincts, just as it did to assign a Hispanic officer to the South Bronx or Spanish Harlem. On the other hand, it did seem odd that the NYPD would engage in purposeful segregation of officers based on race.

As African American police officers began to hit the streets, the black community obviously welcomed their presence. On the other hand, the way in which they were welcomed in the precincts was more complex. As you would expect, some old-timers were less likely to be welcoming than the younger officers, some of whom went through the police academy with African American officers and in some cases had been in the armed services (including Vietnam) with these same officers.

The racial integration of the NYPD was brought home in graphic fashion in a six-month span when two sets of officers, one African American and one white, were killed at the hands of the Black Liberation Army (BLA). On July 21, 1971, as I was working anticrime with my partner Richie Sabol, across the Harlem River at the Polo Grounds Project, Officers Joseph Piagentini and Waverly Jones were executed while in uniform responding to a dispute there.

Six months later, on January 27, 1972, police officers Rocco Laurie and Gregory Foster were both executed in the East Village by members of the same Black Liberation Army. These two sets of black and white police officers were four of the many police officers across the country who were killed during this time by the BLA, as part of that group's war on society—specifically, the most visible symbol of an orderly society, the police. Many speculated at the time that these officers were specifically chosen because they were, in fact, integrated teams of one white and one African American officer.

The hiring of officers of any race stopped for almost five years in the late 1970s as a result of the fiscal crisis in New York City. In 1979, the department began hiring again to try to make up the loss of almost ten thousand police officers in the prior five years. With these new hires came an even stronger push to recruit more minorities, especially African Americans.

A similar reception awaited many of the new female police officers who entered the NYPD beginning in the early 1970s. Beginning in 1973, very large classes of female police officers began to graduate from the police academy. Again, many veteran officers showed some resentment, myself included. However, younger officers, like my brother, Ciaran, who may have had female classmates in their academy class, were more readily accepting.

For me, the most notable impact of these minority officers was the self-policing impact they had on other, mostly white male officers. A white police officer was less likely to use offensive racial language, or even worse, abuse his power, toward a minority member of the community, especially a prisoner, if a minority officer was present. Similarly, a male was less likely to use gender-insulting language if the person in the police car next to him was female. In no way am I suggesting that bad language and bad conduct were eliminated as a result of these new minority officers, but things did improve. And to be sure, there was no shortage of black or female police officers who also engaged in crude language or misbehaved badly. The bottom line is that there were some extremely positive benefits from having a more diverse police department.

In the early 1980s, I had the opportunity to work at police headquarters for the chief of department of the NYPD, Robert J. Johnston, and so I saw firsthand the effort made by the NYPD, especially under its first African American police commissioner, Benjamin Ward, to recruit and hire more minority officers, with a focus on African Americans. While there was some success in recruiting and hiring more minorities, the numbers paled in comparison to the effort expended. One would have expected, even hoped for, better results.

Many explanations have been offered as to why police departments have a difficult time recruiting more minorities. Some of the difficulty is a result of the disparate rates of prior contacts with the criminal justice system, which disqualifies many minorities. Another reason might be cultural, as in the way a young man explained it to me one night while I was walking my beat in the South Bronx in the early 1970s. When I mentioned to him that the NYPD was hiring large classes and asked if he would be interested, he replied without hesitation that under no circumstances would he ever become a police officer, because he would feel a traitor to his race. He felt strongly that the NYPD and police generally oppress and brutalize the black community, and he could never be a part of such an organization or such a profession. I'm not sure if this was just bluster on his part or genuine feelings, but I have heard that sentiment enough to know there is something to it.

Police Commissioner Ben Ward offered another realistic explanation in the mid-1980s. Racial tensions were especially high in New York

City during that time, and many black leaders denounced the NYPD on an almost daily basis. Ward pointed out that it wasn't helpful to constantly berate the NYPD while he was trying to recruit more minorities. What young man or woman wants to join an organization whose members their community views as racist or brutal? Ward was not trying to deny that brutality or racism existed, but he felt that one of the ways to help bring change was for young minority men and women to join the organization and help make change from within.

In the early 1990s, while assigned to the Office of Management Analysis and Planning, I began to notice a phenomenon regarding the assignment of police officers by race. As I mentioned earlier, assigning officers based on their race to precincts where the vast majority of residents were black made sense, given that there were so few black police officers to begin with. You really want to assign officers where they will benefit the community most, including providing positive role models for young children and teenagers. But as greater numbers of minorities, especially African Americans, are hired, the expectation is that they will spread out to other precincts.

Unfortunately, this was not the case, especially in the region called Brooklyn North, a area encompassing a large number of police precincts with a majority of African American residents. While white and black officers were assigned to these precincts on a relatively proportionate basis, many of the white officers transferred out at a higher rate than their black counterparts once they had enough time in rank to do so under their contract and existing department policies. Blacks, on the other hand, stayed longer, and there is some evidence that some black officers from other, nonminority precincts requested to be transferred to these precincts.

Once police officers haves enough time in rank, they can generally request a transfer to an assignment of their choice. The end result is that a certain amount of self-segregation occurs, which runs counter to the desires of the department and good public policy. Workers' rights supersede the larger goals of the department and public policy.

I ran into this phenomenon again in Philadelphia and Miami. In Philadelphia I made a conscious effort to get more white police officers into traditionally black neighborhoods and more black officers into traditionally white areas, especially when new recruits were graduating from the police academy. I just felt it was the right thing to integrate the various districts more fully. I firmly believe that in a well-integrated system, officers don't get "too comfortable" in their own ethnic zone, feeding off their biases and feelings regarding this or that member of an opposite group. It has been my experience that an integrated platoon of officers has the self-policing effect on the officers I mentioned earlier.

Unfortunately, in Philadelphia the same pattern emerged; some police officers, through a variety of methods, self-segregated into their own groups. This did not mean of course that districts were entirely one group or another. Rather, the tendency was for officers to prefer to work with their own racial or ethnic group. So you still had some integration among officers but not to the extent that the numbers would have suggested.

In Miami, a much smaller city than New York or Philadelphia, the same self-segregation occurred. Three police areas cover the entire city: North District, Central District, and South District. The vast majority of African American police officers will be found assigned to the North District, the largely African American area of the city, while the vast majority of the Hispanic officers can be found in the South District, the geographical area of Miami with the majority of the city's Hispanic residents.

While the issue of self-segregation is not a death knell for effective policing, I believe it defeats the positive goal of a well-integrated police force, not just in numbers but also in actual assignments and deployment. For example, if you had a city in which the population broke down 50 percent white, 20 percent Hispanic, and 30 percent African American, and the police force consisted of 50 percent white officers, 20 percent Hispanic officers, and 30 percent African American, you can argue, correctly, that the police force is made up of the right racial and ethnic mix—that, in fact, the police force reflects almost perfectly the population it serves. However, if the vast majority of white officers work together in their area and the vast majority of African American officers work together in their particular area, I don't think you can make the case that you have a well-integrated police force.

Is self-segregation stasis, or is it just a stopping-off point on the road to full integration? Americans recently elected an African American, Barack Obama, as their president. President Obama is biracial, with a white American mother from the heartland, and an African father. Some say that President Obama is postracial, that race is not a factor—that in America, with his election, we have moved beyond race. That thought lasted for only about the first two weeks of the Obama administration.

President Obama's new attorney general, Eric Holder, the first African American to hold the position, gave a talk on race at a Black History Month celebration in Washington, D.C. Holder's speech was an unwelcome dash of cold water in the faces of those who had been warmed by the notion of a postracial society. Holder may have been impolitic in his remarks and could have found less provocative words to describe his observations. Nonetheless, his thoughts, in my opinion, were correct. We have made a great deal of progress, but we are not there yet. As Holder correctly pointed out, we face a great deal of reluctance and a great deal of uneasiness in dealing with the issue of race. Unlike Attorney General Holder, I would not have chosen the word *cowards* to describe those who are reluctant. Just describe them as they are: reluctant.

About five months later, in July 2009, our postracial president got himself involved in a racial imbroglio during a prime-time press conference when he referred to the Cambridge Police Department as having acted "stupidly" in the arrest of a distinguished African American Harvard professor, Henry Louis Gates. Gates, returning from a fourteen-day trip to China, had difficulty entering his home in Cambridge; apparently the front door's lock was damaged. With the assistance of his cabdriver, Gates forced his way into the home. A nearby neighbor's attention was drawn to the two men breaking into the house, and, being a dutiful citizen, she called 911. Sergeant James Crowley of the Cambridge police responded to the call. When he confronted Gates in his home, words were exchanged, and the situation between the two grew heated. Gates was arrested for disorderly conduct, a charge that was later dropped.

Four days later, a media feeding frenzy had broken out, with opinion makers lining up on either side of the argument. Supporters of Gates alleged that Sergeant Crowley was a racist, evidenced by the fact that he had arrested a man in his own home. Supporters of Crowley maintained that the officer was just doing his job and should have been thanked rather than verbally abused by Gates. Far too often sides were chosen, it appeared, largely by race. It was an unfortunate situation that was blown out of proportion. But it did highlight the fact that race is still a critical issue in our society. No amount of wishful thinking or idealistic positing of a postracial society has changed that fact.

The Gates incident took me back thirty-five years to when I first read Alexis de Tocqueville's *Democracy in America*. The French historian wrote glowingly about America and its unlimited potential. However, he identified what he considered to be America's Achilles' heel: the problem of the races. Tocqueville believed that the separation of the races would continue into the future and that this separation would be the critical factor in limiting the country's progress.

I think we have proven Tocqueville wrong, but not completely. We have made tremendous progress in the area of race relations, especially over the last half century. With the election of the first African American president of the United States, some argued, wistfully, that America had transcended race and that those who were fixated on race were stuck in the past. President Barack Obama, as both a candidate and president, did a masterful job of staying out of the politics of racial identity. But the Gates case showed all too clearly that even a dexterous postracial president can be dragged into the cauldron. Race is still an issue.

I have now spent forty years in policing, two-thirds of my life, and I have seen tremendous change. Progress has sometimes been tough and sometimes very emotional, but it has always been good. The past gives me hope for the future.

INDEX